WRITING IN 1907, almost fifty years a[fter his] death, Thomas Seccombe noted an [aspect] of William Hickling Prescott's gr[eatness] which succeeding generations of [scholars] agreed. "Prescott," Seccombe wrote, [belonged to] a race of which it is, perhaps, no exaggeration to say in the twentieth century that there is a probability of its becoming . . . completely extinct. . . . I refer, of course, to the great race of stylist historians."

That Prescott belonged to this great race of historians there can be no doubt. Printed and reprinted (almost every year even now, one hundred years after his death, sees new editions of his works) Prescott's histories continue to offer readers dramatically romantic vistas of the sixteenth-century Spanish world and continue to contribute to the wide popularity of the author of *Conquest of Mexico*. In his lifetime, Prescott received international honors and renown, ranking with Macaulay and other great writers of England and the Continent. His books were acclaimed masterworks, and he knew and enjoyed immediate and widespread popularity.

Yet behind the books lies the story of equally remarkable achievement and success. In his forties and afflicted with near blindness when he began to publish his histories, the aristocratic, proper Bostonian, who possessed the means and leisure to dedicate himself to the profession of a man of letters, deliberately sought distinction in a career that touched two continents and spanned more than two decades.

From the record of author-publisher relations, much of it given here from unpublished letters and documents, sources not used in conventional biographies of Prescott, C. Harvey Gardiner has drawn a full-length portrait of Prescott as an author and has gauged his contribution to the cultural history of his time. The complex character of Prescott, his dealings with his four American and two British publishers, his image of scholarly authorship, his wariness of what he termed the "slippery" trade,

(Continued on back flap)

PRESCOTT AND HIS PUBLISHERS

PRESCOTT

AND HIS PUBLISHERS

C. HARVEY GARDINER

Carbondale

SOUTHERN ILLINOIS UNIVERSITY

PRESS

For Kitty

ACKNOWLEDGMENTS

ACKNOWLEDGMENTS are extended to many: to Roger Wolcott, great-grandson of William Hickling Prescott, for generous access to his manuscript holdings; to Massachusetts
Historical Society, Director Stephen T. Riley, and staff
members Warren G. Wheeler and Winifred Collins; to
Harvard College for access to manuscript collections in
the Houghton Library, and to Carolyn E. Jakeman; to
Little, Brown & Company, and especially Charles B. Blan-
chard, for access to company records; to Boston Public
Library and especially Sarah W. Flannery and the staff
of the rare book collection; to New York Public Library; to
the Hispanic Society of America and especially Clara
Louisa Penney; to Harper & Brothers for permission to use
manuscripts; to J. B. Lippincott Company, and especially
President Howard K. Bauernfeind, for access to company
records; to the Historical Society of Pennsylvania; to the
Manuscripts Division of the Library of Congress; to the
library of the University of Illinois and to Professors
Royal A. Gettmann and Gordon N. Ray; to the Newberry
Library and Ruth Lapham Butler; to the Huntington
Library and the British Museum for access to manuscripts;
to the library of Southern Illinois University and staff

vii *Acknowledgments*

members John Clifford, Ruby Kerley, Harold Smith, Alan M. Cohn, Earl Tannenbaum, Flora Breniman, Betty Lingle, Ferris S. Randall, and Verna Rees; to the Graduate Council of Southern Illinois University; and to the Graduate School of Washington University.

Director Vernon Sternberg of the Southern Illinois University Press has contributed personally to the production of this volume in a manner that has enriched the product of another author-publisher relationship.

Acknowledgments are tendered, too, for permission to employ quotations from *The Correspondence of William Hickling Prescott 1833–1847* (Massachusetts Historical Society, 1925); *One Hundred Years of Publishing* (Little, Brown & Co., 1937); and Rollo Ogden, *William Hickling Prescott* (Houghton Mifflin Company, 1904).

C. Harvey Gardiner

Carbondale, Illinois
September 27, 1958

CONTENTS

ILLUSTRATIONS

between pages 166–67

PRESCOTT AND HIS PUBLISHERS

CHAPTER ONE

PRESCOTT AND THE SLIPPERY TRADE

In the winter of 1837/38 the debonair, handsome, brown-haired Boston socialite-historian William H. Prescott, a bit beyond forty years of age, published his first book simultaneously in England and the United States. Planning a career of scholarly activity that included the prospect of more books, Prescott assessed his initial experiences with publishers so "that, in my future calculations and bargains I may have something to guide me with the slippery 'trade.'"[1] His blanket indictment of those with whom he would be forced to do business if his manuscripts were to be converted to books stemmed from a combination of circumstances, specific and general.

Some of his doubts and suspicions about publishers derived from the experiences of author friends, men such as Jared Sparks and George Bancroft. Sparks' skepticism about publishers early included Richard Bentley, with whom Prescott was doing business in England. "I have not a high opinion of him," he wrote Prescott. "Next to Colburn he has the character of being the most familiar of any publisher in London with the small tricks of his trade."[2] In a day in which the professions of publisher and bookseller commonly were one, James Fenimore Cooper, with both European and American experience inspiring his words, declared, "These booksellers have no souls."[3] A student of nineteenth-century publishing has recently stated that "in 1820 neither author nor publisher wholly trusted the other."[4] This statement touches a truth that persisted in mid-century decades, as illustrated in the publishing career of William H. Prescott.

A party to changing times in America which witnessed the emergence of the first generations of modern giants among both authors and publishers, Prescott, a man of impeccably meticulous tastes, was confused by his first experience in a rapidly and basically changing area of American life. For the first time in America, some authors, with widening reputations that assumed national and international proportions, were earning respectable livings by their pens. Likewise, some bookmen who had previously combined the publication of a limited number of titles of their own with a bookselling operation that included numerous titles from other publisher-booksellers decided to specialize, dedicating their all to publishing. And as publishers and booksellers tended to separate, the new species of publishers enlarged their operations—with more titles, more advertising, more agents, bigger editions—and in so doing converted themselves from strictly local operators to houses with regional and even national outlooks and reputations.

But only part of Prescott's doubts about the publishers stemmed from the novelty of his experience with them, his limited knowledge of their business, and the changing nature of the publishing industry.

Some of Prescott's attitude toward publishers derived from the nature of the man Prescott happened
to be.

Of the many factors that made a historian of William Hickling Prescott, one of the most significant
was his mingled awareness of and pride in his own
heritage.[5] His grandfather, Colonel William Prescott, had carved a niche for himself in American
history as a commander at the Battle of Bunker
Hill. Decades later, the grandson gave the warrior's
sword a place of honor in his study and did his ut-
most to advance a monument-building program in
honor of that patriot. The military man's son, William H. Prescott's father, gained fame in another
way, as a leading legal mind, as a legislator, as a
judge—first in Salem, Massachusetts, and then in
Boston. The bigger community, ideal for William
Prescott—the name persisted through the generations—and his expanding professional prospects,
gave full rein to the catholic intellectual tastes he so
purposefully fostered in his son.

Destined to win his prominence as man of letters
and historian, William Hickling Prescott was born
May 4, 1796, in Salem, Massachusetts. The family
moved to Boston in 1808. For more than a half-
century of his sixty-three years of life, therefore,
Prescott was first and foremost a Bostonian. Judge
Prescott's reputation, financial success, and personality enabled his family to move in the best social
circles of that New England metropolis. The teen-
age son was trained in the social graces at home and
in the classical tradition at the private school of the
Rev. Dr. John S. J. Gardiner.

With more potential than demonstrated ability,

Prescott entered Harvard in 1811, as a Sophomore, and pursued his studies in a manner which suggested that the social nature of the young man had to be served as much as did his intellectual growth. No great intellectual passions developed to compensate for Prescott's obvious dislikes, but increasingly William and his family took it for granted that after Harvard he would follow in the footsteps of his father in the legal profession. Fate disposed otherwise.

One evening, during his Junior year, young Prescott, in the act of leaving the commons, was struck in his left eye by a crust of bread hurled during a rowdy moment such as was all too common at Harvard in that period. In time this event became the turning point in his career. The sight of the injured left eye was lost, and sympathetic nervous and rheumatic conditions so weakened his right eye as to make use of it uncertain. He completed his college career in 1814 and initiated the study of law before the full effect of the eye condition became apparent.

Coincident with the realization that the son could not follow his father's profession, rest, travel, and medical treatment for the young Prescott received increased attention from his family. In 1815, the nineteen-year-old, with uncertainty written across his future, visited his maternal grandfather in the Azores, after which he journeyed to London and Paris in search of medical advice. Pain mounted, augmented by homesickness and seasickness and the pessimistic opinions of the best oculists. The youth spent days and months confined to darkened quarters. Away from home and in misery, he sufficiently passed into the valley of darkness that he purchased and used for writing purposes a noctograph, a wired device designed to guide the writing of a blind person. At the moment of its acquisition in London, Prescott could not have anticipated the role the noctograph would play in the writing of his books.

After two years in Europe, he returned to his father's house, physically ill and emotionally upset. Unable to pursue the legal career that required so much recourse to printed statutes and opinions and unable to move with his accustomed grace and assurance in society, young Prescott became a recluse. After a while the crisis passed; and, in addition to mingling in society once more, he sought an area of activity for his boundless energy and ranging interests. Read to by his sister, Prescott so widened his love of literature that he decided to seek a career as a man of letters, possibly in the realm of literary criticism.

In 1821, Prescott's first significant publication appeared in the august *North American Review*. For the next decade he averaged slightly more than one article a year in that Boston literary journal. Both his reading interests and his literary efforts identified him with Western European literature, his chief attention being given to England, France, and Italy in the fields of poetry, drama, and the novel. His love of beautiful expression, an important ingredient of his eventual genius, derived from his love of good literature. So, too, the ranging interests he had in literature may have helped him to embrace such broad themes as became his standard fare in later years.

Yet, even as his essays inclined him toward literature, his search for a theme on which he might

launch himself on a large-scale scholarly project
moved him from that field into history. As he turned
his back on literature as his major focus, Prescott
also shifted to a new geographical area. George
Ticknor, busy on a lifetime study of Spanish literature, was building the kind of library that invited
Prescott's attention. More than anyone else, Ticknor
drew Prescott toward Spain and Spanish themes.
Once there, the historian-to-be fixed on the period
of Ferdinand and Isabella.

Ready, in January, 1826, to dedicate himself to
Spanish history at the dawn of modern times, Prescott knew countless problems. Systematic, long-term
endeavor such as a major project demanded caused
him to hire the first of the indispensable reader-
secretaries he was to know through all his remaining years. His negotiations with booksellers were
aimed at building the library required for his research. Slowly, at first, but surely, he disengaged
himself from review writing. At thirty-one years of
age, Prescott, scrawling, "I subscribe to the 'History of the Reign of Ferdinand and Isabella,' " [6]
moved seriously and almost completely into the field
of his future greatness, encouraged and supported
by the unfaltering assistance of a wide range of men
—Ticknor and others in Boston, bookseller Obadiah
Rich in London, diplomat Arthur Middleton in
Madrid, and many others in numerous places and
conditions of life. A questing mind, a love of truth,
a literary bent, an understanding father, and helpful friends—all joined with physical disability to
evoke the accident of intellectual genius.

From the 1820's to the close of his life on January
28, 1859, Prescott centered his creative powers in the

history of Spain in the old world and the new in the
late fifteenth and sixteenth centuries. In the realm of
subject matter, as in his physical world, Prescott
had obstacles to overcome, for one of the finest, yet
subtlest, measures of his eventual greatness was his
establishment of the popularity of Spanish themes
for the English reading public. Born into an American outlook that included pro-English, anti-Spanish
sentiments based on deep-seated attitudes derived
from Elizabethan days, Prescott contributed to the
miracle of helping to establish a separate and distinctly American estimate of Spain. His works, in
the aggregate of their objectivity and completeness,
did much to bestir the American mind from auto-
matic acceptance of the Black Legend assessment
of things Spanish which so negated as to malign the
record of that nation.

Within Prescott's lifetime his three major works,
upon which his reputation continues to rest, *Ferdinand and Isabella, Conquest of Mexico,* and *Conquest of Peru,* were acclaimed masterworks both at
home and abroad. Three days after the release of
the first work, an anonymous reviewer wrote in a
Boston newspaper, the *Boston Weekly Messenger,*
December 28, 1837, "To the lovers of literature and
of scholarship, this book has a peculiar charm."
Writing in Boston's own *North American Review,*
for January, 1838, Prescott's intimate friend William Howard Gardiner commended the history for
its "admirable order, and due proportion," for its
"epic or dramatic interest," and for its "authenticity . . . supported, at every step, by ample references to the best original sources." Francis William
Pitt Greenwood, a classmate of the historian in the

Harvard class of 1814, wrote in the *Christian Examiner and General Review* for March, 1838, "We but repeat what we hear from the universal voice of our reading community, when we say that this history is an honor to its author, and a most valuable addition to the literature of his country." John Pickering told the readers of *The New-York Review* in April, 1838, that "the author is so thoroughly master of his whole subject, that he is enabled to detect many errors and omissions of those eminent historians, whom we have been accustomed to look up to as our guide and authorities." Prescott's friend George Bancroft, the historian, insisted, in the *United States Magazine and Democratic Review* of May, 1838, that "the mind of the author reflects objects without distorting them . . . no breath of prejudice dims, no bigotry tarnishes."

Such opinions, voiced by friendly Americans—most of whom were Bostonian acquaintances of the author—might be discounted heavily were those of foreigners not in the same vein. In London, *The Spectator* for January 6, 1838, declared the history "places the author next to Hallam amongst our living historians." In the *Edinburgh Review,* January, 1839, Spanish intellectual Pascual de Gayangos wrote that "Mr. Prescott's work is one of the most successful historical productions of our time."

Six years passed, and in the closing weeks of 1843 Prescott's second history, his *Conquest of Mexico,* was ready for the reviewers. A friend, G. S. Hillard, exclaimed in his review in the January, 1844, issue of the *North American Review:*

It is a noble work; judiciously planned, and admirably executed; . . . It will win the literary voluptuary to

its pages by the attractiveness of its subject and the
flowing ease of its style; and the historical student
will do honor to the extent and variety of the research
which it displays, and to the thoroughness with which
its investigations have been conducted. We can confidently predict for it an extensive and permanent
popularity. . . . It will take its place among those
enduring productions of the human mind.

A month earlier, in the December, 1843, issue of the
British *Quarterly Review,* H. H. Milman had asserted: "Mr. Prescott may take his place among the
really good English writers of history in modern
times; and will be received, we are persuaded, into
that small community, with every feeling of friendly
and fraternal respect." In the April, 1845, *Edinburgh Review,* S. M. Phillips prefaced his consideration of the Bostonian's second work with the words,
"Mr. Prescott has long been honourably known as
author of one of the most valuable historical works
produced in the present age." Prescott had so completely penetrated the inner circles of British literary acceptance that it became mere routine for
Phillips to add, "We doubt whether any intelligent
reader has laid down that now before us, without
acknowledging it to be one of the most delightful
narratives in his recollection."

As a footnote to Prescott's immediate popularity
it might be added that Mrs. H. W. Longfellow, con-
fiding her opinion to her journal, similarly insisted,
"It [*Conquest of Mexico*] has the fascination of a
romance and cannot be left. . . . Mr. Prescott seems
to have seen it all with his own eyes as he makes his
reader." [7]

When the *Conquest of Peru* appeared in 1847, the

critics routinely certified the fact that the master had another work ready for the public. Francis Bowen, a Boston friend of the historian, reminded the readers of the *North American Review,* October, 1847, "There is a witchery in Mr. Prescott's style," adding that it possessed "the vivacity and freshness of the contemporary observer and narrator." Abroad, the September, 1847, *Quarterly Review* asserted expansively, "Spanish America is fortunate in her historian." A remarkably similar note in the *Blackwood's Edinburgh Magazine* for July, 1847, stated that "Mr. Prescott has added to his well-merited reputation by his narrative of the Conquest of Peru." By way of summation, the reader was reminded that Prescott had "produced three long and important historical works, conspicuous by their impartiality, research and elegance; entitling him to an exceedingly honourable position amongst writers in the English tongue, and to one of the loftiest places in the as yet scantily filled gallery of American men of letters."

In New York, Philip Hone jotted in his diary the statement, "Prescott has established his claim to rank as *the* historian of the United States." [8] Within one decade a literary nobody of 1837 had scaled the scholarly literary heights that carried with them, for Prescott, repeated accolades as one of the world's finest historians.

Popular with the reading public as well as with the critics, Prescott's works were repeatedly reprinted during his lifetime, prompting the author's persistent relations, at home and abroad, with numerous members of the "slippery trade." The short-lived American Stationers' Company of Boston published

Ferdinand and Isabella in the winter of 1837/38, following which Little, Brown & Company of the same city published the work numerous times in the years 1838–44. With his *Conquest of Mexico,* Prescott shifted his American publication arrangement to New York and Harper and Brothers. Following the success of the new history, the old one was also transferred to that house, from which, in turn, also came the *Miscellanies* and the *Conquest of Peru.* After somewhat more than a decade with the house of Harper, Prescott transferred his publishing allegiance back to Boston, to Phillips, Sampson, and Company, which publishing house, after introducing the earliest volumes of *Philip the Second* in 1855, quickly reissued all the earlier works as well. From their press came *Charles the Fifth* and Prescott's last work, the third volume of *Philip the Second.*

In the twenty-two years of its publication during Prescott's lifetime, *Ferdinand and Isabella,* bearing the imprints of four American houses, appeared in the United States in more than twenty impressions. At least one printing appeared every year in the United States between 1837 and 1859, with the exception of 1842, 1847, and 1855. On numerous occasions, more than one impression appeared in a given year. The later works, with mounting popularity for Prescott and, consequently, larger editions, likewise ran to numerous printings during the author's lifetime. Such circumstances promoted continuing ties between Prescott and his publishers.[9]

In England, some circumstances were similar and some dissimilar—the mounting popularity and successive editions resembled the American experience, while the number of publishers and certain of the problems between author and publisher were different.

Behind Prescott's works of recognized worth, past and present, lies the significant area of the author's relations with his publishers. The contracts, memoranda, financial settlements, and voluminous correspondence between the historian and his four American and two English publishers serve as the materials for the story behind his books. In detailing that story, we may, it is hoped, enlarge our awareness not only of the nature of William Hickling Prescott but also of the world in which he lived. Herein lies the story of the stereotype plate, a new factor on the changing publishing scene. Offered, too, is a case-study of mid-nineteenth-century publishing agreements. Likewise present is the exasperatingly persistent problem of international copyright.

Prescott's relations with his publishers demonstrate the lengths and depths of author concern about the physical side of his intellectual product as he actively insists on his own ideas of book design and book manufacture. Eager for acceptance and reputation, Prescott also was party to new and widening concepts of promotion and distribution. Some of the fruits of literary success were financial, with Prescott's career an instance in which literary and scholarly considerations were always accompanied by financial aspects of authorship. And because the man was so much a social being, he never was simply a scholar. His relationships with his publishers, therefore, were never so completely formal and business-like that they precluded the warm, personal side of author-publisher relations possible in a day devoid of agents and editors.

In Prescott's career is a view of the publishing business in a variety of forms—the complacent bookseller-publishing operation in restricted locale and the dynamic printing-publishing activity of the promotion-minded houses conscious of the national scene. Prescott's ties with his American publishers fall within the transitional period which established the dominance of New York City over Boston and Philadelphia in the American book world. Here is the tie between a scholarly gentleman of aristocratic temperament and money-grubbing booksellers and publishers of a different social world. This is a case study of an author's ceaseless quest for beauty and quality of product in a period during which cheap, pirated printings of contemporary authors denied such prospects to classics priced at 10 and 25 cents per volume in competition with Prescott's works priced at $2.00 and $2.50 per volume.

Prescott's enjoyment of this previously unmentioned side of his life is evident in his letter to the Harpers on January 22, 1846, in which he insisted, "As I have got beyond . . . sending and receiving love-letters, I find the most agreeable part of my correspondence is [of late with] Publishers."

The historian's awareness that the competitive and commercial aspects of the publishing business commonly led to the production of cheap and tawdry books underscored his insistence that a fine book could not remain such in the estimation of the public unless it appeared in fine form. To that end, he expended much effort and money and demanded that his publishers do likewise. One of the best means of assuring basic compliance with his outlook lay in the systematic and regular conversion of his manuscripts into stereotype plates independent of, and generally prior to, his negotiations with his publishers. For Prescott, the stereotype plate became the catalyst to ever-widening author-publisher relations.

———•———

CHAPTER TWO

THE STEREOTYPE PLATES

ONE OF THE OLDEST of the duplicating processes intended to reduce cost and speed printing, stereotyping was winning wide acceptance in the United States in the 1830's, a century after its introduction by William Ged of Edinburgh and almost two decades in advance of widespread British use of the process. Basically, stereotyping calls for the making of a mould of each type-page. Into each mould is poured molten metal which, upon cooling, forms a solid plate, reproducing the original type. Many refinements followed, including that of 1846 by which moulds of papier-mâché permitted the adaptation of stereotype plates to rotary machines, but all of Prescott's matrices, manufactured between 1837 and 1858, appear to have been of the old type for use on flat-bed presses.

Stereotyping made printing cheaper. A very modest amount of type enabled a printer to produce an entire book, because as soon as one stereotype matrix was completed the type could be distributed and employed again in the next plate. In addition, the plates could be used indefinitely, thereby cutting drastically the cost of any subsequent printing of the

same work and augmenting the speed with which it
could be produced.[1] As the artisan yielded to the
machine to make printing increasingly a process and
less an art, stereotyping became a boon to the expanding and changing publishing industry.

To the author—and in Prescott's case it was he
and not the publisher who financed the stereotype
plates for his works—stereotyping meant, at least
initially, something quite different. Never possessed
of the economic compulsions of an author depend-
ing upon his literary income for his daily bread, and
at the beginning of his publishing career not in the
least given to the thought that his book would call
forth successive editions, Prescott embraced the new
process for other reasons. As a man of fashion, fastidious in his dress, a connoisseur of fine food and
drink, and generally *au courant* with polite social
practice, it was not difficult for this Boston author to
adopt a trend which was increasingly fashionable
in American publishing circles. At a moment when
authors commonly held publishers suspect, the employment of stereotype plates, by narrowing the
range of the publisher's freedom of action, served
automatically to allay such suspicions. In other
words, the use of stereotype plates by an author
rendered publishing a less slippery trade. And at the
same time it also served to harmonize author-publisher relations by replacing uncertainty with cer-
tainty. Any author resorting to stereotype could
impose some precedent-making standards upon his
publisher. With stereotype plates, broken type could
be minimized; with stereotype plates no crowding of
lines could occur. Indeed, by means of stereotype
plates the author could establish patterns for such

major areas of book production that the publisher could well nigh be forced to reflect the tone of the outlook of the author in much of the remaining manufacturing process. With numerous reasons for his embracing the use of stereotype plates, Prescott had two decades of varied experiences with them, among them some unanticipated ones.

"I wish to consult you fully," Prescott wrote to Sparks on February 25, 1837, when he contemplated his first book, "as to the best way of getting out the book—the size of the volumes etc.—I count on you for all the information relative to the mysteries of the trade." William H. Prescott, having spent the last ten of his forty years quietly researching and writing in his father's Bedford Street residence, was ready to commit his manuscript on Ferdinand and Isabella to print.

Turning to Jared Sparks was a natural thing, for few, if any other, of the literary men of Boston could match Sparks' knowledge of the problems and pitfalls of publication in the late 1830's. A Harvard graduate of the class of 1815, the year following Prescott, Sparks had early joined Prescott in helping to found Club, the social-literary group composed of two dozen vigorous young minds of the emergent Athens of the New World. Club's brief experiment in 1820 with its own publication paled beside Sparks' handling of the editorship of the majestically authoritative *North American Review* for a half-dozen years—years during which he sharpened his facility for evaluating manuscripts and during which he learned to organize and get fat numbers of the review through the press, issues containing almost a dozen articles by Prescott. More recently, since surrendering the editorship of the "old North," Sparks' successive historical works had widened his acquaintance with the ins-and-outs of American publishing.

At that moment, just as Club-member William H. Gardiner previously had done, Sparks was evaluating the thick "Ferdinand and Isabella" manuscript when Prescott's frank plea for further assistance reached him in Cambridge. The accompanying dinner invitation served to bring Sparks, Longfellow, and William Amory to the Prescott table on Tuesday, March 2. Making the most of the occasion, the disarmingly gracious host capitalized upon Sparks' experience. Among other points Sparks emphasized was the idea that Prescott should have his manuscript stereotyped. By the next morning Prescott, having given the suggestion further consideration, concluded in a letter to Sparks, "The more I think of the stereotyping the better I am pleased with the arrangement—if I can secure the services of a good midwife to bring my bantling into the world."

Helped by Sparks, he next turned to another successfully published author, George Bancroft, the first volume of whose *History of the United States* had left many readers hungering for more on the same noble theme. In producing that successful scholarly history, Bancroft also had offered the reading public a beautifully printed and attractively bound book. So the historian of Spain, mulling over Sparks' helpful hints, penned a letter on March 6 to Bancroft, who was still rejoicing over the inauguration of fellow-Democrat Van Buren as president. In Prescott's letter of March 6 to Bancroft in which he asked whether he should stereotype or print in the usual way the work he already had planned for three stout octavo volumes, Prescott indicated his preference. "Will you have the goodness to let me know, in a few words," he wrote, "what your stereotyping costs you, and what agreement you have made with Bowen?"

Having put to Bancroft the probing personal kind of question one could address only to an intimate, Prescott also directed a similar inquiry to Sparks. Sparks, hard at work readying his *Life of George Washington* for publication, even sent his contract to Prescott, presumably at the latter's request.

A month later, the historian's contract of April 10, 1837, with the American Stationers' Company called for his furnishing the stereotype plates from which they would print their edition of 1,250 copies.[2]

Turning to Folsom, Wells and Thurston of Cambridge with his bulky work, Prescott contracted for the manufacture of his first set of stereotype plates. Directly descended from the University Press of Cambridge, which William Hilliard had founded in 1800, this press was an important reason why Boston, in the first half of the nineteenth century, was renowned as the producer of the finest books in America. Owner-management changes were frequent, as in 1842 when Charles R. Metcalf, Omen S. Keith, and George Nichols became the owners, with Marshall T. Bigelow succeeding Keith in 1843, but consistently high quality work, stemming in large measure from the continuing influence of scholarly Charles Folsom, marked the operation of the Cambridge establishment from the 1830's into the 1850's.[3] With the single exception of those for his *Miscellanies,* all the Prescott plates were produced in Cambridge, first by Folsom, Wells and Thurston, then Metcalf, Keith and Nichols, and finally Metcalf and Company. The interrelation of all these printing establishments is evident also in their common use of the title, Printers to the University. The quality of their work, the fairness of their prices, the timetable of their operations, as well as their nearness to Prescott's base of operations, commended them to the historian.

From the half-title page of volume one through the closing printer's notice in the third volume, the job represented somewhat more than 1,600 pages. For the initial set of plates, complicated and made more costly by continuing corrections by the author, Folsom, Wells and Thurston received $2,143.90.[4] By early autumn the plates were finished. Studying a proof off them, Prescott singled out the errata which impelled corrections in the plates. Throughout the stereotyping, Charles Folsom, who rendered such continuing services across the decades that he deservedly won the sobriquet "Cambridge Aldus," helped Prescott perfect the plates. Finally, all was in readiness for the printing of the book.

Amid harmonious relations all around, the presses ran off thirteen hundred copies in two impressions. Then the American Stationers' Company, caught in the trough of national depression, quickly collapsed, less than six months after the initial appearance of Prescott's book.

Salvaging his stereotype plates, which, indeed, had never been in the publisher's hands, since they were used in Cambridge by the firm of printers that had manufactured them, the historian looked about for another publisher. No such contingency had prompted his recourse to the plates originally, but the author now had an additional reason for believing in and insisting upon them for all time in the future. Nor was this the only instance of its kind, because Prescott's last American publisher also went bankrupt.

In its first article, the contract of May 14, 1838, with Little, Brown & Company stipulated that their edition of seventeen hundred copies would be printed from Prescott's plates. With all presswork on the stereotype plates to be performed by Folsom, Wells and Thurston, the stereotype plates were to remain in their possession in Cambridge unless written consent by Prescott permitted their removal to some other press. Any damage suffered by the plates while serving the purposes of Little, Brown & Company would be chargeable to the publisher.[5] Year after year the plates were used by the Cambridge printers.

With the *Conquest of Mexico* ready for publication and the author desirous of doing business with a publisher who offered the widest distribution, Prescott contracted with the Harpers of New York for a first printing of five thousand copies, the edition to be printed from stereotype plates provided by the author. To John Lloyd Stephens, possessed of his own interests in Latin America, Prescott wrote on March 29, 1843, as follows: "I am now . . . up to my eyes in Stereotyping." [6] June and July not only found that work continuing, it saw Prescott pointing out errata in the finished plates, as when he wrote to printer Metcalf on July 31, 1843: "Please to correct these *errors* in the plates. On the top of page 306, change the figure V to VI.—Number the pages *355* & *452* and also insert the pages *277* & *278* which were omitted in one of my copies from the stereotype plates." Sometimes a later communication from the author retracted corrections previously made on the stereotype proofs.

The correction of plate proofs was one of the many tasks allotted Edmund B. Otis, reader-secretary to Prescott between 1842 and 1846, the most productive period of the historian's total career. Like others who served in that capacity—he was eighth in a line of ten—Otis was a college man in his twenties who, on graduation, combined some remunerative labor with Prescott with further study for the launching of a professional career. Otis, like those for whom the record is fuller, probably received four hundred dollars a year for five hours of work per day, the hours to be designated by the historian. For Otis, the daily stint became an exceedingly regular period, beginning at 9 A.M. In addition, the employer was liable for food expenses, outside Boston, in excess of three dollars weekly.

In the process of converting manuscript to stereotype plates, Prescott played widely varying roles, but essentially he was a book manufacturing generalissimo, somewhat removed from the fray of actual production. On occasion, no pre- or post-stereotyping problem was too minute for his personal attention. But his identification with this activity stemmed from many things: his involvement in digesting materials or writing a draft of his next work, the condition of his eyesight, his general health, his social inclinations and involvements, and a certain impetuosity of character that stamped him pleasantly unpredictable.

By late June the author habitually had made his annual summertime trek to Nahant. At most a momentary interruption to his routine, this shift of scene cast Prescott even more completely in the role of literary generalissimo—firing memos and letters to the printer in Cambridge and to the secretary-reader in Boston, with passing attention accorded channels of communication that included the mails, express service, and personal messengers. A typical operation is the following outlined to printer George Nichols in a letter of July 20, 1843.

> I shall send up today the remainder of Book VI which will be left at Little & Brown's for Mr. Greenleaf to carry to Cambridge tomorrow at 12 o'clock. This book contains, according to my calculations, 230 pages. I have already received 80 of them, and there now remains sufficient to last you till next Thursday, the day before which, on Wednesday, I will send you a fresh supply, equal to a hundred pages.

Prescott's calculation was uncannily accurate, for the pertinent part of the third volume of the *Conquest of Mexico* contains 229 pages.

Much of the same routine was in order when his late spring and early autumn junkets found Prescott enjoying life at Pepperell. The following communication to Nichols, on September 25, 1843, is typical.

> My mother is in town & will return to Pepperell on Thursday morng 7 ocl. So if you have not sent the proofs from the Plates to the House in Bedford St., I shall be glad if you can do it by Wednesday in season for her to bring the copy to me.

On occasion, and specifically with the *Conquest of Mexico,* Prescott found himself a victim of pressures. He was caught between the publishers on the one hand and the conversion of manuscript to stereotype plate on the other. Having concluded his work with the manuscript of his history in March, 1843, Prescott inaugurated what was intended to be a leisurely process of converting it to stereotype. Weeks later, the contract of late April with the Harpers did nothing in itself to upset that expectation. Of course it was the unwritten expectation of both author and publisher that the new book would be ready before the year ended. Indeed, the state of communications and transportation in the interior of the country suggested it would be highly advisable to launch the book some weeks before Christmas. When the promotion-conscious New York house began to talk of issuing one volume per month, beginning in September or October, some element of pressure on the stereotyping schedule arose. In mid-June the contract for the English edition was agreed upon, and Bentley, knowing that he had no legal exclusive right to publish the book in England, understandably insisted that he have a fortnight's advantage over the American publisher, lest some American copy reach England and serve to inspire a competing English edition for his in London. At first glance, a two weeks margin for Bentley appears to be a mere trifle, but it must be remembered that he expected to use proof sheets from the stereotype plates, with their transportation requiring still another ten days to two weeks. So it was that the early season American edition, which had to be preceded by the English edition for which the stereotype proofs were to serve as fair copy, gradually so shortened the time for producing, proofing, and correcting the stereotype plates that Prescott found himself unpleasantly hurried. One such experience was, for Prescott, one too many.

The experience was agonizingly distasteful to him, and as he apologized to the stereotypers, who seemingly bore up under it well, Prescott was obviously upset. As a man whose disposition and manner of living cried out for freedom of action, he never subjected himself knowingly to controls imposed from the outside, even though he made, broke, and remade many tight regimens for himself. Accordingly, the unpleasant experience of 1843 led him to resolve that in future contracts he would insist upon safeguards against the prospect of such unseemly haste being thrust upon him and his stereotypers a second time.

Prescott paid for his stereotyping in terms of friendship as well as dollars, paving the way, even as one book was finished, for the production of the next. For example, he wrote George Nichols on October 5, 1843: "I am much pleased with the appearance of the volumes [*Conquest of Mexico*]. They show the excellence of the plates. . . . I am truly obliged by the thorough revision & re-revision you have given the work. But instead of the imperfect copy I shall ask you to oblige me by accepting one of the N. York edition with the plates & maps when it comes out." The friendly sentiments bestowed upon the printer by the author obviously were reciprocated, because Nichols, proud of his identification with Prescott's latest work, was treasuring one of the copies of proof run off at Cambridge.

Indeed, the historian exhibited a tendency to praise his stereotypers at the expense of his publisher. Begrudgingly admitting to his absent friend Edward Everett that his New York publishers had published his second work in a style that matched his first book, he revealingly added, "Yet the merit of the typography belongs to the Cambridge printers." [7] When the presswork was taken out of their hands, Metcalf, Keith and Nichols meticulously struck their names off the plates before shipping them to the Harpers. Prescott, neither told nor anticipating this, engaged in an angry flurry of correspondence with his publisher about the absence of the names of his stereotypers before he learned the truth.

The reception given the big edition of the *Conquest of Mexico,* plus the expiration of his contract with Little, Brown & Company, led the historian next to contract with the Harpers for the publication of *Ferdinand and Isabella.* After making certain that all were in good repair, he sent, via Harnden Express, and with a covering letter dated November 19, 1844, not only the plates for the text but also the five plates of engraved portraits which had graced recent issues of that work. In such fashion Prescott implemented his insistence that the New York printing resemble one of the last Boston editions.

In both its contents and its pre-publication history, Prescott's third book differed from its predecessors. The author had unusually clean copy for his *Miscellanies,* because, after all, it consisted of previously published essays. Bentley, first to work with the slightly altered essays, sent Prescott proofs of successive portions of the forthcoming volume. These Prescott quickly shuttled to the Harpers, to whom he wrote on June 24, 1845: "I send you the proofs of the 'Miscellanies'—the first 96 pages—as far as I have received them. . . . I will send you more, as I receive them." Less than three weeks later, with another ship in with English proofs, Prescott hurried a second batch to New York, which he described in a letter of July 10 as "looked over by me—essentially correct." At the end of the first week of August, according to a Prescott memorandum dated August 7, seven weeks after the initial shipment to them, the Harpers held a full set of the London proofs.

Meanwhile, publisher and author had exchanged views on the subject of stereotyping. "How would you like," Harper and Brothers wrote Prescott on June 10, 1845, "for us to publish the work *on shares?* —We to advance all the funds necessary to get the volume stereotyped (in Boston), and published in the style desired, and pay you one-half of the profits." Already unhappy in a half-profits arrangement with Bentley in London, Prescott replied as follows: "I don't much like the idea of publishing on Shares." He added:

> I should prefer to stereotype the book at my own expense—& to own the plates and sell you any number of copies that you may . . . require.
>
> Or secondly, . . . sell whole affair outright for $2000 . . . to be pd in 1 yr of publication.

As a last resort, Prescott would accept the Harper suggestion.

As finally agreed, in compromise fashion, the

Harpers produced stereotype plates in New York City from Bentley's proofs of the *Miscellanies* under an agreement by which author and publisher divided the expense between them. Accordingly, when informed at time of completion that their total cost was $449.60, Prescott forwarded his payment of $224.80 in a letter dated August 7, 1845. Though satisfied with the volume, Prescott, for the first time, was not in complete control of the basic text of one of his books. Several circumstances explain this deviation from his normal desire and procedure.

The control, by the Harpers, of the copyright on one of the items included in the *Miscellanies,* the study of Charles Brockden Brown, must have induced some of his willingness to go fifty-fifty this time. Also, had Prescott insisted upon their manufacture in Cambridge, he might have had to bear the shipping expenses as well as responsibility for delay in the appearance of the American edition of a work which was soon to be available in London. Likewise, he probably remembered the pressures on him in stereotyping the *Conquest of Mexico.* This possibly encouraged his acceptance of a formula which clearly eliminated the prospect of any such recurrence. However impelling such reasons were in 1845, they soon dimmed before Prescott's persistent urge to have complete control of the plates behind his literary offspring. After switching his publishing affiliation back to Boston a decade later, Prescott bought out the half-interest held by the Harpers in the plates for the *Miscellanies.*

Prescott invariably turned to the manufacture of his stereotype plates before he reached terms with a publisher, and thus eliminated completely the prospect of any editorial revision of his manuscript. He did so with a standard of values which he carefully maintained. "I have arranged with the Printer," he told the Harpers on December 12, 1846, concerning his *Conquest of Peru,* "to have stereotype plates made of it so as to correspond precisely with the other works."

More than eight years elapsed between the appearance of the *Conquest of Peru* and that of the first volumes of *Philip the Second,* years during which, in the absence of the production of new plates, considerable attention was bestowed upon old ones.

On December 10, 1853, the Harper establishment suffered devastating fire. Ten buildings burned, and amid the million-dollar loss every one of the thirty-four large-size Adams presses were destroyed, along with all plates then upon them. Prescott was doubly concerned: for the future of the publishing company for which he had come to have real affection and also for the physical safety of his numerous and invaluable stereotype plates. The complete sets for all four of his books were in New York. Fortunately, no set of Prescott's plates was in immediate use; they reposed, instead, safely in the storage vault under the pavement.

In reply to the historian's direct query, the Harpers wrote him on December 28, 1853: "The plates of all your works, we are happy to inform you, are *safe;*—and we intend to reprint from them as soon as we can possibly find presses & paper." Prescott penned his pent-up relief several months later, in a letter dated February, 1854: "I am very glad to understand by your letter that my stereotype plates are all safe." To replace the burned stock of Pres-

cott titles, the author urged his publisher to print
the number of copies destroyed without any thought
of paying additional royalties to him.

Rather than because of misunderstandings with
his New York connection or because of their recent
fire, the promise of bigger royalties for his forthcoming *Philip the Second* lured Prescott back into
Boston publishing circles in the middle of 1854. The
contract with Phillips, Sampson, and Company
called for Prescott's producing the stereotype
plates, from which the publisher would print the first
and second volumes of the new history. Subsequent
volumes of the work, as yet unwritten, would also be
converted to stereotype by the historian.

The initial publication of a new title by the Harpers had led to the shifting of the plates for an earlier
work to that firm. Now the stereotype plates of
Ferdinand and Isabella, the *Conquest of Mexico,*
and the *Conquest of Peru* were to be transferred to
Boston for use by Phillips, Sampson, and Company
within one year of the initial publication of the first
volumes of *Philip the Second.* Within that same
period the plates for the nonhistorical *Miscellanies*
were to be put at the disposal of the Boston publisher
by the author. Phillips, Sampson, and Company
promised, in regard to all the plates so entrusted to
them, to bear full responsibility for them above and
beyond reasonable wear and tear.[8]

The pledge by Prescott concerning the *Miscellanies* necessitated one of two courses of action with
reference to the Harpers: a division of the set of
plates he owned jointly with them (plus the production of the half he did not own) or the purchase of
the Harper half-interest. Prior to the completion

of his new Boston agreement, Prescott explored the issue of the stereotype plates for the *Miscellanies* with the Harpers and found them both friendly and co-operative. "We shall be happy," they wrote to him on July 29, 1854, "to dispose of our interest in the plates of the 'Misc' at a reasonable rate—say the price charged for stereotyping at Cambridge." Within forty-eight hours of the signing of the new contract with the Boston house, Prescott was negotiating the purchase of the Harper interest. For the sum of $224.80, the historian acquired the publisher's half-interest in the plates. Simultaneously, the New York house granted Prescott the right to use the one item in that collection of essays on which the Harpers held the copyright.

With the completion of the *Philip the Second* plates in the spring of 1855, Prescott turned his thoughts to the plates that he would soon order from New York to Boston. To his friend and confidant Jared Sparks he put his problem as follows in a letter of July 6, 1855:

> I shall not take my works from the Harpers until the autumn; and before doing so it seems to me that I am entitled, under a clause in my contract with them, which I enclose [it provided for indemnification by the publisher for damage due to use], to claim some compensation for the damaged condition of the plates. I suppose there can be no doubt they ought to have touched up the plates occasionally while in their hands. As this has not been done they are now very much defaced; and Metcalf tells me it will cost $75 a volume to repair the broken letters. This I suppose would be considered something more than ordinary wear and tear.

As I understand that you have had occasion to make such a claim yourself, & have had it allowed, I should be much obliged if you would give me your opinion on the subject.

In view of the fact that the Harpers had the plates for nine volumes, under four titles, this represented the sizable sum of $675 for plate repairs. Having resorted to stereotype originally upon the hearty recommendation of Sparks, the historian was turning in the right direction for advice.

Expressing his desire that the plates be readied for shipment to Boston, Prescott raised the issue of plate damage with his publisher. Seeking an exchange of views on the subject, he was confident, as he wrote to the Harpers on July 24, 1855, that his publisher would "do what is right by me."

The plates of the *Conquest of Mexico,* in fifty boxes, left New York for Boston early in September, to be repaired there for Prescott at the Harpers' expense, it being understood, the Harpers agreed in a September 6 letter to Prescott, that they would stand behind "such repairs as have arisen from careless usage." As fast as they could box them, the New York house promised to ship the other plates. Fifty-two boxes of plates for *Ferdinand and Isabella* left the Harpers' hands the following day, September 7, as did thirty-six boxes of plates for the *Conquest of Peru* on September 12. On September 20, the last plates, those for the *Miscellanies,* were readied for shipment to Boston.

Under the watchful supervision of the original manufacturer of all of the plates except those of the *Miscellanies,* the desired repairs were effected in

Cambridge. For them, Harpers honored Prescott's draft in the amount of $63.50. The wide disparity between this charge and Metcalf's estimate possibly derived from that printer's too hasty glance at some of the latest printings of Prescott's works. The small damage charge also indicated that the plates had not been subjected to careless handling by the Harpers.

With the completion of the stereotype plates for *Philip the Second* and the initiation of the movement of the earlier plates to Boston, Prescott had turned to the writing of the brief post-abdication career of Charles V. Concluding that limited labor, he contracted for its publication by Phillips, Sampson, and Company in what became an unusual stereotyping arrangement. Prescott's addition to Robertson's previously published history of the Spanish monarch constituted less than two hundred pages in a total of approximately seventeen hundred pages of material, in consequence of which Prescott apparently had less reason than usual to desire control of all the plates.

The plates manufactured by Metcalf and Company of Cambridge were paid for as follows: Prescott provided at his expense those serving his original contribution, and he and the publisher divided the expense for the Robertson portion of the work. However, the contract provided, according to Prescott's memorandum of January 14, 1856, that, should Prescott come to want his usual complete control of the plates, the historian could purchase the publisher's interest.

By the spring of 1858 the third volume of *Philip the Second* was so near completion that Prescott began to convert it to stereotype form, once again using the facilities of Metcalf and his associates. A leisurely pace was insured by Prescott's precautions as he recovered from his February stroke of apoplexy and as the entire nation wallowed in a financial depression that delayed publication. By mid-August the stereotype plates for the thin third volume of the exhausted historian's last and unfinished work neared completion.

Because of such variables as eyesight, general health, age, social involvements, and historical labors, the stereotyping quotas set by Prescott fluctuated widely from book to book and even from one part to another of the same work. With the numerous limitations of a first effort, the stereotyping of *Ferdinand and Isabella* stretched from spring well into the autumn of 1837. His second work, with its stereotyping initiated in April, 1843, scheduled the conversion of ten pages of manuscript into stereotype daily. On June 2, 1843, Prescott informed his publisher: "My first volume you can have when you wish, except the preface & contents. . . . My second volume will probably be stereotyped by the last of July; the first half of the third volume will be stereotyped by the last of August—but the whole work will not be completed till the latter part of September or the first of October." However, pressures from his publishers forced a revision of schedule, and Prescott appealed to the stereotypers, Metcalf and Company, in an undated letter in July for thirty pages per day, adding, "I can take care of them . . . we have no more days to lose, I assure."

With the *Conquest of Peru,* Prescott proceeded to push fourteen pages through the stereotyping process daily, according to a letter to the Harpers of December 21, 1846. All must have gone well because, eight weeks later, on February 26, 1847, Prescott reported to the Harpers: "My printing goes on swimmingly. I am someways now in the second volume."

Eight years later the older, wearier, and weakened historian could not maintain that pace. For the first volumes of *Philip the Second* he also planned to transform manuscript into plates at the rate of 14 pages per day, but the burden was too much for his eyes, and he reduced the daily schedule to 10 pages. Whereas the initial schedule for the 2 volumes totaling approximately 1,300 pages would have required about 90 work days, the revised production program demanded 130 days, about 6 weeks additional time, or so Prescott reported to Bentley in a letter of December 5, 1854. Although his desire to give the finishing touches to his plates never diminished, Prescott's physical capacity to do the job declined perceptibly in the 1850's.

However, only when he stopped writing history did Prescott free himself from his interest in and concern about stereotype plates. Every American contract had called for stereotype plates; and every English one, except that for the relatively trifling *Miscellanies,* implied publisher access to sheets from those plates.

For example, in March, 1837, at which time Prescott, dedicated to stereotyping *Ferdinand and Isabella,* had contracted for its publication neither in America nor in England, the historian wrote his agent in London, "Should you not be able to make an agreement with a good publisher, I would strike off a number of copies from my stereotype plates, and send them in sheets to London." [9] This intended use of the plates beyond the Atlantic never materialized, but it early indicated Prescott's intention of using them anywhere and everywhere to his best advantage.

Six weeks later, with both his American and English publishing needs covered by contracts, Prescott informed Richard Bentley: "As the work is to be stereotyped here, I propose also to forward to you by the Liverpool packet every week the proof sheets as they shall be struck off." [10] Months later, on October 4, 1837, Prescott proudly informed his London publisher: "I have now performed what I proposed . . . my printer . . . has forwarded the last parcel of *Ferdinand and Isabella* to London. I hope they will be found of the service I anticipated in saving the English printer time and trouble." Thus, with his first book, Prescott established a practice he persistently followed—that of sending proof sheets off the stereotype plates as the fair copy for the English printer. This was always the primary relationship between the stereotype plates and the English editions. But though proofs from every plate crossed the Atlantic to speed English editions, no Prescott plate ever sailed the ocean. And even though he came to depend upon such proofs regularly, Bentley never followed them so closely as to duplicate their lineation and pagination. So used, the stereotype plates helped the English publishers, but they never guaranteed the measure of author control over the London printings that he exercised over the American ones.

Incidentally, no record exists of any shipment of proofs ever failing to reach its London destination, but Prescott so scheduled the shipments as to eliminate the prospect of delay and inconvenience such a mishap might occasion. His practice of sending the proofs piecemeal partially served that end. As an added safeguard, the author sent duplicates of the first shipment with the second, duplicates of the second with the third, etc. When two copies of a certain batch of proofs moved almost simultaneously toward England, they did so as a matter of precaution, by different vessels. Such procedures eliminated the headaches any lost part of the manuscript could have produced. The record is sufficiently erratic that one concludes that Prescott had no one and only addressee for those packages—some went direct to Bentley, while others only reached the publisher via the author's London agent, Colonel Thomas Aspinwall. Nor did the batches of proof always travel as ordinary packages aboard ship. They often were ensconced in the diplomatic pouch, thanks to Prescott's numerous and influential contacts within the diplomatic establishment.

Because the *Miscellanies* represented a simple republication, with minimal editing, of previously published essays, the usual relationship between American proofs and English editions was broken. It served Bentley's purposes just as well for corrected copies of the printed articles to come his way. Such he received from Prescott.

Never as popular in British publishing circles as in American in those years, stereotype plates were adopted by Bentley for Prescott's works only as the

copyright furor of the mid-1850's, with promise of
bitter competition, required cheaper printings for
the editions he needed in the London market.

With *Charles the Fifth* and Prescott's shift from
Bentley to Routledge as his second and only other
English publisher, the long-established routine persisted as Prescott sent the new stereotype proofs
across the Atlantic. So it was, too, when Routledge
outbid Bentley for the third volume of *Philip the
Second,* for the historian informed Routledge on
September 20, 1858, "I now accede to your proposal
and send by this steamer the sheets of the 3d vol."
Prescott had penned his last line to an English publisher concerning proof sheets.

With tight schedules between dates of publication
in England and America commonplace rather than
unusual, and with the author trying from a distance
to minimize error in the London editions, Prescott's
stereotype plates played a significant role in relation
to the London editions. They helped foreign publishers get his titles out in fine style—a major consideration with Prescott—and at reduced expense—
a major consideration of every publisher. This very
measure of co-operation extended Bentley and Routledge possibly intensified the historian's unconcealed
disgruntlement over his meager English earnings.

Then, too, the exact number of copies of each book
produced from the original stereotype plates cannot be ascertained, but the record of their use is remarkable. The plates for *Ferdinand and Isabella*
remained with the Cambridge printers between 1837
and 1844 for the production of eleven impressions
by the American Stationers' Company and Little,

Brown & Company, one of which the latter house sent to Paris in 1842. Transferred to New York City and the custody of the Harpers in time for their 1845 impression, the plates remained there until 1855, and saw use almost every year. Returned to Boston, for the use of Phillips, Sampson, and Company, the plates were used by that company regularly every year, beginning with 1856, down to the death of Prescott. The year 1859, with its depressed economic conditions, also witnessed the demise of Phillips, Sampson, and Company. The author's heirs contracted for the use of the plates by J. B. Lippincott Company of Philadelphia, by whom they saw repeated use until September, 1873,[11] a life of more than thirty-five years.

The pattern of use of the other sets of stereotype plates in America resembled that of those behind the first book. Those for the *Conquest of Mexico,* manufactured in 1843 in Cambridge, were used initially in New York City. After somewhat more than a decade of heavy use there, they were returned to Boston for use by Phillips, Sampson, and Company, beginning in 1856. After the death of Prescott these plates, too, went to Philadelphia and the custody of the Lippincott firm, by whom they were used until 1873.

A decade after the manufacture in New York in 1845 of the plates for the *Miscellanies,* Prescott bought out the Harpers' half-interest and transferred them to Boston. There Phillips, Sampson, and Company used them between 1855 and 1859, after which they, too, immediately went to Philadelphia. In Lippincott's hands they were used until

1875. Needless to say, the stereotype plates of these essays did not experience the same heavy use as did those for the histories.

Manufactured under the watchful eye of the author in 1847, the plates for the *Conquest of Peru* also were first used by the Harpers. In 1855, the year which witnessed both the last Harper and the first Phillips, Sampson, and Company impressions, they were returned to Boston. Shifted to Philadelphia after the death of the author and the dissolution of his last Boston publisher, the plates were used by Lippincott until 1874.

The plates for *Philip the Second,* two volumes in 1855 and the third in 1858, saw use in Boston and Philadelphia, with Lippincott employing them through 1873. The 1856 plates for the Robertson-Prescott *Charles the Fifth* duplicated the pattern of the *Philip the Second* plates, with Lippincott using them until 1875.

The varying lifetimes of these sets of plates had little relation to use. If such had been the case, the lesser-used plates for the *Miscellanies, Philip the Second,* and *Charles the Fifth* might have known longer lives. On the other hand, the oldest and most heavily used plates—use based on popularity, not age—for *Ferdinand and Isabella,* the *Conquest of Mexico,* and the *Conquest of Peru* deserved retirement before they achieved it, for the ragged state of many of the late impressions of those titles from the original plates is apparent even to any untrained critic of printing.

Prescott, economic man as well as historian, allowed the stereotype plates to pose a long-term dilemma for him. From a very early moment, his dissatisfaction with the text and notes of his various titles led him, as historian in search of scholarly perfection, to make many corrections, and to desire even more, in the expensive plates. However, his investment in stereotyping early drove him to the realization that only minor changes could be effected—the kind that simply extended in brief fashion a note that was open at the bottom of the page or the rare change in the text manipulated in exactly the same number of type spaces as the old text had required, as he noted, for example, in a letter of September 2, 1843, to Nichols.

On this score the difference between English and American editions is recorded as early as the autumn of 1839 in a letter addressed to Bentley: "I am anxious that your editions, which are not fettered by stereotype, should come out as complete as possible." [12] Also, when Prescott sent Bentley a sheaf of corrections and additions preparatory to the issuance of a new London edition, the author blandly indicated some of them "were too long to be worked into stereotype, and of course will not appear in our American copies." [13]

That the stereotype plates represented a kind of strait jacket that persistently troubled Prescott is evident in his frustrated desire to correct his *Conquest of Mexico*. "For the next error, Vol. III p. 55, note," he wrote the printer Nichols on September 14, 1843, "I would strike out the remark on Clavigero, but stereotype forbids as that would leave a gap. Could you not substitute Italian words of Clavigero? This would destroy the point of the note but would corroborate the text. Any matter will do, on a pinch, so long as it is not a blunder to fill up a chink

in the notes.'' This solution appears in the published
book, but no large-scale revision was possible in his
American editions, and only one book, the *Miscellanies,* for which he manufactured added plates to
cover his review of 1850 of friend Ticknor's book,
ever knew a significant change through addition. In
consequence of this, later English editions of his
works, quite often produced on separate type set-
tings, were textually superior to their American
counterparts because they could take into account
any and all corrections and additions.

With the passage of time and the increased number of unused corrections on hand, Prescott anticipated the day when, having worn out the original
stereotype plates, he could offer the public an author's authorized and revised edition of all his works.
Needless to say, such did not come in his lifetime.
With his heirs lacking his interest in scholarly perfection, but sharing his interest in dollar income
from plates long since paid for, they simply continued their use.

In the end, however, the promise of revision and
the mass of notes that facilitated it became a reality
in the hands of the author's last reader-secretary,
John Foster Kirk, when he, freed from the economic
compulsions and scholarly activities which kept Prescott loyal to the original stereotype plates, prepared
the revised editions which Lippincott gave to the
reading public in the 1870's.

Meanwhile, the stereotype plates behind the six
Prescott titles did much to eliminate a major area
in which author-publisher misunderstandings might
easily have developed. Indeed, Prescott's resort to

stereotyping was a primary, though intangible, contribution to the easy relations he knew with every one of his publishers. The plates not only reduced printing costs for the publisher, they also enabled the author to negotiate for the earliest edition bigger royalty payments than usual which, once established, were maintained to the author's advantage. As they lessened tensions, increased income, sped up later printings, and guaranteed an imposition of author standards on the publisher by virtue of their being manufactured prior to any agreement with a publisher, the stereotype plates were indicative of Prescott's interest in book manufacturing and harbinger of the complex publishing agreements to which he became a party.

———◆———

CHAPTER THREE

THE PUBLISHING AGREEMENTS

ALTHOUGH HE LIVED in a boisterously nationalistic period in American history, Prescott appreciated fully the importance of American acceptance in European, especially English, literary circles. Accordingly, he wanted simultaneous publication of his books in England and America. In the twenty-one years of his publishing career, between 1837 and 1858, Prescott entered into contractual relations with four American and two English publishers, and had additional negotiations with two other London houses. The publishing agreements varied greatly, from unspecified numbers of copies in an edition to first editions of twelve thousand copies, from flat guarantees of royalties to the bird-in-the-bush prospect of half-profit arrangements. Some agreements provided for publication of a single title for a single year, unless renewed; others involved as many as five different titles in different sizes over a period of years.

At home and abroad Prescott wanted his books published in beauty and dignity. An astutely capable handler of his own interests in America, Prescott almost always had indispensable assistance from

able agents in London. In America, Prescott enjoyed
relatively good relations with his publishers and
had some financial assurance because of the protection given a national under the American copyright
law. In England, however, he suffered disappoint-
ments, both legal and financial, because of the absence of international copyright. The following
account of Prescott's publishing agreements, a complicated and pivotal phase of author-publisher relations, is established on a title-by-title basis. This
permits immediate comparisons between the domestic and foreign contracts for a given work. In
addition, a chronological approach to the books offers better appreciation of the changing aspect of
the agreements across two decades of expanding
author popularity.

Prescott approached the problem of publication
much as he did that of historical writing. He turned
first to those who were at home in the labyrinth of
manuscript collections and to those who produced
well-received histories—men such as Pascual de
Gayangos and George Bancroft. So, in respect to
publishing he counseled with editors and authors'
agents—persons such as Jared Sparks and Colonel
Thomas Aspinwall. With Prescott, the unendingly
dependent aspect of the scholarly life was underscored by the fact that the historian was addicted
to his Boston. Under the circumstances, the author,
interested in all areas of book manufacturing, was
compelled to employ an agent abroad while he negotiated personally with domestic publishers.[1]

Although no written contract ever served to link
them, Prescott found an ideal agent in London publishing circles in the quiet of his Bedford Street

study one day early in 1836 when he was visited by
Colonel Thomas Aspinwall, a fellow New Englander
on leave from his consular post in the English capital. Aspinwall's knowledge of London was buttressed, as far as playing author's agent was concerned, by professional services which he had rendered Washington Irving in the British literary
market. To such advantages, Aspinwall, in pursuit
of Prescott's interests in England, could add that
peculiar pride so easily attached to the worthwhile
achievement of a fellow-citizen of Massachusetts.

In the course of negotiating an English contract
for the publication of *Ferdinand and Isabella,* Aspinwall, while not meeting his severest test, did
come to comprehend the many-sided outlook of Prescott. At one moment, the author placed his fullest
faith and confidence in his agent, as when he wrote,
"I shall abide entirely by your judgment." [2] At the
next moment he rained such a series of suggestions
upon Aspinwall as to indicate the agent had neither
ability nor authority. In one early letter Prescott
stated his preferences to Aspinwall as follows.

> If no arrangement has been concluded, I should prefer
> to dispose of a single edition (retaining the copyright
> for subsequent editions) to a respectable publisher, on
> as good terms as possible, but without any compensa-
> tion, if he will give none. Thirdly, if that cannot be
> done, I should prefer to dispose of the entire copyright
> on the best terms possible, and without compensation
> if he will give nothing. In the last event, I should be
> willing to be interested to an amount not exceeding
> one half in the publication of a single edition, retain-
> ing the copyright; and if that cannot be effected, I

am willing to give half the copyright, to a respectable publisher and be equally interested with him in publication. I should give the preference to these several alternatives in the order in which they are stated.[3]

Meanwhile, Aspinwall was finding it difficult to interest any English house in Prescott's manuscript.

Although Aspinwall's initial optimism diminished greatly in the face of successive rebuffs by the Longmans and Murray, the author's optimism remained strong. "Of a dozen publishers [in London] I should hardly know to which to give the preference," he wrote his agent.[4] And, reaffirming his acceptance of any terms reached by the Colonel, Prescott added, "But with the exception of Longman or Murray I am not willing to be interested with any bookseller in the publication, which must be got up at the sole risk and charge of the publisher."[5] It was Prescott's first book, and while a certain naïveté attended his ideas about the terms he desired, it must be remembered that as a long-time student of European literature, in the course of which study he had noted the products of various British publishers, the historian was far from quixotic in his preferences.

While Aspinwall carried the pre-publication copy of *Ferdinand and Isabella* to yet another publisher, Prescott suggested a way out should every house turn its back on the book. He would send a hundred or even two hundred copies of the sheets off the American stereotype plates for London distribution, hoping, with the employment of such an entering wedge, to effect swiftly other and better arrangements. Such a procedure was not unheard of, since it had been the means by which Bancroft and Sparks, among others, had initially introduced their American writings into England.

The third London publisher to whom Aspinwall turned, Richard Bentley of 8 New Burlington Street, eliminated that prospect by accepting the work for publication. Upon receipt of word of that happy event, Prescott hurriedly penned appreciative letters to both men. To his agent he wrote on May 5, 1837, "I approve of and concur in any contract you have made or may make with Richard Bentley." [6] Bentley either belonged in, or had been instantly promoted to, the select circle of London publishers Prescott deemed respectable.

Prescott's first English publishing agreement, dated March 20, 1837, permitted Bentley to produce an edition of unstated size for which the publisher would bear all expenses. Control of the presumed copyright—and presumption it was because no arrangement then existed between the United States and England on the subject—remained with Prescott. To strengthen Bentley's uncertain position, it was agreed, though not stipulated in the contract, that American publication of the work would follow English publication, a practice intended to free the Englishman from an early rival edition in London. Net profits would be divided equally between publisher and author. Like all subsequent contracts between them, this one was a written agreement, phrased by Bentley to the satisfaction of the author and his agent.

A combination of confidence in his London agent and rejoicing over his own recently concluded American arrangement for publication hurried the author into correspondence with his English publisher. In a characteristically long letter, he showered offers and suggestions and questions about stereotype proofs, the position of the notes, publication schedule, illustrations, and copyright upon the sophisticated Bentley, whose professional experience over a couple of decades included so many American authors that he was recognized as the leading English publisher of American authors.

Though he surely sensed that he had an uncommon author on his hands, the busy publisher ignored his newest American correspondent for months. It was January 9, 1838, before Bentley's first letter to Prescott reached Boston. By that date Aspinwall had received a presentation copy of the American edition, and Prescott, intoxicated by soaring American sales, was promising Bentley better illustrations in a letter dated January 9, "should the History go to a second edition in London."

Between the agent and the publisher in London and the author in Boston, a widening stream of correspondence developed. Some of it was mere duplication, some of it confusingly self-defeating, as the future would indicate. Time would also regularize the channels and divisions of labor which were then so new that they were punctuated by trial and error for a while.

With the receipt of his first English income, in February, 1840, Prescott fashioned with Aspinwall an informal business arrangement which, without formal written contract, became the basis of their continuing relations. "With respect to my commission," Aspinwall wrote to Prescott on February 29, 1840, "my feeling is much like your own." He added:

My exertions for the accomplishment of your wish to
have the work published here were not prompted in
the slightest degree by any thought of the "luck
penny" that might come afterwards, nor since it has
been generously placed at my discretion by your kind
confidence, do I find it an easy matter to allow the
pere de famille to have a vote in determining the
amount. But as it so happens that I have mouths to
feed and as you will feel your delicacy returned in
some degree by my treating the present as an affair
of business I venture to state that the usual rate of
commission in ordinary cases of this nature is ten per
cent on the proceeds of books published on half profits.
You will accordingly find on the next page the account
so far made out on that principle.

The commission principle thus established continued
throughout the long period that Aspinwall served
Prescott in London.

No trace of misunderstanding, financial or otherwise, ever ruffled the author's relations with his
agent, although time alone gave Prescott the experience and understanding of transatlantic affairs
that permitted the most efficient employment of his
agent. On the other hand, enough confusion occurred
in Prescott's relations with Bentley so that the author's need for his agent persisted, even in the long
periods between contract negotiations.

In America, Prescott's interest in book design and
manufacture joined with his loyalty to his home-
town to insure his personal participation in the negotiation of his American contracts. A major question, however, was to which publishing house should
he turn? The relationship between author and publisher was in an ill-defined formative state at that

time. It was not enough simply to conclude that the work belonged to Boston. There were many companies, some sufficiently established to harbor traditions, others so new as to be imaginatively daring. The names of some called to mind frivolous, ephemeral literature—the trashy novels of the day; while other names were synonymous with serious, even grave, literary undertakings. Most publishers garbed in drab black cloth the books which they compounded of such inferior paper and printing as to deny them any real application of artistic concern.

In the showdown, Prescott, torn between Hilliard, Gray & Company and a newer organization, American Stationers' Company, tossed his lot in with the latter. A recently-founded venture sparked by a number of book-minded men inclined to emphasize quality, the new publishing house seemed the ideal means for launching in the American market the luxury item Prescott's work promised to be.

The contract of April 10, 1837, called for an edition of *Ferdinand and Isabella* of 1,250 copies, with all expenses except one to be borne by the publisher. Prescott supplied the stereotype plates and engraving plates and received $1,000 under the terms of the agreement. Since Prescott was able to walk a few short blocks and communicate with his first publishers in person, very little correspondence exists for this relationship. Consequently, our knowledge of what surely was a written agreement is fragmentary and indirect. However, it was a short-lived agreement.

No record exists of unpleasant relations between the historian and his first Boston publisher. Conceived and born in the trying economic conditions

of the Panic of 1837—and then, as now, books were
such luxuries that the publishing industry was unusually vulnerable to depression—the American
Stationers' Company was doomed to early failure.
In the absence of the firm's records, any assessment
of the relationship between Prescott's book and that
event is conjectural, but nonetheless, given the unusual success of *Ferdinand and Isabella,* one suspects that the Prescott title postponed rather than
hastened the collapse which was a matter of record
in the spring of 1838.

When the collapse came, the American Stationers'
Company had in print a hurried second edition to
satisfy public demand for the work. At this point,
Prescott, with the mid-spring stock of that second
edition fast diminishing, hastened to find another
publisher. In C. C. Little & Company, forerunner of
the present firm of Little, Brown & Company and
one of the first booksellers to stock *Ferdinand and
Isabella* at the moment of its debut, he found that
publisher. (Little & Company became Little, Brown
& Company in 1847, by which time this 120-year-old
publishing house had ceased publishing Prescott's
works. For the sake of simplicity, the modern style
of Little, Brown & Company is employed throughout
this account.)

Descended from Hilliard, Gray & Company, for
whom Prescott earlier had entertained such high regard that he had considered them for his initial
Boston arrangement, Little, Brown & Company was
a new local establishment. Both Charles C. Little
and James Brown, the partners, had learned the
book business with Hilliard, Gray & Company. With
the dissolution of the old firm of that name in June,

1837, and the establishment of a new one bearing the old name at a new location, the time had come for Little and Brown to strike out for themselves. Their partnership "for the purpose of publishing, importing and selling books" operated from the address of the old Hilliard, Gray & Company, at 112 Washington Street.[7] Prescott's second contract with an American publisher was signed with them on May 14, 1838.[8] The following were the principal provisions of the agreement.

After the completion of the sale of the remainder of the copies produced by the American Stationers' Company, Little, Brown was to be allowed a five-year period during which they could print and publish 1,700 copies of *Ferdinand and Isabella,* for which right Prescott would receive $2,975. Their exclusive rights obtained until November 1, 1843, and until then the author promised Little, Brown the use of his plates to print both the text and the illustrations.

Pledged to maintain the work in three octavo volumes, the publishers promised no impression would number fewer than 250 copies. The high standards of the author were written into the provision "that the paper shall be as good in sizing and quality as the paper of the first edition, and worth six dollars a ream; and that the binding and execution shall be in every way equal to the first edition of said History, said Prescott to be the judge."

Figured at $1.75 per copy, the payments due Prescott were to be made by promissory notes executed at the moment each impression was struck off and payable in six months. Payment for the last lot of the 1,700 copies was to be due no later than November 1, 1843. Failure on the part of the publisher to give Prescott such notes at the time of each impression or failure to pay the notes within thirty days of the dates payable would permit the author, if he so desired, to void the contract immediately.

The better to protect Prescott's basic stake in the stereotype plates, it was agreed they would remain in the possession of Folsom, Wells, and Thurston except when, upon express order by Prescott, they were to be turned over to Little, Brown. While in possession of the plates, the publishers assumed responsibility for any kind of damage that might befall them.

The work was to be printed, as previously, by the trio of Cambridge printers, unless Prescott consented to the employment of some other printing establishment. The author and his publisher also established the wholesale price of $6.00 for the work in lots, the price at which review copies would be furnished for journals and newspapers selected by Prescott which the publishers felt did not deserve free copies, and the price at which copies might be remaindered to the author.

Diligently trying to get additional engravings from England, Prescott promised his new Boston publishers they could have at cost any he so obtained. One copy of each one hundred copies issued was to go to the author, or if he did not desire such additional copies, he was to be credited with $4.25 for every such copy he failed to take. Reserved to Prescott was the exclusive right of publishing in Europe and the right to abridge the history. Little, Brown would receive preferential consideration in the publishing of any such abridgment if they offered him as much as any other house.

In case of dispute between author and publisher, a three man arbitral board was to be appointed, each party naming one, and the two so designated then selecting the third member.

Down to November 1, 1843, Little, Brown had the right to exceed the total of 1,700 copies if demand called for the publication of a greater number. In such circumstances any excess number was to be issued in lots of not less than 250 each, subject to all the conditions established for the original 1,700 copies.

In the absence of the text of the historian's contract with the American Stationers' Company, it is impossible to indicate exactly how much this agreement with Little, Brown of 1838 repeats and reflects his depression-ridden experience with his first American publisher. However, economic uncertainty, as well as author desire, surely prompted such provisions as those which saw Prescott continue to control his stereotype plates and protect himself against assignment of contract to another publisher and against cut-rate remaindering, something to be anticipated if a publisher sought operating capital or tottered on the brink of bankruptcy. The acceptance of his work also no doubt prompted the elastic terms which permitted the new publisher to exceed the minimum agreement. Prescott prepared himself for both depression and prosperity, the failure of a second publisher, and the continuing success of his book. Time demonstrated that many of these precautions were unnecessary. For example, no record exists of any difference that necessitated the naming of arbitrators; and every printing was accompanied by prompt payment of royalties.

In 1841, the rumor that *Ferdinand and Isabella* was about to experience competition in America led Prescott and Little, Brown & Company to fight fire with fire with an abridgment of the history. Explaining the matter to his Spanish aide, Gayangos, Prescott wrote: "I am obliged to make this abridgment (which however will occupy me but three or four weeks) in self-defense, as the work has found such a sale here that I found it would be abridged for me by a literary adventurer, and I did not care to let anybody but myself mangle the features of my own bantling." [9] Facing the necessity of converting three octavo volumes into one of duodecimo size, Prescott decided to design the abridgment "for youth & schools," which, as he wrote to Francis Lieber on June 3, 1841, induced his "stunting and dwarfing the ideas as well as paragraphs down to the calibre of schoolboys."

On May 27, 1841, Prescott and Little, Brown & Company executed a detailed contract for the abridgment. The historian was to provide the plates for text, illustrations, and maps for a book of a minimum of four hundred pages. Little, Brown & Company, with an exclusive right to the work for five years, dating from receipt of the plates, promised to publish 4,000 copies, with no impression less than 1,000 copies. Prescott was to receive by means of promissory notes payable in 9 months from the dates of the various impressions, 20 cents per volume, or a total of $800 for the 4,000 copies. In addition, he was to receive 1 copy for each 200 copies published. The wholesale price, in lots of 100 or more copies, was established at 80 cents per copy. The minimum of 4,000 copies could be exceeded indefinitely, in impressions at least of 1,000 copies each, by further payment to Prescott at the rate of 20 cents per volume. As in the earlier contract between the historian and the same publisher, this agreement could not be assigned to another publisher without Prescott's consent, and provision was made for the arbitration of differences. Reflecting his constant pursuit of quality of product, Prescott was to be the judge whether or not the publisher attained the size and quality of paper demanded by the historian's insistence that his abridgment equal that made of Bancroft's history. Financially and artistically both author and publisher were happy when the diminished threat of competition, fading before the onslaught of publicity that Prescott himself would release an abridgment, enabled them to scuttle the abridgment contract, which they did on March 27, 1843.

In the meantime, feeling that the threat to the three-volume history was general, Prescott concluded a second half-profits contract with Bentley on July 3, 1841, for an English edition of the contemplated abridgment.

The agreements of 1841, the only ones signed by Prescott which did not produce a published book, intensified his awareness of the business side of bookmaking. Further significance attaches itself to the episode because through the victory in which the historian out-bluffed a would-be competitor he saved the American field for his beloved octavo editions.

In 1843, when the contract of 1838 with Little, Brown & Company drew to a close, Prescott had finished his *Conquest of Mexico*. He therefore had added reason for opening negotiations with publishers. In an essentially small operation, which lacked a system of wide distribution, Little, Brown, with 8 successive impressions of 500 copies each, had marketed 4,000 copies of *Ferdinand and Isabella.* Prescott possibly wondered what that sale might have amounted to if his publisher had possessed the apparatus for national promotion and distribution. For the new book, at any rate, he concluded he would start from scratch in a widened search for a publisher. In so doing, Prescott looked beyond Boston, doing so all the more rapidly because of an assist by a successful author who knew exactly the publisher for Prescott. That author was John Lloyd Stephens.

Previously acquainted, Prescott and Stephens, out of mutual interest in Latin America, had become warm friends. With the publication of Stephens' *Incidents of Travel in Central America,* the Bostonian began a letter to Stephens, a particularly long one in which he expressed himself admirably, with the words: "I cannot well express to you the great satisfaction and delight I have received from your volumes." [10] Almost overnight the book established itself as a best-seller, with a phenomenal sale of 20,000 copies within three months. (Incidentally, Stephens, also working through Colonel Aspinwall, sold more than 2,500 copies in England through publisher John Murray.) [11] Prescott was doubly impressed—by the added dimension the New York archaeologist gave the American Indian and by the wonderful demonstration of publisher activity which riveted the name of Harper and Brothers in his mind.

Returning some borrowed books and sending Prescott a copy of his new work, *Incidents of Travel in Yucatan,* Stephens wrote in March, 1843:

> I have spoken to the Messrs. Harpers about the pub-
> lication of your next work. They are desirous to un-
> dertake it and of course offer their usual best terms
> i.e. half of the nett profits, or they will allow you to
> have it stereotyped in Boston, and to keep the plates
> under your own control, they pay the cost, and will al-
> low the same rate per copy that would be allowed by
> your Boston publisher. They consider that with their
> capital and business connexions they have the means of
> making larger sales than any other publishing house
> in the country. . . . It is my belief that they would
> sell of such a work as yours at least 2500 copies more
> than any other house, and I feel persuaded that after
> a year's trial of them with the new work you will find
> it to your interest to put Ferdinand and Isabella into
> their hands.[12]

Warming immediately to Stephens' proposal, the historian gave his unofficial agent an extended state-ment regarding his new work—the subject-matter, length of manuscript, and capabilities in the market. Of Little, Brown & Company he wrote: "My pub-lishers here have always used me well, and although I have made no agreement with them, they probably expect to have the publication of my work, and I should feel bound in honour and disposed to give them a preference, but it cannot be expected that I should give them the business at a great pecuniary loss to myself." [13]

Prescott thus subscribed to the principles of "trade courtesy" so common in author-publisher relations in pre-Civil War years. Without benefit of any written agreement regarding his forthcoming

books, the publishers in general considered Prescott
as Little, Brown's author until he initiated steps to
the contrary. Such gentlemanly conduct between
publishers and genuine affection between author and
publisher did not preclude, however, demonstrations
of interest by one's publisher in manuscripts in the
making. Quite possibly, the failure of Little, Brown
& Company to prod Prescott with queries about his
next book—and it was no secret—led him to believe,
all the more, that the firm lacked the aggressiveness
called for in publishing circles.

Prescott's thinking about the second history,
sketched for Stephens so the archaeologist could explore the matter with the house of Harper at the
same time he himself did so with Little, Brown &
Company, included a desire by Prescott for a royalty
of $1.50 per copy in a contract calling for 8,000 or
more copies, with $6.00 to be the retail market price.
Accepting the volume approach to income, Prescott
was willing to have his royalty per copy cut from
$1.75 to $1.50, but percentage-wise, as he sought a
reduction of retail price from $7.50 to $6.00 for a
three-volume work, he actually was increasing his
royalty from 23⅓ to 25 per cent. Publisher capacity
to insure the wide distribution needed to attain the
volume that would make such an arrangement attractive became the crux of the issue. In the 1840's, as
now, the relationship between the publishing and
the manufacture of books was resolved variously by
different houses, but it is evident that Prescott felt
that Harpers, possessed of their own manufacturing
establishment, could produce more profitably and
sell at lower prices than had Little, Brown & Company.[14]

Stephens put the proposition to the Harpers, and Prescott carried it to Little, Brown & Company. The two houses were not far apart in their reaction to the historian's proposals, but he decided to turn his back on Boston in favor of New York, "not so much for the difference of first amount offered . . . but for the eventual sales." [15] In all this, Stephens was much more than mere relayer of messages, for the financial and artistic success of his own Harper-published books spoke to the Bostonian with telling eloquence.

"I send you the contract drawn up conformably, I believe, to the desire in your note," Prescott informed the Harpers on April 25, 1843, about the agreement whose full text is not known. Refusing their offer of $15,000 for the copyright, he sold them a one-year right to produce an edition of 5,000 copies of the three-volume *Conquest of Mexico* for $7,500, with the understanding that they might exceed that number at the same rate of $1.50 per copy for the author. As usual, Prescott's desire to maximize his control over the book included his providing stereotype plates, which, indeed, he had put into production before reaching terms with his publisher. Despite the fact that a contract for a book was in large measure a business matter to be decided on its financial merits, it grieved Prescott to favor the upstart metropolis on the Hudson over the Athens of the New World, a sentiment he penned fellow-Bostonian Edward Everett when he wrote, "I am sorry to transfer the work to New York." [16] At the same time, Aspinwall busied himself with the *Conquest of Mexico* in London.

Numerous factors complicated Prescott's approach to contracting his second work in England. With his English income from *Ferdinand and Isabella* disturbingly low, he preferred a different kind of arrangement for the second book. On more than one count he quietly questioned Bentley's financial integrity, and felt that more fairly computed his London earnings would have approximated $4,000 instead of barely exceeding $1,500. Prescott's belief that Bentley cut the net profit, hence the author's share, by entering enormous charges against the book was reinforced by the historian's conversations with Charles Dickens in Boston in 1842. Dickens insisted that Bentley scarcely could have spent one-fifth the sum that he had charged against *Ferdinand and Isabella* for advertising.[17] Though Dickens' views may be heavily discounted, for he and Bentley had been parties to one of the bitterest chapters of author-publisher relations in the mid-nineteenth century,[18] he obviously deepened Prescott's doubts and suspicions. Prescott concluded that since he had made so little money on one half-profits arrangement, another formula should be tried. At any rate, when Prescott instructed Aspinwall to open negotiations, Prescott informed Bentley, on April 1, 1843, "I should prefer an outright sale to having it published on shares."

To Aspinwall, Prescott unburdened himself. A second work by an author surely would have a larger audience, in consequence of which the author reasonably could expect greater income. For a good copyright in England, he felt his *Conquest of Mexico* was worth £1,000, but, in the light of reality, he could neither give such assurance nor expect such income. Facing squarely the insecurity attending the

English publisher of an American work, he suggested that he would accept £450 or more for his work. If the best offer was below that figure, he would revert to the prior pattern of half-profits. Even though he preferred to ignore Bentley completely, he sensed that he could not easily free himself from the New Burlington Street house. However improperly, Bentley had already advertised the second work. And furthermore, would the author not be victimized in the future regarding his continuing stake in *Ferdinand and Isabella* if he refused to treat with Bentley for the new book? But it was not to be simply an open and shut case in favor of Bentley, because others definitely were to be asked to make offers for his *Conquest of Mexico*.[19]

Sharing his author's high regard for both Murray and Longmans, Aspinwall agreed that Prescott was somewhat at Bentley's mercy, as he wrote to Prescott on April 17, "I think with you that Bentley is first to be dealt with." In the belief that such information laid before English publishers would induce them to make more generous offers, Prescott next informed his agent of the details of his new contract with Harper and Brothers. But even so, though Aspinwall "knew both Mr. Murray and the Messrs. Longman would be ready and eager at any time to publish any Work" by Prescott, he preferred to work in an unhurried fashion upon Bentley first.[20] A cagey veteran in his profession, Bentley soon wheedled from Aspinwall Prescott's desired selling price. Bentley next created a furor when, announcing he would pay as much for the new work as Longmans or Murray, he suggested that Aspinwall determine what those offers might be.

In a furious and tedious exchange of notes, agent and publisher somewhat forgot the book as they hurried communications back and forth on the meaning of the preference Prescott intended to accord Bentley. The publisher accused Aspinwall of so twisting it as to reduce preference to mere priority; the agent, in turn, argued that Bentley equated preference with virtual monopoly.

Bentley did his best to assure himself the new book at the lowest possible price. His premature, unauthorized advertising of the *Conquest of Mexico* had been one such effort. Now his insistence that Aspinwall canvass the trade to learn the figure Bentley had to match was another. Had Bentley succeeded in getting Aspinwall to so "use" the other London houses without their having any real prospect of getting the new work, they would have been so justifiably enraged as to boycott Prescott in the future, a not undesirable thing from Bentley's viewpoint, since it would guarantee his obtaining any third Prescott work. Plainly put, Bentley knew a good author when he saw one, and Prescott was a good one; so why not use every wile to monopolize him? There existed also the possibility of driving a wedge between the author and the agent.

On one occasion Bentley wrote Aspinwall, "I should beg to refer the point to him [Prescott] for his consideration."[21] Aspinwall barked back, "Mr. Prescott's instructions to me urge despatch, disclose his views and wishes most fully and give me absolute authority to carry them out."[22] Hoping to minimize the price at which he could obtain the *Conquest of Mexico,* Bentley pointed out that, at the moment, he was more than £200 out of pocket on

the third edition of *Ferdinand and Isabella,* by which
he tried to couple the prospects of a second book
with the performance of the first. The other side of
his two-edged argument merely underscored, by
virtue of the fact that the first work had gone to
three editions, the author-agent insistence upon a
good price for the *Conquest of Mexico.* Since neither
side held all the cards, the contest continued.

By the end of May, Bentley put himself on record:
"I have no hesitation in declining to purchase the
copyright of the new book at the price named by you
viz. £1000." [23] And, as he prepared to turn to other
publishers, Aspinwall sent Prescott copies of the
recent exchanges between himself and Bentley, adding: "His main object appears to be to avoid for
the present all direct negotiations between him and
myself exclusively and still to reserve an option as
to taking the work after I have obtained offers from
some other publisher." Concluding his comment on
Bentley with reference to the financial accounts on
Ferdinand and Isabella, Aspinwall crisply concluded,
"Credat Judaeus." [24] The London agent prepared
to turn to Murray and the Longmans.

Next, on June 6, Aspinwall sent the following
communication to Murray.

I take the liberty of enclosing for your consideration
a description of the Conquest of Mexico, a new work
by Mr. Prescott, the author of Ferdinand and Isabella.
It will appear in the United States about the month of
November.

He wishes to dispose of the copyright. Should you
feel inclined to treat for it, I shall be happy to meet
you at your office or here as may best suit your convenience.

Three days later an identical communication went to the Longmans. The studied delay represented a factor of preference in favor of Murray. Indeed, Murray's unsatisfactory reply was in Aspinwall's hands before he sent the offer to the Longmans. Aspinwall must have been startled to read, in a letter from Robert Cooke of Murray's dated June 8: "The author has already asked Mr. Murray to name the terms he feels disposed to publish it upon and from which Mr. Murray cannot deviate." "There is no copy right in the work," the Murray reply continued:

> and there is no law to prevent any one from reprinting it in this country.
> If Mr. Prescott would like to consign copies of the work to Mr. Murray's care at a certain price, he will be very happy to undertake the agency for him. *This is the way adopted by Mr. Stephens and Mr. Murray and which has been satisfactory to both parties.*
> Or if Mr. Prescott prefers it and will send Mr. Murray the sheets of the book as it is printing in New York, he will print at his own risque and expense the work in this country and divide the profits with the author, . . . otherwise than this, in the present unprotected state of the law and the depressed state of literature, he cannot do.

Murray had said nothing that would support Prescott's desire to switch his publishing arrangement to the house on Albemarle Street.

Like Murray, the Longmans reacted rapidly to the prospect of making an agreement with Prescott. Mr. Thomas Longman rushed to Aspinwall's office and "offered either to take the work on half profits, to sell the American sheets on commission, to print on half profits, or on commission from the stereotype plates, or to pay £300 down and 200 more on the sale of 1500 copies." Aspinwall dismissed the offer at once, and returned to negotiations with Bentley, who now looked better than before because no other house looked as good.[25]

Bentley, informed that Aspinwall was about to contract with another house unless he agreed to take the *Conquest of Mexico* at £650, went to Aspinwall's office late on June 16. "After many arguments, upon his right to a preference, dullness of trade, state of international copyright, dangers of piracy, etc., etc.," Aspinwall reported to Prescott, "he consented to give his notes at six, nine and twelve months from the date of publication for £650 provided he shall be put in possession of the work, so as to publish it here a fortnight before it makes its appearance in the United States." [26]

When, finally, Bentley cast the arrangement into written form, something he always did in his agreements with Prescott, Aspinwall apparently felt impelled to inform Prescott how, in the future, they might profit from their own errors. "I hope you will excuse me for suggesting to you," Aspinwall told Prescott, "the expediency of writing as little as you possibly can to publishers or other persons here concerning any work you may wish to sell in Great Britain. The publishers take advantage of it to your prejudice and in some degree, also to the embarrassment of the selling agent." [27]

With his contracts complete for *Conquest of Mexico* on both sides of the Atlantic, Prescott busied himself more fully with the tasks of getting stereotype plates to New York and proof sheets to London and with co-ordinating the schedule of the two editions. All went well. Bentley's edition appeared on October 24, 1843, and the Harper edition, in stuttering volume-at-a-time fashion, between December 6 and 21.

Months before the expiration date for the five-year agreement with Little, Brown & Company for *Ferdinand and Isabella,* Prescott had begun to explore the possibilities of cheap serial publication of the work. This commonly-employed publishing technique in mid-nineteenth-century America often aimed at selling a standard work to a less scholarly and a lower economic class of readers than those attracted to hardbound books at $2.00 to $2.50 per volume. Of course it developed that the reader who bought the book in serial publication at 25 cents per number, often issued weekly or bi-monthly, commonly paid as much, if not more, than if he had acquired the standard book edition. A further proof that serial publication, which was a mixture of publisher desire to broaden his market and publisher awareness there was a wider market among the more literate and more numerous common folk of the day, appealed to a different segment of society is seen in the studied inclusion of illustrations in every number of such serialized works.

The matter of more numerous illustrations led Prescott into correspondence with Frederick Catherwood, the well-known artist, who had recently been associated with Stephens' successful books. However, a decision was delayed by Catherwood's absence in London and by Prescott's attention to his second work. When no decision was reached concerning a thirty-six-issue release of *Ferdinand and Isa-*

bella, Prescott decided to extend the arrangement for that work with Little, Brown & Company.

The extension of the Prescott-Little, Brown & Company contract, without reference to a specific time period, permitted the author to terminate it at will. Henceforth, each and every impression would consist of at least 500 copies, a number easily dictated by the experience of 8 successive printings. The influence of the agreement of 1843 with the Harpers for the *Conquest of Mexico* is reflected in such terms as those which found Prescott satisfied with a royalty of $1.50 per copy, it being understood that the wholesale and retail prices would be $4.80 and $6.00, respectively. Six weeks following this agreement, on March 25, 1844, the Boston house completed the one and only impression published under this arrangement.[28]

While the last impression of the first history by Little, Brown was being sold, Prescott, released by the issuance of his *Conquest of Mexico* from focusing most of his attention on it, renewed his interest in the idea of serial production of *Ferdinand and Isabella,* and had it intensified by the Harpers' show of interest. The following letter from the Harpers to Prescott on April 25, 1844, went as far as a publishing proposal.

> We would be pleased to issue your "Ferdinand and Isabella" in numbers on the following conditions: You . . . furnish . . . stereotype plates . . . now used by Little and Brown and also (in addition to those already published in the work) 36 engraved illustrations as proposed by you, at your expense.
>
> We will publish from these plates and engravings not to exceed 24 numbers at 25¢ each at retail, and

not to exceed 16⅔¢ at wholesale. For one year, for 3,000 copies Harper to pay $1 per copy to William H. Prescott, at same rate for additional copies.

For those sold in muslin binding Harpers to pay Prescott $1.50 per copy.

The employment of the original stereotype plates, forcing the proposed serial version into octavo form, would insure a quality product distinctly above the cut of most such publications. The total price for the twenty-four numbers, retailed at twenty-five cents per number, matched that of the regularly published edition. However, Prescott's royalty of one dollar for each twenty-four-number-copy represented but two-thirds of his accustomed income. Obviously, serial publication was more attractive to publisher than to author. In addition, revised estimates of the cost persuaded Prescott that it would be better to issue *Ferdinand and Isabella* entire, as in the past. On October 28, 1844, he wrote to the Harpers as follows.

I find but fifty copies remaining here of the last edition of "Ferdinand and Isabel," and it will be now necessary to make a new contract. You remember, no doubt, your proposition to me last spring to take fifteen hundred copies on precisely the same terms that you took the "Conquest of Mexico," so soon as the present edition should be disposed of. Although you have not withdrawn that proposition, yet, as several months have elapsed, you may have changed your mind, and I shall not avail myself of it, till I hear from you that you now wish to abide by it. I shall ask Little and Brown proposals and bring the matter to an issue.

In less than three weeks such an exploratory exchange ushered a new contract into existence, providing for an early edition of fifteen hundred copies of the first history by Harpers, on financial terms duplicating those for the *Conquest of Mexico*. Providing engravings of English origin at cost and insisting upon the standards of the earlier editions, Prescott shipped the stereotype plates to New York City and sent a letter dated November 19, 1844, covering the matter.

The break with Boston was now complete. Behind Prescott lay the only instance in which he ever considered the invasion of the mass American market with a serial publication. Behind him, too, was any need for an agent in his dealings with the New York house, because he conducted these last negotiations, through a combination of correspondence and conference, entirely by himself.

For his next book, the *Miscellanies,* Prescott began correspondence with Aspinwall on November 15, 1844. He proposed that Aspinwall see whether Bentley or Murray would be interested in publishing in book form, to match the style of his histories, a group of biographical and critical essays which he had published previously as individual items in the United States, chiefly in the *North American Review.* "Possibly they may not be willing to give a farthing," he wrote Aspinwall. "But you will probably think best to ask something, as I shall still have to select and dress them up a little."

Aspinwall immediately turned to his new task, and on December 9 reported an agreement with Bentley, according to which Bentley "could only publish the essays upon the plan of half profits." [29] The ease with which Aspinwall reached this third agreement with Bentley induced him to tell Prescott on February 3, 1845, "I was glad to be permitted by the latitude of your instructions to deal with Mr. Bentley a little more easily in the present occasion, than I did on the preceding one."

Despite the fact that the arrangement put still another title into the style of contract which in the past had contributed to suspicions and disgust, Prescott was pleased with Aspinwall's work. "The papers may not be worth much," he wrote to him on February 27, "but they are worth as much now as they ever were."

As he put himself to the task of selecting six hundred pages of material, Prescott had no clear idea what the volume of essays should be called. In more respects than one, this strangest of his books was unlike his histories. To his friend Edward Everett, a former editor of the *North American Review*, the historian confided, "I am about to commit a folly, which you will think savors of mental blindness; that is, the publication of some of my periodical trumpery, whose value, or rather little value you know." [30]

No complete answer is available for the question, why did he publish it? Wordy and uneven—adverse judgments rendered by Prescott's contemporaries as well as all interested parties since then—the work could only detract from his good name. On the other hand, his good name would serve to market it, and so it did. Contributing nothing to his reputation, it added slightly to his literary earnings.

Harper and Brothers first learned of the forthcoming volume of essays in England through a printed announcement by Bentley, but, in the absence of word from Prescott, discounted the idea. It was late May, 1845, before the historian raised the issue in correspondence with the house of Harper. Their immediate reply on May 27 was, "We should be proud to be the publisher of the work in this country." Just like his English publisher, Prescott's American publisher apparently accepted the book without even inquiring about the contents. On both sides of the Atlantic there was a marketable magic about Prescott's name.

On June 10, less than a week after Prescott suggested that they ponder the matter of an offer for the essays, Harper and Brothers wrote him: "How would you like for us to publish the work on shares? We to advance all the funds necessary to get the volume stereotyped (in Boston), and published in the style desired, and pay you one-half of the profits."

The half-profits proposal, seldom used in America and rarely so by the Harpers,[31] was not without relationship to the publisher's skepticism about the success of the volume. Countering the Harpers' suggestion, Prescott, cool to the half-profits idea, came up with alternatives of his own in his letter of June 16: "I should prefer to stereotype the book at my own expense—and to own the plates and sell you any number of copies that you may . . . require." "Or secondly," he continued, "sell whole affair outright for $2000 . . . to be paid in one year of publication." As a final alternative, he would agree to a half-profits arrangement.

The Harpers replied on June 30, "The getting up of the work is to be at our expense—to be reimbursed out of the profits." For Prescott, the half-profits idea had come to America. In mid-August, the book appeared in England, followed by an American edition in December, this being the longest interval between the English and American editions of any of his works.

Obviously satisfied with the Harpers as his publisher, Prescott knew, in 1845, that certain authors were hostile in varying degrees to that house. A blistering denunciation of the house of Harper published that same year by Theodore Sedgwick Fay was a matter of common knowledge.[32] However, when Francis Lieber expressed doubts about doing business with them, Prescott detailed to him his relations with Harper and Brothers in a letter dated August 6, 1845, as follows.

I make very simple and explicit contracts with them and have no complicated accounts, advances &c. They agree to take a certain number of copies of a stereotype work, & pay me so much a copy—one dollar, fifty cents therefor. [Good for the pair of Prescott histories, this explanation does not hold for the *Miscellanies.*] They have paid me punctually. My contracts give them also the right to print as many more copies as they please, within the specified time, they paying at the same rate as before. This put me to a certain extent in their power, as they certainly may cheat me in regard to the number of copies they strike off. But I do not think there is much danger of such a gross fraud in a house of their standing and character, and where it must be known to the four partners, and to some of the subalterns in the establishment,—at least if carried to any extent. This would be supposing rogues to be more plentiful than usual, even among publishers. I have found, too, that the report of the Harpers from persons who have dealt with them, and know them best, has been, almost always, favorable to their integrity. I have had the opinions of such men as

Catherwood and Stephens, who have dealt with them
long and largely, & who think them shrewd and sharp
in their bargains, but faithful in the execution of
them. They have no chivalry, and will not send you
a horse or a butt of wine, as Scott's publishers did
him, if your book should make a fortune for them. I
should recommend you to be precise in your *written
contract*—and to leave as little in said contract, as
possible, to contingencies. Downright sales for an edition are the best thing. But it is not easy for an author
to do the best, always,—only the best, his publisher
will agree to. I should add in conclusion, that Mr. Fay
of Berlin thinks very ill of the whole concern. His
case is a difficult one to explain—& he has another
pamphlet on the anvil, he writes me, anent the matter.
I should easily believe they could be guilty of considerable blunders in their rapid wholesale way of
doing business. But I should be very slow to suspect
them of intentional fraud.

As a matter of fact, Prescott thought first of the
Harpers for his next book, *Conquest of Peru,* which
was completed three years after the publication of
the *Conquest of Mexico* and only one year after the
appearance of the American edition of the *Miscellanies.* In early December, 1846, he alerted both his
London agent and his New York publisher. "It is a
long time since I have heard from you," he wrote
the house of Harper on December 12 in an unusually
detailed letter, "and I now write to announce the
completion of my 'History of the Conquest of
Peru.'" He continued:

It will make, as well as I can estimate, between 10 and
1100 pages. . . . I have arranged with the Printer to

have stereotype plates made of it so as to correspond
precisely with the other work. . . . The printing will
be completed by the first of April. . . .

I am willing to offer you the work on similar terms
with those you gave me with the ''Conquest of Mexico,'' you to pay me for copy-right $.50 per volume on
all copies you publish. You took five thousand copies
of that with exclusive right of publication in the U.S.
for one year. I would sell you this work in the same
ratio, that is, seven thousand five hundred copies,
making the same number of volumes which you
bought of the other. As the work will be four dollars,
instead of six, and would have a better sale opened for
it by the other I should hope you might get rid of the
same number of volumes of it in the same time, but I
am willing to extend the right of publication to two
years, instead of one, that there may be no doubts on
that head. It would be easy to arrange the date of publication if you accept my terms, which I would make
in all respects, except those already stated, like those
in our contract for the ''Conquest of Mexico.'' I
should, however, be more particular to have the paper
of a heavier quality than that in your last editions,
and indeed, this should be attended to more carefully
in the future ones of Mexico, as the work, I am convinced, suffers from it.

In seventy-two hours the Harper reply was moving toward Boston. ''We have received,'' they wrote
on December 15, ''your esteemed favour of the 12th
inst., containing proposals for the publication of
your work on the 'Conquest of Peru,' to which we accede.'' Of the Prescott-Harper contracts, and this
was to be the last, many things might be said, but
none more remarkable than the speed by which
Prescott and the Harpers came to agreement.

In essence, Prescott had stated the contract terms. It remained for him merely to send two copies of the formal document to New York with the request that the publisher sign them and return one to him. Leaving blank the price at which the author could buy additional copies of the work, he expressed the hope in his December 21 letter to Harpers that it could be fixed at $1.40. He was to complete the stereotype plates and forward them to New York in time for spring publication, an event which in itself would be different, since the American editions of all three previous works had appeared in December.

While the American agreement for Prescott's third history was thus so acceptably resolved, Aspinwall methodically played his part in London. "I know not what terms," Prescott wrote his agent, "we may expect from the British publishers."

> Do you think it would be too much to *ask* for it as much as you did for the "Mexico"? That was I think a thousand pounds. You however are the only judge of what is best to ask, and whatever you ask or receive, be assured I shall be entirely satisfied as I always have been with all you have done for me—and grateful to boot. I only hope it will not cost you the trouble that the other work did. I should much like to have a book brought into the world by the classic press of John Murray, but on the whole, considering my friendly relations with Bentley and that he has my other historicals, I should give him the preference if he comes I think we may say within a hundred pounds of any other publisher.[33]

In a rambling, friendly paragraph Prescott thus expressed his hopes and confidence. In part it was so

because of the strength of the tie, now moving into
its second decade, between him and Aspinwall; and
it was in part in this vein because the battle over the
contract in 1843, plus continued proof that England
was no gold mine for him, had given Prescott an air
of quiet resignation.

Less than ten days after Prescott's instructions
and ideas reached him, Aspinwall wrote the author,
"I have sold your History of the Conquest of Peru
to Mr. Bentley for £800 on the same terms as to payment that we were agreed upon in the disposal of
the Mexico." [34] It was the easiest contract negotiation between Aspinwall and Bentley for any of the
Prescott histories. Aspinwall did not obtain the full
£1,000, but that figure had been established simply
as the kind of initial asking price from which one
expected to retreat somewhat. For a two-volume
work, Bentley was paying £150 more than he had
given Prescott for the larger *Conquest of Mexico.*
The historian's widening reputation explains some
of that success; some of it, too, seems born of the
mutual respect gradually established between a
value-conscious stubborn Yankee agent and an
equally obstinate and businesslike publisher.

Following the appearance of his *Conquest of Peru,*
the pattern of Prescott's relations with his publishers changed greatly. The popularity of his works
and the rapidity with which they had emerged between 1843 and 1847 combined to make his publishers
eagerly hopeful. American readers scarcely had time
to acquire copies of the *Conquest of Peru* before
Harper and Brothers asked Prescott if he cared to
discuss arrangements for his next history. With re-

gret they must have read the reply in an undated letter, probably September, 1847: "It is quite uncertain, from the state of my health if [there] is another Historical work. If I do, the completion of it will be necessarily so long delayed that I should not be wishing to enter into any arrangement, for its publication at present." Eight and one-half years were to pass before a new work appeared bearing the name William H. Prescott on the title page, and before that the tie with the Harpers was broken. Meanwhile, however, the relationship between Prescott and his publishers continued in the realm of accountings for royalties on new impressions of the various titles.

In England, the picture was different, because with the outright sale of his interest in his *Conquest of Mexico* and *Conquest of Peru* Prescott's continuing interest in them was simply in the realm of their popular and scholarly acceptance. However, both *Ferdinand and Isabella* and the *Miscellanies,* published on the half-profits arrangement, inspired further negotiations, which Bentley initiated.

In the spring of 1847, between the conclusion of the contract for the *Conquest of Peru* and the publication of that work, Bentley asked Prescott if he were interested in liquidating his interest in *Ferdinand and Isabella* in favor of its publisher.

The idea of disposing of his English stake in the first history had never occurred to Prescott, and he said as much to Bentley in his letter of May 13. "It is a subject of which I had not previously thought, but, on consideration, I am satisfied that such an arrangement, if it can be satisfactorily made, will be attended with some obvious advantages to both you and myself, though I never part with my copy-rights here." And Prescott added:

> I have written accordingly to Col. Aspinwall, to give him my views of the matter; and he has power from me to arrange it definitively with you, if you can agree on terms. I am the more willing to do this, as I am satisfied you would never desire to bring out the book in a manner that would discredit the author or the subject.

While Aspinwall and Bentley were exchanging views on the new matter, the *Conquest of Peru* was published in fine style, the publisher put an added half-dozen copies at Prescott's disposal, and he showered his Boston author with other books from the Bentley press. Some of this was part and parcel of the pattern of increasingly friendly relations between publisher and author; some of it, too, might have been intended to facilitate the negotiation regarding *Ferdinand and Isabella*.

Prescott instructed Aspinwall to ask £600 for the author's half-interest, a sum which Bentley refused to pay. He countered with an offer of £250, which he later advanced to £300. With publisher and agent so far apart, the negotiation broke down, and Aspinwall reported to the historian on July 3, "I have endeavoured to dispose of the copyright . . . without success." Detailing the exchange between himself and Bentley, he asked Prescott to inform him if he had shifted his views on the matter. As far as Prescott was then concerned, Bentley had both started and stopped the negotiation; there was nothing more to be done.

The author's relations with his English publisher on publishing agreements came to approximate those with the house of Harper, reduced to successive financial accountings and comments on them. However, Prescott's trip to England in 1850 permitted, at last, a face-to-face meeting of two men whose contacts up to that time had been restricted to a dozen years of correspondence.

It was not until May, 1854, that Prescott was prepared to negotiate for the publication of his next book, *Philip the Second*. With Aspinwall no longer in London to help him, Prescott intended to negotiate both the American and English contracts himself.

Interested in marketing a large first impression of the first two volumes of *Philip the Second*, at a royalty of 50 cents per volume, along with cheaper editions of the older works, the historian outlined his proposition to the Harpers in a letter dated June 29. The July 3 reply from New York stated: "We will accept your proposition for Philip the Second, with this modification, namely, that the note for $5000 shall not be given until we have sold 5000 copies of the work. . . . We shall be happy to publish the cheap editions of your former works, and to guarantee the sale of 3000 copies of each in the usual way." Prescott, wanting more liberal terms than those which, by that time, had become routine between him and the Harpers, told them that their reply was unacceptable. To that, the house of Harper replied on July 10: "We are afraid that we shall not be able to change our offer . . . very materially." Part of the company's inability to meet Prescott's terms, it was intimated, stemmed from the fact that

the insurance money that they expected because of
their fire of December 10, 1853, was still involved in
litigation. The letter of July 10 closed with the hon-
est admission that "we should greatly dislike to part
Company with you."

A few days later the break anticipated by the publisher materialized. Terming it "one of the most unpleasant letters I ever wrote," Prescott added, "it
would be too great a sacrifice of my interests for me
to decline proposals which secure to me the certain
payment of fifty thousand dollars." [35] The competing offer at which the historian hinted not only ended
the tie with New York, it re-established one for Prescott in his own Boston.

Hearing that Prescott might consider offers for
both his new and his old works, Francis H. Under-
wood urged his employer, Moses Dresser Phillips, of
Phillips, Sampson, and Company, to call on the historian at his summer residence at Lynn. Prescott
indicated he would welcome overtures from the Boston house, while also giving Harper and Brothers
an opportunity to renew the old arrangements and
make an offer for the new work. Phillips outlined his
proposal to the author. [36] It was the promise held
forth by Phillips that precipitated the severance of
ties with the Harpers in July, 1854.

The contract of August 5, 1854, between Prescott
and Phillips, Sampson, and Company was at once the
longest, most complex, and most financially promising agreement the author ever executed. [37] In general,
it provided for the publication of the new work,
Philip the Second, and provided for the publication,
in quick succession, of all the older titles in both
octavo and duodecimo. Although the Boston firm

admittedly was not of the proportions of Harper and Brothers, the program it undertook was conceived on the same, if not larger, basis. With time ultimately defeating the operation of parts of the agreement—depression delayed the implementation of it, and Prescott was dead and the company out of business before the initial six-year period elapsed and likewise before any duodecimo editions could be produced—a distinction must be made at once between the theoretical prospects and the real operation of the arrangement.

For the first two volumes of *Philip the Second* Prescott was to furnish stereotype plates, with the publisher pledged to produce 12,000 copies of each volume, in octavo, within three years. For the total of 24,000 volumes, Prescott was to receive $12,000, half in cash on the first day of publication and half by note payable in six months. For the right to publish additional copies of the first two volumes, either within or beyond the stated three-year period, Phillips, Sampson, and Company promised to pay Prescott at the rate of 50 cents per volume, in cash semi-annually. For later volumes of that title (Prescott conceived the work as running to five or six volumes in all), the author was to grant similar three-year exclusive rights to the publisher in return for $6,000 for 12,000 copies of each volume, payable on the first day of publication in the manner of the first two volumes, i.e., half in cash and half by note payable in six months.

Led by *Philip the Second,* the other Prescott titles were to fall in line quickly. Within one year of the date of the contract—hence by August 5, 1855—Prescott was to get the stereotype plates for *Ferdinand*

and Isabella, the *Conquest of Mexico,* and the *Conquest of Peru* into his new publisher's hands. Their exclusive right to produce octavo editions of the older histories found them agreeing to pay the historian 50 cents per volume, in semi-annual cash settlements. Within the same interval the stereotype plates for the *Miscellanies* were to be transferred to Boston, with the publisher allowed to publish any number thereof, paying royalty of 50 cents per volume, in cash, in annual settlements.

Once the older histories and the volume of essays had followed the new work into octavo form, author and publisher were to turn attention to cheaper duodecimo editions. Within one year of the initial publication of the first volumes of *Philip the Second,* which experience fixed as December 10, 1855, Prescott promised to provide the Boston house with stereotype plates for duodecimo editions of all four older titles. For exclusive right to publish 3,000 copies of each history each year for a period of six years, Phillips, Sampson, and Company promised Prescott $6,000 per year for those six years, with the company liable to that amount whether the works were published in those numbers or not. For all duodecimo volumes in excess of 3,000 copies annually, the publisher promised the author 25 cents per volume, payable in cash in annual settlements. For the *Miscellanies* the six-year right to publish in duodecimo found the publisher pledged to produce 2,400 copies in all, for which Prescott would receive $600, all to be paid during the first two years following initial publication. The publisher's right to continue the octavo and duodecimo editions beyond the six-year period, at 50 and 25 cents, respectively, per volume to the author, rested upon the whim of the historian who had the right to terminate the arrangement at will.

The closing portions of the contract provided for retail prices for all titles—new and old—of $2.00 per volume in octavo and $1.00 per volume in duodecimo. The publisher's rights were limited to the United States, and they could neither assign nor transfer them without Prescott's consent. The author wanted twenty-five volumes of the first edition of each volume of *Philip the Second* gratis. Additional volumes of any title, in octavo, he could buy at 66 cents each, with the duodecimo priced at 33 cents per volume for him. With the termination of the arrangement, the stereotype plates were to be returned in as good condition as on receipt, reasonable wear and tear excepted. No timetable for future volumes of *Philip the Second* was established.

In January, 1856, a subsidiary agreement between Prescott and Phillips, Sampson, and Company was reached, providing for the publication of the Robertson-Prescott *Charles the Fifth*. Unlike the other contract between them, it provided for Prescott's stereotyping, at his expense, his continuation of Robertson's work, a division between author and publisher of the stereotyping expense for the rest of the work, and a fifty-fifty division of all net profits. According to Prescott's memorandum of January 4, in case the agreement was broken, Prescott not only retained his plates and the copyright on his continuation but had the right to buy the publisher's half-interest in the jointly-owned plates at half the total original cost.

Any analysis of the contract would substantiate Prescott's view that it promised him a minimum of $50,000. Flat guarantees of $12,000 for the first two volumes of *Philip the Second,* $36,000 for duodecimo editions of the earlier histories over a six-year period, and $600 for 2,400 copies of the *Miscellanies* in duodecimo added up to $48,600, without taking into account such prospects as continuing income at 50 cents per volume on octavo editions of the older titles and $6,000 per volume for each and every additional volume of *Philip the Second.* Thus, the Prescott-Phillips, Sampson, and Company agreement contradicts the statement that "contracts in the last century lacked the complexity of present-day agreements and reflect the comparative simplicity of doing business in those days." [38]

Conditions arose which prompted Prescott to a generous revision of these terms a few years later, but as he made his last American publishing agreement, optimism on the part of both author and publisher called for long life and prosperity for both. Meanwhile, in the simultaneous English negotiation the factors of speed and happy agreement, so prominent in the American arrangement, were lacking.

With Aspinwall no longer available to him, Prescott, out of friendly ties with Bentley and a file of correspondence indicative of his agent's past handling of his affairs, logically concluded that he could negotiate a contract with the New Burlington Street house for *Philip the Second* via transatlantic mails. Taking into account the jeopardy a publisher might be placed in by an adverse decision on copyright by the House of Lords, Prescott wrote on May 16, 1854: "I offer it to you at the rate of One Thousand Pounds per volume; that is two thousand pounds for the two volumes first to be published, and one thousand pounds for each succeeding volume of the work.'' That price presupposed the author's ability to give his publisher a good copyright, but with that highly uncertain, Prescott continued his statement, ''In the other alternative of my being only able to send you the proofs in advance, I will furnish them to you for five hundred pounds a volume for the two first volumes and two hundred & fifty pounds for each succeeding volume of the work.'' In either instance the author wanted payment by means of the publisher's notes, one-half due six months after publication, the remainder on a nine-months note. Because of his numerous friends, Prescott added, ''I should stipulate to have twenty-four copies of the work of the largest size published given to me without charge.'' The author was so certain that his terms were both fair and acceptable that he insisted upon an answer by return mail, with it understood that he would view any modification of his proposal as equivalent to rejection. Either Bentley would take it quickly, at his price, or Prescott would turn to other English publishers.

Bentley, caught between judicial uncertainty as the House of Lords pondered a case of interest to the whole English publishing industry and Prescott's insistence on his terms, yielded to his author, stating in a letter of June 1, ''The terms you have proposed to me come in such a form, as not to admit of my applying to you for any modification of them, and I therefore at once accept them.'' But even as he did so, Bentley could not refrain from remarking that the price was unreasonable if a court decision reduced his advantage to mere priority on American sheets. Time soon demonstrated that Bentley's fear, far from groundless, undermined what appeared to be a sound agreement between the historian and his publisher.

Bentley composed the agreement and sent it to Prescott in late July, 1854. Two portions of it drew comment from him in a letter to Prescott dated July 21: the provision for Bentley's paying £800 at 5 per cent discount at six weeks from date of publication, with the remaining £1,200 payable at 4, 6, and 9 months, and the publisher's search for a margin of security by insisting upon "a clear priority of Six weeks before publication in America." And even before Prescott could reply, Bentley wrote to Prescott on August 11, "The opinion of *a majority of the Judges,* has determined the question that a foreigner cannot hold copyright in Great Britain." The publisher's worst imaginings had materialized.

Prescott's reply dated August 19 stated: "It will now be better to have the contract drawn up in a different form, specifying the sale of the advance sheets at the price agreed upon." At the same time, the historian reminded the publisher that should he be reluctant to make such a contract the work could be offered elsewhere.

Bentley, ill and enraged, did not avail himself of the author's offer to release him. He countered with the suggestion that publication of *Philip the Second* be postponed. For Bentley, the situation reached proportions of chaos when Routledge began to put cheap editions of Prescott's works on the English market. The exchange of letters which followed reveal a delicate bit of negotiation.

I am sorry to be again obliged [Prescott wrote to Bentley on October 18] to return the contract which you have sent me unsigned. The only objection I have to make to it is in regard to the last clause, over which, as you will see, I have drawn my pen. I am wholly at a loss to comprehend how there must have been such a misapprehension on your part respecting the terms of our agreement as to have led you to introduce a stipulation by which I should be bound to return a portion of the sum that I am to receive in case the work should be published by other parties in London within a month after its publication by you. No engagement of this sort appears in our correspondence, nor was it inserted in the former contract which you sent me. You are to pay me for sending you the sheets of the work in advance of its publication *here*. Of course I am bound not to furnish such sheets to any other parties; but I cannot be expected to assume that risk of the work being reprinted in London from your own edition by another house. This risk is the natural consequence of my not being able to give you a copyright; and it is precisely because you have to incur this risk, that you pay me £500 instead of £1000 per volume.

Bentley improved the situation when he wrote on November 9, "The Agreement for Philip the Second, with the omission of the clause struck out by you has been signed by me, and is herewith enclosed, together with its counterpart for your signature." But even as he did so, he continued with a species of pleading that suggested that his action and his desire contradicted each other.

Signing the latest version of their arrangement,

Prescott stated in his letter of November 26, "I am much obliged by your prompt reply; and indeed there was no time to lose, as I go to press to-morrow." And, he added:

> It gives me great pleasure to have completed the arrangement by which you are to continue the publication of my historical works. Now that the arrangement is completed, I may truly say that I have never tried to dispose of the Philip to any other English publisher; and if I have received proposals from that quarter they have never been of my seeking. If you think the £500 may prove burdensome, I can only say that not only was I offered the terms I proposed to you but I have good reason to believe that I could have got better terms than I have asked of you for the remaining volumes. I hope however your fears will not prove well-founded. If you adopt the practice which exists among our booksellers, you could, I should suppose secure a sale to a certain amount in advance by obtaining orders from booksellers before publication.

At the close of the year, Prescott and Bentley were once more in agreement despite the lingering fears of the publisher which included the imminent threat of cheap reprint competition in a period that found most Crimean War-conscious English readers satisfied to read newspapers. Indeed, the wartime situation, with its higher taxes, and the prospect of Bentley's edition appearing at the tail-end of the literary season prompted him in a December 14 letter to Prescott to suggest postponement until the autumn of 1855.

For the transmission of proof sheets to London, Prescott fell back upon prior practice and got them into American diplomatic pouches. In this manner they came to the hands of Colonel T. B. Lawrence, attaché of the American legation in London. Needless to say, Lawrence was inexorably drawn into the role of limited agent for Prescott in the English capital. Accommodating Bentley on the score of a favorable moment for the launching of the new work, Prescott agreed on the postponement with his American publisher and announced that Bentley should get his edition out before November 15.

Just when everything seemed under control once more to the mutual satisfaction of American author and English publisher, Prescott learned, via rumor, that Bentley was on the verge of bankruptcy. Concerning this delicate issue, Prescott, in search of facts, turned to the London bookseller Rich for confidential information.

Prescott brought the ugly issue into the open in a letter of May 29, 1855, to Bentley, in which he stated: "I think it was due to the long and friendly relations which have existed between us, that you should have advised me of the change in your circumstances. As my distance from you keeps me in ignorance of the real state of things, I have requested my friend Mr. Sturgis—a member of the house of Baring, Brothers Ltd.—to see you on the subject; and whatever arrangements he may think proper to make, I shall entirely approve of." Driven by involved circumstances, Prescott resorted to another agent on the scene in London. Nor was Sturgis' new duty destined to be a one-day affair.

Inaugurating his service to Prescott with the call upon Bentley, Sturgis touched off another show of pique and indignation. Bentley told Prescott in his letter of June 22, "I think it would have been more in accordance with the long-continued friendly terms of our correspondence, if, when any injurious reports about me reached you you addressed yourself to me direct.'' With startling rapidity both author and publisher thought the other inconsiderate. In truth, Bentley's affairs had turned bad, but after tottering on the brink, he was beginning to muddle through successfully. If Prescott would but accede to his request that he come to England, and thereby secure a better legal position for the publisher in the matter of English copyright of the American's work, his prospects would be better still.

Declining the invitation to go to England, Prescott suggested that the contract for *Philip the Second,* without recourse to alternatives, either be executed or rescinded. ''I beg you will communicate your decision,'' he wrote on July 9, ''to my friend Mr. Sturgis, who has kindly consented to take charge of the affair for me.''

Bentley countered with a more pressing invitation to the author to come to England, buttressing his own request with the opinions of his legal counsel, F. N. Devey, who was supported in them by solicitors James Willes and Alfred Turner. Detailing his case, Bentley concluded a July 26 letter to Prescott: ''If after full consideration of the reasons I have herein urged, you should still remain of the same mind, that is, *not* to come over to England, as I have advised, then in that case I at once accept your offer to rescind the Agreement between us.'' Prescott resisted Bentley's urgings and, considering the contract broken, asked on August 11 that the sheets in Bentley's possession be returned through Mr. Lawrence.

With eighteen months wasted in the negotiation with Bentley, Prescott, without a publisher in England and on the verge of publication in America, faced a dilemma. Sturgis, knowing of the pressure of time, rushed to sample the London market in advance of specific orders from Prescott. The offers that once had been so high were now otherwise. Routledge offered only £100 per volume for the receipt of sheets and Prescott's promise that he would have a six-weeks margin prior to American publication. With the prospect so dismal, Sturgis reopened negotiations with Bentley and planned to turn as well to Murray, as he informed Prescott in his August 31 letter.

In the ensuing free-for-all in London, Bentley emerged the victor, completing an arrangement with Sturgis for the first two volumes of *Philip the Second* on October 16, by which he agreed to pay £250 for the two volumes. Prescott had tumbled, in his expectations, from £1,000 per volume to £500 per volume and then finally to £250 for the pair of volumes. It was an appropriate moment for agent Sturgis to say, as he did in a letter to Prescott dated October 17: "Perhaps when some more volumes are ready, you will try the experiment of whether residence here during the process of publication will secure a copyright, & so make up for the small sum obtained for the two present volumes."

Late autumn found both the Phillips, Sampson, and Company and the Bentley editions of *Philip the Second* released, with Bentley issuing demi- and crown-octavo editions simultaneously in his effort to hold the English market. And almost immediately Bentley joined the reading public in his country in wondering when the remainder of the work would be ready for publication. "Am I right in supposing that the remaining portion of the Work is far advanced? and may probably appear during the coming year?" he wrote Prescott on November 6. He was wrong on both counts.

Prescott took the probing inquiry in stride, answering on December 16:

> You ask me when my work will be completed. I should be glad to have you tell me. If I were to ask you when Sebastopol was to be taken or when John Bull & Monsieur—whom he is hugging so closely just now—will go to loggerhead again, you would find it as easy to answer as it is for me to answer you. I write to please myself, and because I love labor. But then it must be a labor of love, or I could not write at all. I am at present tolerably industrious, and propose to continue so, if my health serves me.

Almost a half-year passed before Bentley renewed his expressed hope that more of *Philip the Second* would soon be forthcoming. In a letter of May 7, 1856, he coupled the query with the reminder that should the historian decide to come to England his copyright could be established.

When Prescott finally deigned to talk of manuscript to be published, he surprised Bentley by introducing a totally new theme, the publication of his continuation of Robertson's *Charles the Fifth*. Outlining what he had done to that old masterpiece of English historical literature, Prescott indicated that it would appear in America sometime after November 15. His letter of August 4, 1856, to Bentley continued: "If you would like to have the work I shall be obliged by your letting me know what you are willing to pay for it on the delivery of the sheets. . . . This vessel will take out letters from me to two other houses making the same offer."

Bentley's quick reply of August 18 read, "I should estimate the commercial value of this work at about £100 for the priority of publication."

True to his word that the work would go to the highest bidder, Prescott informed Bentley on September 15: "I am sorry you did not give me a better bid than £100 for the continuation of Robertson's Charles V, as it falls considerably below the offer of the Messrs Routledge, to whom of course I have been obliged to deliver the book."

The Routledge offer actually exceeded that of Bentley by only £10, a trifling sum, insufficient in itself to explain the switch of the historian to a publisher who previously had pirated his works. In his irritation at the thought, expressed by Bentley, that Prescott should canvass other publishers merely to determine the sum that he should pay, the author probably would have turned his back on the New Burlington Street house for a single shilling. Furthermore, it should be added, Prescott had met Routledge in America in 1854 and had been somewhat impressed by him. Indeed, it had been that meeting that had inspired Prescott's initial demand for £1,000 per volume for the *Philip the Second*.

By mid-November, 1856, Routledge had four separate editions of the *Charles the Fifth* before the English public. Pleased though he was, Prescott realistically admitted in his November 17 letter to Routledge, "I do not count however upon any brisk sale for you. Charles V is an old fellow."

Though grieved at losing one of Prescott's works, Bentley remained on friendly terms with the author, sending him gifts of books, and occasionally probing with queries such as the one of January 8, 1857: "Do you think of publishing two Volumes of 'Philip' together, next? I hope you do." When no answer was forthcoming, the publisher repeated his question and statement of hope on February 17. Eventually Prescott replied on March 9: "When I have a volume ready for the market I think I should publish it without waiting for its fellow." By the autumn of 1857 Prescott felt sufficiently advanced with his work to hazard the word that the spring of 1858 would find the next volume completed. This rare instance of his pinning himself down in advance to something approximating a timetable was not fulfilled, since Prescott had an apoplectic stroke in February, 1858.

However, with the spring of 1858 Prescott began the stereotyping of his almost completed volume but hesitated to enter into contract negotiations, hoping that through delay some ray of hope might pierce the dismal state of affairs marked by the absence of international copyright.

During the second week of the last August of his lifetime, Prescott opened negotiations for the third volume of *Philip the Second,* via correspondence, with both Bentley and Routledge. To Bentley he wrote on August 13, "Should you pay the sum originally arranged for each of the first two volumes (£500) I should be happy to take the risk of a month's priority of publication in England." And to Routledge, the historian indicated in a letter of

August 12 that, with no time for negotiations, he would accept the highest initial bid offered him.

Wanting to re-establish himself as Prescott's publisher, especially in reference to a work of which he had issued the earlier volumes, Bentley, though harassed by the realization that his edition would inspire a cheap reprinting by Routledge, wrote to Prescott on September 3, 1858, ''If you will give me a clear two months' priority, I will give for this priority the sum of Four Hundred Pounds.''

With Bentley offering £400 and wanting two months' priority and Prescott desiring £500 for one month's priority, the author and publisher were once more so far apart that the historian again turned to Routledge. On the same day, September 20, he wrote his refusal of Bentley's strings-attached offer and his acceptance of Routledge's offer of ''260 guineas for the advance sheets of the 3d volume.'' It was understood that the remaining volumes of the work also would go to that publisher at the same price unless the establishment of international copyright warranted Prescott's insistence on the original £1,000 per volume with which he had opened the entire negotiation four years earlier.

The third volume of *Philip the Second* appeared in both England and America in December, less than six weeks before the historian's death. The man who always had more to write and who looked expectantly into the future, leaving his last work unfinished, had concluded his last contract.

Prescott's publishing agreements across a period of more than two decades knew certain consistencies and inconsistencies in both the United States and

England. In both countries, for all his works his agreements were in part an expression of his desire to put physically attractive as well as intellectually superior books before the reading public. In both countries, through all the years the economic side of the historian was subordinate to the scholarly and artistic urges in his nature. Such factors served to stabilize much of his approach to publishing arrangements. Meanwhile, in each country there was also an element of instability that affected the Prescott contracts. In America, the changing circumstance of Prescott's expanding reputation and the new concept of expanding publishing operations induced his flitting from house to house and from city to city. Behind the American shifts was a search for harmonization of author and publisher outlook. In England, the changing circumstance that provoked his shift from Bentley to Routledge was rooted deeply in the precarious state of copyright. For Prescott it represented unending frustration.

No other mid-nineteenth-century literary theme surpasses the copyright issue as touchstone to understanding the great difference between our times and those of a century ago. Now the matter of copyright is so regularized as to be taken for granted. Then, copyright, in its international aspects, was the persistent concern of many authors and the bane of any author as prominent as Prescott.

———◆—◆———

CHAPTER FOUR

COPYRIGHT

NUMEROUS REASONS inspired Prescott's awareness of the property rights attached to his published works. As a historian whose very leisure to practice his craft depended on propertied wealth, which he in time came to administer, William Hickling Prescott early was conscious of the status of his literary products as property. In addition, his father's identification with the legal profession, plus the fact that he himself studied some law, underscored the almost intuitive awareness of the historian of his legal rights and the protection due his books. However, in the course of decades of dealings with American and English publishers, Prescott paradoxically demonstrated little real interest in the basic copyright problem.

The American copyright law of February 3, 1831, in response to agitation spearheaded by Noah Webster, had extended the original term for American citizens from fourteen to twenty-eight years, with privilege of renewal for fourteen years, giving an author a total of forty-two years of protection. Preliminary to winning such protection for his literary products, the American writer had to deposit, prior to publication, a printed copy of the title page of his work in the clerk's office of the district court of his home district.

Under that law, on seven separate occasions, protective steps were taken by Prescott. Six times he personally took out the copyright, walking into the Boston office of the clerk of the District Court for the District of Massachusetts. On these occasions, among other formalities, he deposited a copy of the title page of the work registered. Since Prescott did not live beyond the twenty-eight-year period of even his first book, the matter of copyright renewal did not fall to him. Every copyright eventually was renewed, beginning in 1865, in the names of various heirs. With the appearance, likewise after his death, of specially edited editions permitting new copyrights, which also knew subsequent renewal, the full story of Prescott's works under copyright reaches far beyond the scope of the present study.

A new era in the legal protection of literary property had opened in Europe shortly before Prescott prepared to publish his first book. In 1836 the government of Prussia passed a law which provided that any country could obtain copyright there for its nationals by granting reciprocal privileges to Prussians. This invitation to international copyright agreement became a reality in 1837 when the members of the German Confederation concluded a convention on that subject. In 1838, in early months of the reign of Queen Victoria, England embraced the idea.[1]

On February 2, 1837, a couple of months before Prescott made his initial American and English publishing arrangements, the new dimension of copyright thrust itself into American affairs for consideration. Thomas Moore and fifty-five other British authors presented a petition "praying Congress to grant to them the exclusive benefit of their writings within the United States." Among the signatories of this petition were many individuals Prescott came to count as friends, among them Charles Lyell, Henry H. Milman, Maria Edgeworth, Henry Hallam, Thomas Carlyle, Samuel Rogers, and Emmeline C. E. Stuart Wortley.[2]

Two days later the British action inspired the presentation to Congress of a memorial by a number of American citizens who supported the idea of altering the American law. The list of thirty signatures, which lacked such names as Irving, Cooper, Bancroft, and Sparks, did include some of Prescott's close friends, among them Henry W. Longfellow and Cornelius C. Felton. In their defense of the right of American authors, they held "native writers to be as indispensable as a native militia." [3]

On February 16, 1837, the select committee, composed of Clay, Preston, Buchanan, Webster, Ewing, and Ruggles, to which the British and American appeals had been directed made its report. Urging "some safe and cautious amendment of the law," the committee introduced a bill for consideration.[4]

Four days later a memorial signed by 152 writers, headed by G. Furman, presented an international copyright appeal to Congress. Although the members of the group presenting the memorial were inconspicuous individuals, chiefly from New York, their very number suggested that the idea was gaining wide currency. The same day the New York document went to Washington, February 20, a similar petition came to the national capital bearing the signatures of nine University of Virginia professors.[5] From Boston to Charlottesville, and from university professor to newspaperman, the appeals came. However, the bill offered by Clay's committee never came to a vote, due in part to public indifference and the pressure of those interests profiting from the absence of international copyright.

When Clay persisted and reintroduced his bill at the opening of the new session in mid-December— just ten days in advance of the release of *Ferdinand and Isabella* in Boston—opposition and support quickly crystallized. Before the year ended a meeting of booksellers, binders, printers, and others concerned with the booktrade in Philadelphia protested the passage of an international copyright law. The opposition created a committee to win signatures to a memorial which they planned to send to Washington. Condemning the proposed legislation, the memorial dwelt on the dangers it offered an industry which involved a capital investment of more than thirty million dollars. With dire prophecy of unemployment and higher prices for books, it closed with the signatures of fifty-two citizens of Philadelphia. In the ensuing three months even more opposition arose in the city of Brotherly Love, because on April 10 a duplicate memorial, bearing 114 names, also went to Congress. Typographical societies in Washington and New York also produced petitions crowded with economic complaint against the proposed liberalization of the American law. On March 28, 1838, a similar protest went to Washington from publishers and booksellers of Boston. Six weeks later still more opposition to international copyright came from Massachusetts.[6]

Support of international copyright came from Boston, New York, and Philadelphia. From the Athens of the New World—one week following the booksellers' petition—sixty-eight men sent a memorial which insisted, ''we are in favor of the proposed measure both because it is essential to the encouragement and development of American literature, and because it is demanded, with much propriety, as an act of justice.'' Among Prescott's friends, the signatories included Edward Everett, whose name headed the list, George S. Hillard, and C. C. Felton.[7] Prescott, with his first publisher bankrupt and possessed of a brand-new contract with a second house, was not a signatory.

The same day, April 24, 1838, also saw memorials favoring international copyright originate in New York and Philadelphia. The New York document bore 136 signatures. The Philadelphia memorial, with 40 signers, had the support of authors, publishers, booksellers, engravers, printers, teachers, artists, and paper dealers.[8]

Tempering the pro-and-con memorials was one headed by Peter S. Du Ponceau and signed by forty-eight others which insisted that the significance of the matter prompted a deliberate and intelligent, not a hasty, approach to decision-making.[9] On June 25, 1838, Senator Ruggles summarized the arguments embodied in both sets of memorials and then concluded that ''the committee have been unable to find sufficient reason for recommending the passage of the bill.'' [10] The Congressional session closed, and the copyright furor waned.

While it is true that Prescott never identified himself with this 1837–38 wave of sentiment in favor of international copyright, it is manifestly unfair to charge, as has one writer, that the defeat of that idea was due to the "coolness of prominent authors like Irving and Prescott." [11] Because it is easy to cloak a writer's total career in the greatness that came only much later, it must be pointed out that in 1838 fewer than 1,250 copies of Prescott's first book had been sold in America and an even smaller number in England. It is also a fact that his book had been contracted for on half-profits in England, and had not been pirated there. Both his limited role on the publishing scene and his favorable position easily combined to induce his indifference at that time.

Never in the course of the next twenty years was there as much agitation about the legal aspects of literary property in America as in the year 1838. However, by Christmas, 1839, two years and six American and two English editions after the initial appearance of *Ferdinand and Isabella,* Prescott, though still unaffected personally by the absence of international copyright, was interested in the issue. Knowing that Senators Henry Clay and William C. Preston would renew the fight for a more just law, Professor Francis Lieber sought to aid his fellow South Carolinian with a memorial from interested persons. Out of long friendship Lieber appealed to Prescott for aid, the result of which was a letter from Prescott to Lieber, November 26, 1839, containing the following sentiment.

> Touching the movement for the introduction of a copyright law, I can truly say, I feel sincerely interested in it; as well I may, now that I enter my fillies for the plate. But, in truth, I am a dull hand in action. . . . Irving is the person, undoubtedly, to

conduct it, but I think there is too much to be said, in order to interest him in it properly, to be managed by correspondence. An hour's talk would do more than a week's writing. Should I, at any time, visit New York, I shall make it a point to see him. But it really requires something more than a passive memorial, and some one should take care of it, and follow it to Washington, to suggest answers and explanations on points which a strong opposition will undoubtedly raise. Where shall we find such a person? Were the trade all as reasonable as Little & Brown, there would be no difficulty. But I fear it will be hard to persuade those worthy gentlemen who live by skimming the cream of other people's wits so easily, to have a conscience. I see a project broached for publishing the new popular works in Newspaper sheets, of such size that each sheet contains two vols., to be afforded at eight cents! It will not be easy to persuade either buyer or publisher of this precious trash that he will be a gainer by a fair copyright law.

Several weeks later Prescott urged Irving to take the lead, stating, "Such a law is certainly demanded by every principle of justice." Apparently expecting rebuff at the hands of American politicians, the historian of Spain continued: "If you [Irving] will prepare a paper, I shall be very glad, when it has been signed in your city, to do all in my power to get such signatures to it here as will give it most weight. . . . I can well understand, from my own feelings how distasteful this sort of work must be to you." [12]

Irving excused himself from leading the movement, but promised his co-operation. Prescott, however, took added steps. "I conversed on the subject with Mr. Webster, before his departure," he wrote Lieber on February 10, 1840, and he promised to support the bill, if introduced in the Senate. The Committee, however, have made such a report on it that I fear nothing is to be passed this session, nor have I much hope in any other. The *apparent* interests of the public are too much in the same seals with those of the publishers, and they, no doubt, persuade themselves that it is a greater good for the country to make the British authors work for us, for nothing, than to put a little money into the pockets of the few, who drive the trade of authorship, among ourselves. As to appealing to higher motives, one must have more faith in the stuff that statesmen are made of, than I have, to think they will weigh against the little calculations of selfishness.

Meanwhile, the liberal Lieber, having penned a lengthy essay on the theory of property in literature, sent a copy of it to Prescott, inviting the historian's reaction and assistance. Liking what he read, Prescott informed Lieber in a letter of April 13: "I have since endeavoured to bring it before the public, through a good publisher. But, I regret much to say, that although I have tried six, beginning with your own Aldus, alias Mr. Brown, I have not been able to negotiate it. Two of the six, only, have condescended to look at it. They will print it, if you will take the risk, and on no other terms." Times were bad for the book business; the theme was an unwelcome one from the point of view of most publishers; and so the author was forced to print his protest at his own expense.[13]

The American law remained unchanged, and the practices opposed by liberals became routine in publishing circles in the 1840's. With the appearance in England of a new title by an established English writer, one could automatically expect an early, cheap edition of the work in the United States. Some American publishers had arrangements with individuals in England whereby the latter, acting as agents, rushed an early copy of the new work across the Atlantic. Even prior to getting the American edition on the market, the American house generally announced its intention of doing so. In time, such announcements were so honored that they eliminated the prospect of competing American editions. This practice, gradually disciplining an unprincipled activity, became known as "trade courtesy."

In the absence of law, the exploitation of the English author's work without remuneration to him was not illegal; hence it was not real piracy. Nonetheless, the practice, which so offended fundamental honesty, was dubbed "piracy." Time and experience produced such a degree of honor among thieves that "trade courtesy" became increasingly frequent, and the American publisher of a certain foreign author —and certain American presses so monopolized individual authors as to have them recognized as belonging to that house—actually made small payments to the author. However, such remuneration never approximated the income that that author might have expected under an enforceable contract. Indeed, the speed of steamships and the popularity of the mammoth weeklies which offered entire novels for a pittance enabled the business of piratical reprinting of foreign works to prosper. American authors scarcely could compete with the abnormally cheap American-produced English works, and the English authors were driven to raging about the exploitation to which they were subjected.

The victimized Dickens, for example, traveling in America, voiced bitter criticism of the American practice. It baffled Dickens that Americans of just sentiment, men such as Irving, Prescott, Bryant, Halleck, and Dana, did not join him in a chorus of protest. However, the Englishman was in error when he wrote "not one of them *dares* to raise his voice and complain of the atrocious state of the law." [14] Not one of those named by Dickens was afraid. Rather, as Prescott himself illustrates, it was a matter of caring rather than daring. Quite plainly, the man who immersed himself in the affairs of six-teenth-century Spain could not view the nineteenth-century copyright issue as heatedly as did the professional agitator for reform in that century. Though a frank admirer in his writings of vigorous men of action—Gonzalo de Córdoba in the Old World and Cortés in the New—Prescott was himself not that kind of man. Prescott, however, was a quiet supporter of justice. Although throughout his literary life Prescott subscribed to the sentiments which he penned in 1839, "I never meddle with the dirty trade of politics," [15] he nonetheless determined his stand on slavery, the Mexican War, and other questions in addition to copyright. Writing to Dickens in 1842, he said: "The copyright I see sticks in your throat. It has stuck long in mine." [16]

However, in the middle and late 1840's, years during which Prescott's increasing reputation and earnings might logically have provoked greater interest in copyright, there is no indication of that interest. Indeed, little such sentiment existed in all the United States. Very little attention focused on the issue when in 1842 the international copyright bill was introduced for the fourth time.

Prescott wrote a half-truth when he informed Dickens in December, 1842, ''The copyright I understand begins to find favour with the bigger sharks, who complain that the smaller ones are running away with their game.'' [17] The phalanx of opposition guaranteed the maintenance of the status quo. Even the long, thirty-three-page memorial engineered by William C. Bryant and others in 1848 in favor of international copyright yielded before the opposition.[18]

Rendered indifferent, in part by his wealth and by his deep aversion to participating in political action, Prescott refused to play any significant part in the battle which counted poets and novelists as staunch defenders of the justice to which the historian gave only lip service. At home, protected by American copyright law, Prescott suffered no inconvenience. Abroad, however, it was a different story.

At the time of the negotiation in England for the publication of *Ferdinand and Isabella,* the concensus of opinion was that an American work could gain English copyright by publication in England prior to American publication. With such in mind, Prescott notified his agent Aspinwall, ''I shall take care to provide that the publication of the work shall be so regulated as to time, as not to interfere with securing a copyright in England.'' [19] And in his first letter to his English publisher, Prescott's concern about English copyright was obvious. ''I have provided in the contract with the publishers who have purchased the edition here,'' he wrote to Bentley, ''that its publication shall not . . . interfere with securing the copyright in England.'' [20] At the time, the matter of copyright in England disturbed neither the American author nor the English publisher. A troubled day eventually came when they rushed letters back and forth across the Atlantic about the facts in the case. Meanwhile, however, no English publisher troubled himself to compete with Bentley's edition of the new American work, *Ferdinand and Isabella,* and it was not until 1843 that Prescott became aware that no copyright of his work was to be had in England.

Early in 1843 in the final stages of helping Madame Calderón de la Barca find a publisher for her *Life in Mexico,* Prescott was sent £25 for the authoress in consideration of the early copy of the American edition which had gone to England to facilitate publication there. Accompanying this payment, the English publishers Chapman & Hall expressed themselves in a March 3 letter to Prescott concerning copyright as follows.

We beg to say that we think you will find on enquiry, that no copyright can be maintained here, legally, for a book first printed in America; and that any English publishers may print any work so published. The only advantage therefore that can be obtained is the receiving early proofs, by which the work can be produced here, before the arrival of American copies, and this priority being obtained, unless the work is very popular, other parties do not think it worth while to print it. But from an *American* copy, it is perfectly open for any one to do so, either in a volume, or in

a newspaper, as is the case with English books in
America.

Having basked in optimism and ignorance about the
rights of American authors in England, Prescott was
jolted by his experience with the Calderón de la
Barca book. To Dickens he had written: "I don't
understand, by the bye, how the circumstance of a
work appearing here just before it does in London
can affect the price of the copyright there. Doesn't
the purchase of a copyright protect the English
publishers?" [21] Chapman & Hall, voicing the generally held British publisher view, firmly told Prescott
that there was no such copyright, a truth faced by
the historian in later years.

Two months later, when Prescott informed his
friend Edward Everett that he had "sold the copyright to Bentley" for his *Conquest of Mexico* for
£650, the astute diplomat, rejoicing with the historian, informed Prescott: "I think you have, on the
whole, done well with Bentley. An Englishman on
the spot, with your reputation as the author of
'Ferdinand and Isabella,' would have done better;
but it is after all not a copyright which Bentley
buys, but merely the anticipation of other publishers
and the protection which exists in the understanding
between the members of the trade." [22]

This up-to-date statement of affairs, on the eve of
the publication of his second book, impressed upon
Prescott the necessity of priority of publication in
England. The *Conquest of Mexico,* published in Eng-
land October 24, 1843, did not appear in the United
States until December, when Harpers brought it out

one volume at a time between December 6 and 21.
This order of publication aimed at from the beginning, now became standard with Prescott. For the
next five years, from 1843 to 1848, Prescott's works
apparently did not suffer from the lack of copyright
in England, although Prescott realized very little
from the sale of his works in England because of this
fact. Moreover, in this interim period Prescott
seemed more concerned about the distribution than
the income from the sale of his books abroad. A
curious bypath in Prescott's publishing career is an
excursion into certain English-language editions of
his first three books in this period.

Based on Bentley's edition of the *Conquest of
Mexico,* a Paris-produced edition appeared at once,
raising some questions that cannot be fully answered.
Robert Walsh, a close friend of Prescott whose long
residence in Paris facilitated contacts there, had
previously put a copy of the historian's first work
into the hands of a French translator, thereby assum-
ing the role of author's agent. Now, on December
12, 1843, he wrote from the French capital: "Galignani undertook at once an edition of your Conquest
of Mexico in three neat octavos. . . . Galignani requested me to furnish him with a paragraph to usher
his edition. You will find it enclosed. The sale of the
American and British copies will not be injured
here." [23] This English-language Paris edition obviously was aided and abetted by Prescott. From the
very beginnings of his career, Prescott had sought
maximum circulation of his books in France, as witness the heavy dispersion of presentation copies
there through Ticknor and his sending, in January,

1842, of a five-hundred-copy impression of *Ferdinand and Isabella* into the Paris market.[24] That had occurred at a time, when, with a half-profits contract with Bentley for that book, it even might have adversely affected his English earnings. With the outright sale of the *Conquest of Mexico* to Bentley, not even the possible curtailment of English income stood in the way of his facilitating the appearance of a fifteen-franc, three-volume octavo English edition in France.[25]

However, the appearance in England of non-Bentley copies of Prescott's works so disturbed the New Burlington Street publisher that he wrote Prescott on May 3, 1844, for the precise dates of the American publication of *Ferdinand and Isabella* and the *Conquest of Mexico*. Prescott scoffed at the idea that American copies had invaded the English market. "I am sorry to learn from your letter by the last Steamer,' he wrote Bentley, "that your copyright is interferred with by Yankee poachers in the Colonies. . . . I am confident that neither my Boston or New York publishers have any hand in the matter. It is not in their way of business to send books abroad on their own account, and they both know it would be a thing I should not overlook, as it is expressly stated in my contract that the British market was my affair exclusively." [26]

Far from adopting the light-hearted attitude of the historian, Bentley cautiously and intentionally delayed publication of the *Conquest of Peru* until immediately after the departure of the regular steamer for America, lest some early copy of his edition redound to his disadvantage. The threat to the

British edition, never strong, quickly faded, and did not demand further attention from the publisher or the author until the spring of 1849.

Compounding Bentley's headaches in 1849, which had included an inordinately dull business season in 1848, which he attributed to the French Revolution of that year, was the rumored reprinting of *Ferdinand and Isabella* by Henry G. Bohn, whose constant practice of issuing cheap reprints constituted a thorn in the side of the more respectable houses of the period. Further legalistic reasoning of the problem of English copyright seemed to be indicated.

The American edition of *Ferdinand and Isabella* had antedated Bentley's edition. Prescott's letter of April 30, 1849, to Bentley argued as follows.

> By a recent decision on copyright in your courts it appears that a foreigner can take one out for a work the publication of which is prior to, or contemporaneous with its appearance in any other country. As it is scarcely possible that a work should appear the same day in countries so distant as England and the United States, the word "contemporaneous" would, I suppose, embrace any reasonable time where it was intended that a work should appear simultaneously in both countries; and as the "Ferdinand" came out in the last week of December here and two weeks later in England this I should suppose would be regarded as coming within the intention of the law. Of this your own lawyers will probably advise you. The construction of the law, as in the cases reported in 1848, appears to me very favorable to the claims of the foreigner. But if it should be otherwise, I do not think it would be advisable to attempt such radical changes in the work as would make it the subject of a new copyright.

To reinforce his own logic, Prescott resorted to legal counsel. The outcome he quickly relayed to Bentley in a letter of May 14, in which he stated:

> Since last writing to you, I have taken the opinion of one of our best lawyers, perhaps the best instructed as to this subject of copyright. He expressed the opinion that the term "contemporary" in the English statute, must cover as much time as would suffice for a book, after its publication in America, to be sent to England & reprinted there. Less time than this would not comport with the intent of the act, which is obviously to secure a copyright to the British publisher who shall bring out a foreign work before it can be received by the trade in the ordinary way and reprinted for publication in England. Now in point of fact "Ferdinand & Isabella" was published by you about three weeks after its appearance here—that is, in less time than a copy of the American edition could well reach England, before steamers were introduced. The first steamer between the U.S. & England did not begin to run, as you may remember, till the May following—1838.

However, Bentley remained uncertain, and he sought legal counsel. The further uncertainty of the six-page opinion of his solicitor, F. N. Devey, a copy of which the publisher sent the author, inspired Bentley's decision to bring *Ferdinand and Isabella* out in popular form at 6 shillings per volume to fend off the threat of piracy.

Reluctant to see his book in any but the finest form, Prescott, nonetheless, bowed to Bentley's decision on *Ferdinand and Isabella,* but he apparently believed that it would be the only title affected. Thus he confided to Bentley in a letter dated October 22,

1849, "I trust, however, that the 'Mexico' and 'Peru,' as the publication was got out several weeks sooner in London than here—will be impregnable." Having made up his mind, Bentley rushed the publication of a crown octavo edition of *Ferdinand,* copies of which he sent to the author in early November. The publisher insisted that with the move to the cheaper edition the threat from Bohn's 3*s* 6*d* reprint would be much reduced if not eliminated, a hope Prescott shared with him. Adapting his artistic sensibilities to the dictate of business, Prescott indicated that he, too, was an economic man. "I trust, as this edition . . . will reach another stratum of purchasers," he wrote Bentley on November 12, "that you will not be a loser. I think, as you keep the larger edition of the work too, that we may snap our fingers at the pirates, and make money on both."

Bentley's first report to Prescott, February 22, 1850, on the running battle with Bohn for the British market indicated that "the new and cheaper edition of your works is selling but not so extensively as I had hoped." More and more the publisher, whose sales were not up to expectation, deplored the lack of international copyright. A draft opinion supplied him by his solicitor and conveyed to Prescott in a letter of March 22, served to reinforce Bentley's fears. "I think, however," Devey, the solicitor, wrote the publisher on May 1, "in publications corresponding in date with Mr. Prescott's Work, the privileges are likely to be confined to Books printed in the United Kingdom, and not to extend to Books printed abroad and published here. This was so considered in Clementi v. Walker and would, probably, be adhered to." With clouds of legal complications gathering, the copyright question surely received attention when author and publisher finally met in England in the summer of 1850.

The next chapter of Prescott's involvement with English copyright was written early in 1851 when Prescott received word that the English pirates were threatening the *Conquest of Peru.* In a mood of depression bordering on despair, Prescott wrote to Bentley on January 13, "The pirates seem to be attacking us on all sides." In the midst of labors on behalf of a memorial from distinguished English literary figures favoring international copyright and his own report that Prescott's works continued to sell in the smaller edition, Bentley's depressed spirit invaded his reaction to the rumor of good prospects for international copyright. "I shall believe it when I see it only," he wrote to Prescott, April 7, 1851.

However, the gloom rapidly disappeared when Bentley gleefully reported to Prescott on May 22 that the question of the right of foreigners to copyright in Great Britain had been decided in the affirmative, reversing the previous "crude and hasty decision." With the sudden switch in their fortunes, Bentley, a fighter in the front ranks of a fiercely competitive profession, announced to Prescott on June 19, "I have proceeded against Bohn in the Court of Chancery."

From Prescott the decision in the Court of Exchequer Chamber elicited the following July 12 response.

I heartily rejoice with you and cannot but think that the decision of so full a bench will be sustained by the House of Lords, should Bohn & Co be disposed to carry up the suit to that tribunal. It certainly affords

a good stimulus to foreign authors, whose works find
a market in England, and it ought to quicken my industry, which has not been up to fever heat certainly
in my own historicals.

That Prescott's interest in the issue of copyright
impelled him to give English publication his close
attention is shown further in his August 19 letter
to Bentley. "I see an advertisement of Murray's in
the last Quarterly showing that Routledge had delivered up his pirated copies of Washington Irving's
works into his [Murray's] hands, which seems a
perfect recognition of the late decision. It is an important decision for you, & for me too." But with the
withdrawal of the pirates, Bentley soon found a new
basis of complaint. His fear, he informed Prescott on
September 26, that the smaller edition of *Ferdinand
and Isabella* would impair the sale of the larger one
had been realized.

However, Prescott looked forward to better days
and was buoyed up by the new tack of the pro-copy-
right element in the United States. On July 20, 1852,
he wrote Bentley as follows.

There will be an effort made here to introduce an international copyright law in the next session of Congress. It will be presented in the form of a treaty to
the Senate—and will have a better chance of passing
than if laid before the House of Representatives, as
it has hitherto been. Mr. Webster has applied to me
to give my views to him on the subject which I shall do.
If this effort fails, I should fear that some retaliatory
measure would be taken by your government.

Paradoxically, as he thus expressed himself in favor
of international copyright, Prescott was harmoni-

ously, even enthusiastically, doing business in America with Harper and Brothers, who were then and for decades to come a leading element in the vigorous denunciation of international copyright.

Prescott's hopes were doomed to disappointment. Webster, more willing than able, was in his grave in less than a hundred days, and the treaty which was subsequently negotiated never became operative. The new approach to the old problem resulted in continuance of the status quo at a moment that particularly disturbed the historian, who was at last far enough along with his *Philip the Second* to see it encompassing five volumes eventually. He deeply longed for a resolution of the existing uncertainty before he published any part of it.

With the opening of contract negotiations for *Philip the Second,* Bentley wrote to Prescott on September 10, 1852:

> In all my arrangements with you I have always been satisfied there was a copyright for American books here provided it was secured by priority of publication; and I have acted upon this conviction, not only with regard to your works but also with Mr. Washington Irving, Mr. Fenimore Cooper, and others.
>
> Should the American Government come to the determination not to enter into an International Copyright Act with England, which I trust is improbable, I do not fear that any retaliatory measure will be sanctioned by the British Government. At all events, I am quite willing to run any risk of any such measures, and to have it embodied in our Agreement for the work.

Bentley might have felt certain of his position, but other American authors, among them Mrs. Harriet

Beecher Stowe, joined Prescott in quizzical uncertainty. In late 1852, according to a letter to Bentley dated October 11, Prescott received a letter from her "containing sundry queries about foreign copyright."

In this period, two of Prescott's most loyal friends, Charles Sumner and Edward Everett, tried to overcome the tide of anti-international copyright opinion. On July 19, 1852, Sumner, in the Senate, took cognizance of two petitions favoring international copyright. One bore the names of such men as James Fenimore Cooper, Jonathan Wainwright, Herman Melville, William C. Bryant, George P. Putnam, and Washington Irving.[27] One name it did not bear was that of William H. Prescott. During the following year, Secretary of State Edward Everett, through Minister John Crampton, negotiated a treaty with Great Britain on the subject. However, the matter which could not win majority support in the two houses of Congress was balked again by the tabling of the Senate.

In the desultory correspondence between Prescott and Bentley about contract terms for *Philip the Second,* none of which work had been finished, suddenly there was renewed attention on the copyright issue when Bentley wrote to Prescott on February 16, 1853: "Again it appears the Copyright Question is to be discussed. The Printers carry it in a short line to the House of Lords, in the hope that the present Lord Chancellor, Lord Trainworth who gave his concurrence to Sir Fredk. P. Misk against us may decide in their favor. We retain Sir Fitzroy Kelley, & the matter will be costly to us at any rate."

Months passed, and more than a year later Bentley repeatedly stated that the decision of the House of

Lords on the copyright appeal had not been pro-
nounced. The suspense was all the more unnerving to
Prescott, who now had two volumes of *Philip the
Second* ready, a circumstance that invited negotiation with publishers once more.

On August 15, 1854, Prescott wrote Bentley an
unusually long letter full of close reasoning that explored every conceivable alternative, all of which
was irrelevant because the long-awaited decision had
removed the issue from the realm of logical speculation. "You will regret to hear,' Bentley informed
him in a letter dated August 11, "that the House of
Peers here has reversed the decision of the Court of
Error; and disregarding the clearly expressed rul-
ing of Lord Campbell, supported by the opinion of
a majority of the Judges, has determined the question that a foreigner cannot hold copyright in Great
Britain." He added:

> This revocation of a principle that I regarded *as
> established,* is a grievous blow to me, from the exten-
> sive dealings I had had with American Authors. But
> in no other case do I so much deplore this event, as
> with respect to your valuable Works. Henceforward
> it seems, or rather it is clear, I must be content to
> share with those who are sure to compete actively
> with me any benefits which may accrue from the sale
> of your works and one of my first endeavours must
> be, not only to reduce considerably the selling price
> of the present editions, but to bring out others on the
> lowest scale of prices that will admit of remuneration,
> to prevent others from underselling me.

Sounding a poignant note of despair, the New
Burlington Street publisher added, "This is a glori-
ous time for unprincipled men or pirates."

The contract negotiations Prescott had carried on

with both Bentley and Routledge were now even more unsettled. As Prescott shifted his position, he epitomized confusion of thought. "It will now be better," he informed Bentley on August 19, "to have the contract drawn up in a different form. . . . I think, however, that a clause should be inserted providing for the possible, though by no means probable case of any of the future volumes becoming entitled to copyright."

But though the copyright decision thus snarled negotiations on future books, it precipitated the hasty issuance of cheap editions of existing ones. One month after the pronouncement of the decision, Bentley had a five-shilling edition of *Ferdinand and Isabella* before the British public, with plans for similar editions of both the *Conquest of Mexico* and the *Conquest of Peru*. Nor did the New Burlington Street publisher have much of a lead over Routledge, who also issued a five-shilling edition of Prescott's first work. It was at this time, under pressures of copyright conditions, that Bentley deleted most of the notes in his editions of Prescott's first book, informing Prescott of the decision in a letter of September 8, 1854.

Groggy in the face of the recent unexpected and costly decision, Bentley clutched hopefully at a straw. In a letter of September 12, he suggested to Prescott: "If I may be permitted to offer a suggestion on the subject, I would submit that it would be most desirable on all accounts to postpone the appearance of your new work, in the hope that this much wished for event [adherence by the United States to international copyright] may happen."

Meanwhile, Routledge tried to make his invasion

of Bentley's domain more palatable to the English public by advertising that Prescott was not financially interested in Bentley's editions. Bentley bought space in London newspapers to contradict Routledge's claim, as in truth he could, since both the first history and the *Miscellanies,* the works for which Prescott's contracts provided half-profits, gave the author a continuing stake in those two titles. Although the decision of the House of Lords technically freed Bentley from the necessity of continuing his payments to Prescott, he nonetheless did so.

To complete the devastation of Routledge, Bentley proposed to Prescott on September 28 that "a statement coming from yourself . . . either addressed to the Editor of 'The Athenaeum,' or better still to myself, would carry a weight with it, which might not be given to the simple assertion of the publisher. Such a statement need not particularize, for it is scarcely necessary to satisfy in this way every impertinent querist." By asking for a general statement from Prescott, Bentley obviously hoped to strengthen his hold on all that author's works, not merely those in which Prescott had a continuing financial interest. Bentley's dilemma was real, because Routledge not only advertised the first history as available, but promised, according to Bentley's letter to Prescott, the *Conquest of Mexico* "in a few days" and the *Conquest of Peru* "very shortly."

Promptly complying with Bentley's request for a statement of the author's interest in his editions, Prescott also reported to Bentley on October 18, 1854: "As to an international copyright treaty, I regret to say that there is not the slightest prospect of one between this country & England. I form this opinion not merely from a general knowledge of the circumstances, but also from conversations with members of the U.S. Senate; who are acquainted with the opinions on the subject that prevail in that body.''

Agreements were reached and rescinded; new proposals were advanced and rebuffed—all resulting from uncertain and undesirable legal conditions. Bentley's solicitor, F. N. Devey, buttressed his own study of the copyright question with opinions he sought from others of his profession. Solicitor Alfred Turner informed Devey in a letter of May 28, 1855, ''I conceive the Foreign Author must in such a case [i.e., to win copyright] reside here to print and first publish under his own direction and having done so launched his Work into the World and registered his right at Stationers Hall he will then be able to assign such acquired right to any one.'' Transmitting a copy of the full opinion of Turner to Bentley, Devey added on May 31, ''I concur with him in thinking that Mr. Prescott can acquire a Copyright in this country, in his Work, by coming here, and residing here during the printing and Publication of it; the Work being first published in this country.'' Next the Prescott-Bentley problem received study by James Willes of Inner Temple. The heart of Willes' three-point opinion dated June 14 read: ''I am of Opinion that Mr. Prescott can acquire copyright in his work by residing in England whilst his work is being printed and published. . . . I am of Opinion that Mr. Prescott can assign his copyright wholly. . . . I am of Opinion that Mr. Prescott can grant a license to publish with limitation as to number or locality or both.''

Encouraged by the unanimity of legal counsel received from Devey, Turner, and Willes, Richard Bentley wrote Prescott on July 26, "I am ready to run the risk of obtaining an advantage, which may be equivalent to copyright on your new Work, with its chance of lawsuits, &c provided you will come to England and remain during the printing and publishing of your Work." Prescott's reply on July 9 summarily dismissed the idea.

Caught in the dilemma that posed loss of author on the one hand and an indefensible legal position on the other, Bentley fought doggedly to win Prescott's sympathetic consideration of his proposal. Indicating his suggestion embraced a confident expectation, not a vague hope, the publisher backed his appeal with references to and quotations from the legal opinions he had acquired. He also faced alternatives, which he communicated to Prescott in a letter dated July 26, 1855: "After this full explanation of the grounds on which I made the proposition to you to come over to England, I hope you will be induced to alter your intention, and consent to come." Bentley added: "If . . . you should still remain of the same mind, that is, *not* to come over to England, as I have advised, then in that case I at once accept your offer to rescind the Agreement between us." Family considerations and personal comfort triumphed over Prescott's interest in English income and copyright. The historian's reply of August 11 contained another refusal to sail the Atlantic.

As a result Prescott reopened negotiations with other publishers, including Murray, Routledge, and Bogue through Russell Sturgis, then his agent in England. It was swiftly evident, however, that under

the double disadvantage of American unwillingness
to adhere to international copyright and the author's
indisposition to journey to England, the agent's
bargaining position was a weak one. When in the
free-for-all bidding for the first two volumes of
Philip the Second Bentley emerged victor, he did so
for a trifling sum. He paid Prescott for the two
volumes the sum of £250. In this manner Prescott's
equity in the volumes tumbled to 12.5 per cent of
the £2,000 which the author and the publisher in the
days prior to the Lords' decision had provisionally
established for the new work.

At last in very tangible fashion, the lack of international copyright became a liability in Prescott's
own experience. Harking back to the days prior to
the Lords' decision, Prescott wrote to an uniden-
tified correspondent on November 15, 1855, that "two
houses in London each offered . . . a thousand
pounds a volume for the copyright—the largest sum
probably ever paid to a foreign author for a single
work, as it was allowed to extend to six volumes."

In late October, 1855, almost eight and one-half
years after his last previous title, a period characterized by one form of copyright difficulty or another,
two volumes of *Philip the Second* appeared in England. Receiving copies of them, the author wrote to
Bentley on November 6 that he thought the work
in such handsome form "that the cheap & nasty
editions of some of the guerilla adventurers" would
take the field with it as well.

Meanwhile, Prescott had picked up still another
idea of a way in which a copyright might be gained
by a foreigner in England. "Mr. Constable, of the
Edinburgh house," he noted in his November 6 letter

to Bentley, "has written to a friend of mine here that he is about to bring out a work written by an Italian, & in order to secure a copyright to it in England had published it first in France—having satisfied himself, after an investigation of the subject, that a copyright can in this mode be obtained for both countries."

Learning that Bentley's beautiful edition was to be joined by "cheap and nasty" editions from the same publisher, Prescott surmised in a letter to Bentley late in November that "no pirate would be bold enough to attempt a competition." Indeed, Bentley felt rather smug about his three editions, at 23 shillings, 12 shillings, and 5 shillings—all of them complete texts—discouraging any piracy. Satisfied with his offering of Prescott's latest book, the publisher did not find the historian's latest idea acceptable. He ridiculed the Constable plan for acquiring English copyright for a foreigner's work, even though he hoped the effort might force revision and improvement of the copyright law.

The new year, 1856, quickly presented an old problem: Routledge had ventured to issue an edition of *Philip the Second.* "Like Galignani and Baudry of Paris" Bentley told Prescott in a letter of February 21, 1856, "he will make his fortune—if he makes his fortune, by pirating the purchases of others. . . . I hope you may be induced to come over to England to see the succeeding volumes of your history through the press, and thus put a stop to the filching of Routledge, and leave his two volumes 'high & dry.' "

Bentley continued to see in the prospect of Prescott's coming to England a measure of salvation that led him to hammer relentlessly at the idea. In the wake of a routine financial accounting to Prescott on their half-profits agreements, he insisted in his letter of May 7, 1856: "Doubtless Routledge must have interfered with the profit derivable from the sale of your Works; but if you came over and thus establish your copyright he would repent of such experiments in future." Instead of going to England, Prescott changed publishers.

With the completion of his supplement to Robertson's *History of Charles the Fifth,* Prescott invited the bids of certain London publishers. With mere priority of publication, in the disturbed state of the copyright, at stake, Bentley offered £100 for the new work. When Routledge, so often and so recently termed pirate by both Bentley and Prescott, offered £10 more, the historian unhesitatingly signed a contract with him.

The historian's change of publisher is difficult, though not impossible, to explain. This period during which he was offered pittances in England for *Philip the Second* and *Charles the Fifth* was one of his most financially rewarding periods in the United States. In the very letter of September 15, 1856, in which he informed Bentley his bid of £100 was insufficient to win a contract, Prescott informed the London publisher that "at my last settlement of six months' sales, my publisher [Phillips, Sampson, and Company] paid me 17,000 dollars." Glorying in his American earnings and disgusted at the low level of his English earnings, Prescott seized the ten additional pounds offered by Routledge.

Bentley, though equally mercenary, bore up like a gentleman. "I will not however imitate his [Routledge's] example although recommended to do so by the advice of others," he replied to Prescott on October 27. His interest in Prescott continued. Bentley sent him recent titles from his press, and hoped, as in a letter of November 13 he cited the example of Mrs. Stowe's crossing the Atlantic to win copyright for her book *Dred,* that the historian could change his mind about traveling to England when next the occasion arose.

Prescott welcomed the issuance of *Charles the Fifth* by Routledge in four separate editions. "One effect," he wrote his new publisher on November 17, 1856, "will be that you must drive every competitor out."

And a year after hearing of the effort to win copyright through France, Prescott was impressed with the prospect of doing so through Canada. He detailed it for London reaction. "The other day," he wrote to Routledge on December 19, 1856, "my publishers [Phillips, Sampson, and Company] received a letter from a London house, saying that it had obtained the opinion of counsel, which satisfied them that if an American would take his book to Canada and remain there—in Montreal or Quebec, for example—while it was published, and sell the copyright to a publisher there, it might then be transferred to a publisher in London, who would thus get a sound copyright. This seems plausible. . . . The house proposed to negotiate with me on this basis. As the letter was addressed to my publishers here, I was not called on to give an answer. I mention this to you that you may satisfy yourself of the feasibility of this way of proceeding; and if you find it safe and we agree on the terms, I should not object to make a short visit to Canada, which I can do in twelve hours—though it would take more than any of the brotherhood would offer me to cross the ocean for the purpose.'' One day after writing in this vein to his new English publisher, the historian sent a similar letter to Bentley, minus any mention of his willingness to adopt the idea himself. Of the two publishers, Bentley gave it more immediate attention. Though unable to obtain satisfactory opinion on the scheme at once, he promised to pursue it.

The last official American concern about the copyright question during Prescott's lifetime came in 1858, when Representative Morris of Pennsylvania introduced a bill before the U.S. House of Representatives. But the nation with perplexing and mounting domestic problems evinced little interest in the issue and the bill received no consideration.[28]

The third volume of *Philip the Second,* published by Routledge after another bidding contest between that house and Bentley, signalized Prescott's last tussle with the copyright problem. Indeed, it broke the friendly tie between Prescott and Bentley. Enraged that Prescott had taken elsewhere the third volume of the work of which he had published the first two, Bentley declared to Prescott on November 9, 1858:

> It has never been my misfortune in a long life to have experienced treatment so incompatible with the usages of men of letters in this country. . . . What I feel I will not express, lest I should use language which I am unaccustomed to employ, even under excitement; but I must leave to tell you, that every one who has read our correspondence agrees with me, that no such thing could possibly occur among English gentlemen.

Upon any future occasion when you may think of publishing in this country, I must beg leave to be spared a renewal of correspondence.

That others may not be led into similar losses, by conduct of the like nature, I shall feel myself justified in submitting this letter either to my friends, or to the public, as I shall deem expedient.[29]

Bentley took the latter course and published a portion of his most recent correspondence with Prescott in February, 1859, after the historian's death. The full measure of Bentley's embitterment is seen in his publication of the correspondence even after he had heard of the death of the author he long had counted friend.

Early in his career Prescott, addressing a friend, indicated one of his lifetime practices when he counted himself within "a quiet little circle that takes refuge from the storm and rather disheartening politics of the day in literature, and meet in a genial and independent atmosphere of our own." [30] Shunning the dirty trade of politics, he refused to co-operate with men in that area of life which alone could produce the kind of law his sense of justice desired. In his experience Prescott, in addition, had been strangely untouched for more than a decade by some of the uglier practices of the period, a circumstance which probably strengthened his acceptance of the status quo. The near do-nothingness of such a prominent writer contributed to the long continuation of a condition which stamped the United States as backward in the matter of recognizing literary property rights. And long after Prescott, Bentley, Routledge, and almost all of his other literary contemporaries had passed from the earthly scene, the copyright confusion persisted, knowing no just resolution until 1891, by which time Prescott's works, no longer protected in the United States, were the subject of cheap and tawdry publication in the author's own land.

However, all was not paradoxical in the author who never said anything to his American publishers while always writing enthusiastically to those in England about international copyright. Out of his love of the beautiful, Prescott demonstrated persistently on both sides of the Atlantic an amazing concern about the details which would help to convert his manuscripts into attractive books. Saying little and doing less about the big issue of copyright, he did a lot and said even more as he contributed ideas and pursued high standards in the production of his successive books.

————•————

CHAPTER FIVE

BOOK DESIGN—AN AUTHOR'S ROLE

ACROSS THE YEARS between early moments of pre-publication planning for his first book and his death, Prescott demonstrated ceaseless concern about the physical, as well as the intellectual, side of his published works. The stereotype plates, produced, significantly, for the author, not the publisher, constituted one important aspect of that concern. Equally important was the historian's recourse to a publisher who handled expensive works even in that period during which absence of tradition more readily permitted a publisher to be daringly imaginative in his book manufacture. In addition, author and publisher must have been challenged by the realization that any book as drab as the usual products of American presses of that day surely would suffer humiliation by comparison with the forthcoming English edition of the same title. Exactly what kind of book the London publisher was producing no one in America knew. That uncertainty, plus the knowledge that English bookmaking standards were normally superior to American ones, caused the Boston author and his Boston publisher to give Prescott's first book, *Ferdinand and Isabella,* the attention that made it something special. So conceived, the first American edition of *Ferdinand and Isabella* served in many ways as a standard to be maintained for all other books by Prescott.

Pleased with the format of his nascent book, Prescott felt constrained, a few days before publication, to write on December 20, 1837, to George Bancroft, who had offered to review it:

> The publishers have felt particularly ambitious to come up to anything that may come from London; and if you approve of the result, pray notice the *physique* of the book—which will help the sale, and is but due to them. I think books got up with as much care in this respect as yours, and mine, and Sparks's, form a favorable contrast to the South, and cannot fail to have some effect in raising the standard in the country.

To Boston-oriented Prescott, "south" probably included everyplace south of Boston, including New York City.

Standing full twenty-five centimeters high, with gold stamped spines featuring the arms of Castile and Aragon, the three volumes of *Ferdinand and Isabella* were bound in tan cloth bearing a floriated design. The smooth-surfaced, cream-colored end papers added another note of rich elegance. Each volume bore a frontispiece portrait: Isabella graced the first, Ferdinand the second, and Cardinal Ximenes de Cisneros the third. The engraving of the queen was the work of J. Andrews, while those of both men had been executed by G. F. Storm. All bespoke the quality of workmanship Prescott insisted upon throughout the work.

The title page, bearing the date 1838 in Roman numerals, signified that release in 1837 really had not been thought practicable by the printer. Possibly only some superhuman burst of author-inspired effort had produced the contradictory circumstance wherein the book with the 1838 imprint won release the last week of 1837.

Reflecting Prescott's desires, the American edition had fine quality paper, wide margins, double-columned footnotes, and separate pagination for the long introductory essay. Volumes one and three carried maps, the former for the War of Granada, the latter for Gonzalo de Córdoba's campaigns in Italy.

In many matters regarding printing that are now usually beyond the concern of authors in their relations with their publishers, *Ferdinand and Isabella* mirrored to a maximum degree the tastes of William H. Prescott. To Jared Sparks, receiving a presentation copy, Prescott wrote on December 25, 1837, "I think you will admit that Queen Isabella herself would have been gratified to have seen herself exhibited in so beautiful a dress."

Just another book, in many respects, to the London publisher, the English edition of *Ferdinand and Isabella* nonetheless was made up in a manner acceptable to its fastidious Boston author. In three volumes, like the American edition, Bentley's version did not distribute the material as equally among them. Some of Prescott's ideas, including his desire that the notes be printed double-column, crept into the London product. Others, such as his hope that the introductory essay be assigned separate pagination, the Englishman ignored. The author seemingly did not realize that footnotes could be printed un-

numbered, and, accordingly, he had not expressed
himself on that subject. Great, in consequence, was
his displeasure when the English edition indicated
its footnotes by symbols.

The author's interest in the total book, an evolving
thing in relation to his first American edition, in-
sinuated itself into his communications with his
agent and with his publisher in England at an early
moment. Even before he had a publisher on either
side of the Atlantic, Prescott informed Aspinwall,
"The work . . . will be executed in as handsome a
style as it can well be done here." [1] And though
genuinely and generally pleased with the first English edition, Prescott never gave his British publisher rest, much less the right to reduce his standards. Condemning the poorer paper, more crowded
printing, and thinner volumes of the second English
edition, he summarized his thinking for Bentley as
follows: "I hope you will never suffer the book to
come out in an inferior dress, as I am convinced the
credit of a good work, as I hope this is, is after all
much affected by the costume." [2] Not long thereafter,
inspired by word of a new edition forthcoming in
England, he entreated his publisher, "I trust you
will get out the book in a style equal to the preceding
editions," following which hope he re-emphasized
the weaknesses of the second edition. [3] In such fashion Prescott attained abroad, as well as at home, the
standards of book design and manufacture he subsequently came to provide for in the very phrasing
of his publishing contracts.

With agents and publishers alike, in both the
United States and England, Prescott approached
every publishing agreement of the 1840's and 1850's

deeply concerned about the general style in which his works would appear. In his reluctant co-operation to produce the seemingly necessary abridgment of *Ferdinand and Isabella* that never saw publication, Prescott jealously guarded his control over his publisher's standards. After a careful statement of them in relation to paper, binding, and general execution, the contract included the phrase "said Prescott to be the judge." [4]

Adhering to the author's admonition that his works know physical standardization, the Harpers produced the *Conquest of Mexico* in the pattern of the first work. Prescott's control of the stereotype plates guaranteed basic elements of similarity—size of type and style of headlines and footnotes. However, the similarity continued in areas controlled by the publishers—quality of paper, ink, and binding. Exactly the same height as the first history, the second one was likewise bound in cloth bearing a floriated design, with gold-stamped spines including the coat of arms of Cortés. Color of binding, which had varied widely with successive issues of the first work, continued to do so, with some lots of the first edition of the *Conquest of Mexico* in dark brown and others in dark green. Further standardization found both histories, *Ferdinand and Isabella* and the *Conquest of Mexico,* offering frontispiece portraits of prominent characters in the history as well as maps which facilitated the reader's following certain significant actions. The remarkable similarity between the second history and the first history attests the establishment of and adherence to a physical pattern of book manufacture by Prescott.

Concerning the same new work in its English edition, the historian pointedly informed Aspinwall, "One condition I should desire to have made, whoever publishes the work, viz: that the first edition shall be got up in a style every way equal to that of Ferd. and Isabel by Bentley." [5] Not content to have his agent relay his demand, Prescott personally laid it before Bentley in a letter of September 14, 1843. Aware of the author's demands, Bentley complied with them, and in so doing produced a first edition of the *Conquest of Mexico* which, in some respects— e.g., better balanced size of volumes—was superior to his first edition of Prescott's earlier work.

On both sides of the Atlantic the *Miscellanies* again demonstrated Prescott's concern about the general appearance of his books. Aspinwall, acknowledging the historian's instructions and reporting on his own activity, reassured him, "I repeated also your condition as to the style and form of the publication." [6] Again reinforcing the labors of his agent, Prescott informed Bentley, "The volume will be got up so as to match exactly with the historicals." [7]

The Harpers heard the same insistent voice about the same book in letters from Prescott dated June 5 and June 24, 1845. Indeed, their prefatory statement to the book, entitled "Advertisement of the American Publishers," read: "The publishers have taken care that the mechanical execution of the book shall be uniform with that of his historical works." Never did a publisher's statement more completely reflect an author's desire.

In his contract with the Harpers for their publication of the *Conquest of Peru*, Prescott repeated his insistence upon paper, binding, and everything else that added up to his concern about the complete book; and in so doing, he expected the new work to emerge in the well-established pattern of his previous titles. As he proposed the negotiation of a publishing agreement for the same work in England, he undoubtedly called much to the mind of Aspinwall with the words: "all in the same style as the preceding work." [8] Prescott could not relax even with word that the English contract had been concluded with Bentley. To Aspinwall he confided his fears about the phrasing of the contract: "I suppose also that he has no thought but of bringing out the first edition of the work at least in as good style as the 'Mexico,' a thing I deem of much importance, though perhaps he did think to mention it in the contract." [9] No vagueness attended his word to the Harpers as he transferred his stereotype plates to them. "I shall depend on your executing your part—the press work, paper, binding, &c, in as good style as you did the first edition of the 'Conquest of Mexico,' " he wrote on April 24, 1847.

By the time of his contract with Phillips, Sampson, and Company in 1854, several things had come to influence Prescott: his earlier insistence upon uniformity of standards for successive works had produced a tradition of quality that might almost be taken for granted; the economic necessity of appearing in England in duodecimo as well as octavo had shaken his previously stubborn stand; the author's stronger interest in the financial terms of his contract tended to subordinate other considerations; and a general physical inability to keep his fingers upon every detail made for a shift in his outlook. Such circumstances represented a conflict of influences, but

his control of the stereotype plates, his identification
with the supply of illustrations, his very presence
in the same town with his publisher—all contributed
to the routine maintenance to the very end of a once
carefully repeated insistence upon the highest of
standards in book manufacture. If Prescott had
lived longer and if the Boston publishing house, instead of going bankrupt, had carried out every pro-
spective operation provided for in the contract of
1854, including the issuance of duodecimo editions,
there would have been a serious deterioration of
Prescott's accustomed standards. As it was, even
though his last contract offered that dismal prospect, it never materialized in the lifetime of the
author. Hence the frank admirer of the octavo and
equally frank disdainer of the duodecimo never witnessed a lowering of his standards in America.

Prescott's pre-publication suggestions and demands frequently were followed by post-publication
judgments on the products of his publishers. To
Bentley he wrote on November 30, 1843: "I have
received a copy of the 'Conquest of Mexico' . . .
The work is got up very handsomely, and agreeably
to my wishes in every respect." And then to indicate
it was not quite perfect in his estimation, Prescott
added:

> I don't know why the page containing the General
> Contents was omitted, as it was destined to show the
> symmetry of the plan. One defect only I notice in
> the Contents of the third volume being printed not
> uniformly with the others, and in an inferior style,
> —not being leaded. This does not look in good keep-
> ing with the rest of the work. But that is a trifle;
> and I am obliged to you for seeing the thing got

through so conformably to my desires. My own page [and he could call it his because of the stereotype plates behind the American edition] has less matter on it than yours, so that the work will have a more bulky appearance. We think that better policy here, though it costs something more.

Even as it accorded general approval, Prescott's criticism touched upon minutiae that demonstrated his reaction was based upon the closest kind of scrutiny. Tingeing his approbation with citation of error, Prescott intended to better subsequent editions and works. Sometimes he jogged his English publisher by comparing his product unfavorably with its American equivalent. "Have you seen," he wrote Bentley on May 30, 1844: "the American edition of the Conquest of Mexico? As there is less on a page the vols. are considerably stouter than the English. Do you think its purchaser would think that he got more for his money if your vols. were thicker, & would it not more than counterbalance the increased cost of paper?"

The results of such needling are best seen in the later publications by that house; some incorporated the author's suggestions and others omitted them with a completeness that was hardly accidental. Undoubtedly the book for which Prescott expressed the most complete acceptance of his publisher's work was the inconsequential volume of *Miscellanies*. Without attendant negative criticism he said of Bentley's edition, "It is very well executed, and matches excellently with the *historicals*." [10] This was doubly logical, for that book posed fewer problems for the publisher and inspired fewer expressions of concern by the author.

With the *Conquest of Peru* in the hands of the reading public, Prescott unburdened himself to the Harpers on June 30, 1847. "The Work," he informed the four brothers in New York, "is executed faithfully, *according to yr contract—in every particular;* and I am glad to see my historical bantling in such a good dress at his christening. As he grows older, pray be careful that he never has a worse one." Prescott's eye-to-the-future admonition stemmed from experience, because Harpers' reprintings of his *Conquest of Mexico* had never equalled their initial effort.

Concerned about the complete book, Prescott logically and persistently applied himself to the specific ingredients thereof. Indeed, it was his demonstrated awareness of the individual components of the book that attached real significance to his interest in the final products of his publishers.

Paper, that most elementary ingredient of the book, constantly drew Prescott's attention, even affecting the publication schedule of his first work. "The paper," he informed Bancroft on November 17, 1837, "caused some delay, the publishers, as well as myself being very fastidious. But we have now got a very beautiful lot from F. Peabody of Salem, sized like any English paper." A few months later the contract with Little, Brown & Company required "that the paper shall be as good in sizing and quality as the paper of the first edition, and worth six dollars a ream." [11] Such an area of author authority, completely alien to modern publishing agreements, is but one of many proofs of the powerful role played by Prescott in his dealings with his publishers. On occasion, as with Bentley's first edition of *Ferdinand*

and Isabella, Prescott became acquainted with still higher standards, as he freely admitted to Bentley, "In paper too and blackness of ink you beat me." [12]

If, on the other hand, later editions employed poorer grades of paper, Prescott not only noticed them, he expressed himself in no uncertain terms. "The new edition," he wrote of Bentley's second edition of his first work, "is made of not quite so good paper, and there is more matter crowded on the page than in the first edition. There is some saving in this, I suppose, though it makes the volumes so much thinner that I should fear the purchaser would not think he had got so much for his money." [13]

Occasionally, as he reinforced his insistence upon quality paper, Prescott requested samples. Writing to the Harpers on September 17, 1843, about the first book they produced for him he asked, "Could you not send me a specimen of the printing and paper?" Like his Boston and London publishers, Harpers also drew criticism by producing later impressions of a work on inferior paper. "I see your latest edition," he told his New York publisher on October 28, 1844, "in the Bookstores. . . . It looks as if it has fallen into a decline; and the paper has a yellow unwholesome look, very inferior & substandard." Behind his blunt condemnation of the new impression is a clear-cut picture of Prescott on the prowl in Boston bookstores, gathering the information with which he fought in defense of his standards. The very regularity with which he chided his publishers about their employment of inferior paper in subsequent printings of his works invites the question for which the answer must remain ever elusive:

did the publishers resort to inferior paper, once the reputation of the work commended it to the buying public, to increase their profit?

Like paper, printing in general, and ink and type in particular, constantly drew Prescott's attention. Satisfied with his Cambridge printers, as exemplified in their repeated production of his stereotype plates, Prescott insisted in early contracts in keeping the presswork for his books in their hands. Indeed, the removal of that work from them was possible only with Prescott's written consent. In printing, as in so many other matters, once a performance satisfied him, it served as the standard for future Prescott works.

When the Harpers insisted upon executing the presswork for the *Conquest of Mexico,* Prescott, reluctant to part from his Cambridge connection, realized that the transfer to New York was necessary if he were to hold his new publisher responsible in the fullest sense for the book. His early insistence upon a sample of the Harpers' printing left no doubt that their right to print the work carried with it an obligation to meet the author's standards. Even as he asked for a sample of their presswork, Prescott sent another copy of his *Ferdinand and Isabella* to the Harpers, with a letter of September 17, 1843, obviously to serve as a model.

In a mixture of compliment and complaint, correspondent Prescott often discussed Bentley's editions. For example, even as he congratulated the London publisher for the blackness of the ink used in the first edition of his first work, the historian hastened to add in a letter dated November 15, 1841, "but the type of your text has seen some service, and does not show as clear and sharp as mine.'' The plea, often repeated, that subsequent English editions be produced from less worn type was always phrased in words of polite request carrying the connotation of bold insistence. The logic of Prescott's insistence regarding type lay in the fact that different typesettings were provided for in the different English editions of his works.

With stereotype plates, rather than type, and those author-owned, there was less basis for complaint regarding the performances of the American printers. Strangely, the man who instantly detected the worn state of English type never faced the fact that his own stereotype plates gradually demonstrated severe signs of wear and tear, repairs upon them by his publishers notwithstanding.

Striving for improved book appearance and reader convenience, Prescott put numerous ideas before his publishers. In pursuit of man-sized volumes in relation to both height and thickness of book, Prescott, tempering both considerations with love of beauty, became an early advocate of the ample margin. The detailed chapter heading, the full running head, and marginal notes—all of which added expense to production—endeared themselves to Prescott as aids to the reader.

The voluminous Prescott notes, which, like text, occasionally assumed unnecessary proportions, posed a publication problem which he faced at an early moment. More than fifteen months prior to his acquisition of an English publisher, the historian informed his London agent, ''The double column for the notes is much to my taste.'' [14] Promptly implementing his desire in his own stereotype plates,

Prescott saw the same style adopted by Bentley. As in all other matters related to the appearance of his volumes, Prescott expressed himself most often and most vigorously in the early years that served to establish precedent. There came a day late in his life, however, when economic compulsions forced a change of outlook upon him. With a cheap duodecimo edition in his hand, he wrote Bentley on December 5, 1854: "There seems to have been a free use of the shears in the notes of the Mexico. Once I should have thought this an unkind cut indeed. But I have made up my mind to yield to circumstances; and so long as one unmutilated 8vo edition keeps the ground, I will not complain."

Out of his early awareness that histories focussing sharply on the careers of prominent men and women would be enriched by portraits of those personages, Prescott demonstrated a deep and abiding concern about the illustrations in his books. In reference to illustrations, Prescott's first test and precedent-making experience was particularly difficult. Because his *Ferdinand and Isabella* offered so many subjects for portraits it called for extensions and alterations of any original list. In subsequent editions, in England and America, the number of illustrations rapidly expanded, at Prescott's insistence.

In his search for the finest engravings for his illustrations, Prescott gradually shifted from America to England. Of his first engravers he held different opinions from the beginning. Storm, a recent *émigré* from England, so delighted him that he had to share his good fortune with Bancroft. "Instead of line engraving, he stipples, which gives a softer and more graceful character to the work," Prescott wrote

to Bancroft on October 4, 1837. Of his second engraver, he wrote to Bancroft on November 17, "I
have been somewhat bothered with the engraver of
my queen, Andrews, who is not near so rapid as
Storm, and I doubt if he will turn me out a better
engraving." Boasting of the fine style in which
Ferdinand and Isabella initially appeared in America, Prescott wrote Bentley on January 9, 1838,
"The most exceptionable part is the plate of Isabella, which from the haste with which the work was
finally brought out, is in an unfinished state." Early
dissatisfaction increased with the appearance of
Bentley's edition, because it introduced Prescott to
the work of Greatbatch, an engraver about whom he
well-nigh rhapsodized. Pleased with Greatbatch and
displeased with Andrews—and desirous that future
English editions carry the likeness of the noble
queen—Prescott urged Bentley to have Greatbatch
execute a fine engraving. Months later, unable to conceal his anticipation of the engraver's handiwork,
Prescott wrote to Bentley on March 27, 1839, "I hope
that ere this, Greatbatch is making love to the good
Queen Isabella." His shift to English engravers set
in at once, and by the mid-1840's they so pleased
Prescott as to lead him to say to Bentley in a letter
of July 15, 1845, on the occasion of his needing a
new plate, "I would not have the heads struck off
anywhere but in London, for they make butcher-
work of this sort of business on this side of the
Atlantic."

In his search for the best in illustrations—first,
fine portraits with maximum historical authenticity
and, secondly, fine engravers—Prescott spent sizable sums of money. As early as 1833 he allotted 50

guineas for portraits from which engravers might produce illustrations, a subject which drew his lengthiest consideration in his first letter to his English publisher. In Spain, Arthur Middleton contracted with artists José Gutierrez de la Vega and José Madrazo y Agudo, the latter Director of the Museum of Paintings and Sculpture, for certain paintings. Middleton himself spent a great deal of time in locating authentic likenesses of Cortés and Cisneros. Much pleased with samples of the work of artist Valentín Carderera y Solano, Prescott ordered almost a dozen portraits of persons related to his Peruvian study and his projected work on Philip II. Working in water color, which the artist indicated would facilitate the work of the engravers on the score of detail, Carderera wanted £3 per portrait. For half-length portraits in water color the price would be £2. In oil, the half-length portrait measuring approximately 14½ x 9 inches would cost £16, and the half-length, life-sized canvases would cost £30 each. All of Prescott's orders fell in the £3 water-color category. And before the artist had completed his commission, Prescott had lengthened the list of requested portraits.[15]

Although Spain supplied most of the artists and portraits for Prescott, an occasional theme involved other areas. A Mexican-executed portrait of Cortés, promising to cost the historian two hundred dollars, drew this retort from him, "Could I not get the head and shoulders at half the price? . . . I have had portraits (two thirds length) of Ferdinand and Isabella copied from the originals in the Royal Palace at Madrid by the best artist in the city, for seventy-

five dollars each."[16] No exact sum can be established as Prescott's outlay for portraits, but it probably amounted to thousands of dollars over the
years.

With the paintings serving merely to assist the
engravers, additional expense centered upon the engravings. In connection with the first American edition of *Ferdinand and Isabella,* Prescott paid Andrews 400 dollars for one engraving and Storm 160
dollars for two engravings. With mounting admiration for English engravings, Prescott turned,
through Bentley, to William Greatbatch, who, among
other things, executed the engraving of Prescott
which served as frontispiece for the *Miscellanies.*[17]
With special concern about that engraving, Prescott
wrote Aspinwall in London on March 30, 1845: "Let
him understand that if the engraving is in your opinion executed in a manner deserving of it you will
give him 8 guineas for me over & above, wh. I dare
say will be 50 per ct. on wht. Bentley is to pay him."
Needless to say, Greatbatch gave the engraving of
the historian special attention, as he noted in a letter to Prescott of May 15, 1845. Prescott, having intended that the illustrations enrich his books, spent
heavily to guarantee that they were historically accurate and artistically beautiful.

Despite the diverse origins of the earliest engravings for his books, Prescott's desire to own and control them as he did the stereotype plates came into
early operation. With the earliest prospect of his obtaining some engravings from England, Prescott
promised, in his contract with Little, Brown & Company, to furnish engravings at the prices he paid for

them. If the abridged *Ferdinand and Isabella* had gone to press, it would have included engraved portraits provided by Prescott.

A few years later, on March 16, 1846, he wrote the Harpers: "Lastly I have to charge you w. the cost of the engravings wh. I furnished you both for the 'Conq't' & 'F & I.' This was also provided in our Contract & I charge you no expense but the price I pd for them in London." Prescott provided the money spent by those who searched for his materials, the money spent on preliminary sketches and paintings from which the engravers worked, and the money spent on the manufacture of the plates themselves. But in his effort to put beautiful books before his readers, Prescott's control of his portraits and his facsimile signatures of great figures of the past—like his control of the text by means of the stereotype plates—was artistically significant and aesthetically rewarding to one who did not attempt to put dollar valuation on every part of his publishing career.

Like all history, Prescott's writings were so rooted in geography that they were enriched by the inclusion of maps. His *Conquest of Mexico,* in which he eventually published two maps, illustrated the deep interest and persistent effort Prescott dedicated to his maps. Wanting to establish the route of Cortés' Honduran campaign, Prescott, as was customary with him, solicited assistance. To George Nichols, in Cambridge, he put the request, in a letter of May 29, 1843, "to see if there is in the library [at Harvard] any ancient map which contains any of the names of the places which I will give you." Neither first nor last in his effort to establish Cortés'

Honduran route with geographical precision, Prescott failed, and so omitted that segment of Cortés' New World movements from his published maps. Those eventually prepared for the *Conquest of Mexico* were based on Humboldt, modified by Prescott's acceptance of Clavigero on some disputed points. But adherence to standards created in his first work is evident in Prescott's insistence that they "be made like those in 'Ferd. & Isabel' noticing only the places noticed in the work itself," as he wrote in letters of June 19 and June 26, 1843, to Nichols.

Satisfied with the maps he had ordered rather than executed, Prescott buttressed his position on the score of their accuracy. "I have examined & read your statements," he wrote George Nichols in an undated letter of 1843, "both general & particular respecting *the Maps*. They are very full, clear & convincing. I would like to have them as vouchers for the fidelity of the Maps should it be hereafter impugned on any point." Any critic of his maps, like any critic of his history, could expect to hear the roar of Prescott's defensive guns.

As he sent the maps for the *Conquest of Mexico* to Bentley, Prescott impressed his publisher with the sense of the significance he attached to them. "The maps are intended each to be fastened by a guard in the middle," he wrote, "so as to lie open like two leaves of the volume, which is much more convenient than folding [as had been the case in his first book]. They are each of the dimensions of two pages. . . . Pray do not omit them, as they are indispensable to following the movements of the Conquerors, which cannot be traced on a modern map." [18] The Harpers, getting the same maps, also received their copy of these views of Prescott in a letter dated September 17, 1843.

In its organization and execution an almost mirror image of the *Conquest of Mexico,* the *Conquest of Peru* was likewise expected to carry two maps. When the proofs of the stereotype plates sent to Aspinwall in London were accompanied by a single map, Prescott explained in a letter dated February 28, 1847: ''I had originally intended to have divided the Map into two parts, but the engraver has brought every place which I had sent into one of the size of an ordinary page, which I think on the whole, preferable.''

With the initial determination of his subject matter for illustrations and maps and with his control of the plates related thereto, it became simple logic for Prescott to determine their locations in his books. On the subject of his forthcoming *Conquest of Mexico,* he instructed his London publisher in a letter dated September 14, 1843: ''The *Portraits* should be arranged— The full length of Cortés (from the Hospital of Jesus)—prefixed to Vol. I.—That of Montezuma to Vol. II. The other portrait of Cortés to Vol. III. The *Map* of the *Route* should be prefixed to Vol. I. That of the *Valley* to Vol. II.—The Fac-Simile to Vol. III.'' ''I will carefully attend to your directions,'' Bentley promptly replied on October 5, ''as to the placing of the Plates & Maps.'' The work, published in London on October 24, 1843, indicates that Bentley followed Prescott's instructions exactly. In America, the Harpers not only received similar instructions, they translated them into reality with their first edition. And when success attended the New York publication of his second work and Prescott decided to transfer the plates for *Ferdinand and Isabella* there for use by the Harpers, the historian indicated in a letter to Harpers on November 19, 1844, "You will see by one of the last editions in wht manner the different engravings & maps are to be arranged in the volumes."

Prescott's detailed concern about the placement of his illustrations never diminished. On November 6, 1855, he wrote Bentley: "I will now state the pages which I think the portraits would face: Philip II—Frontispiece of vol. I. Don Carlos—Frontispiece to vol. II. Margaret—Vol. I p. 371. Duke of Alva—Vol. II p. 252. Map of Malta, vol. II. p. 400. Facsimile of Philip's handwriting at the beginning of vol. I."

Prescott exhibited his illustrations proudly and took more than average care to call the attention of his readers to them. Instead of customary lists of illustrations, naked in their brevity, Prescott commonly offered detailed notes about his illustrative material.

Naturally, the man who wanted illustrations in his books was displeased when, on brief occasions, they were lacking. A combination of circumstances produced this unpleasant reality more than once: dependence upon English sources in a day of slow communications; the often dilatory tendency of Bentley, through whom Prescott channeled such matters; and lack of foresight on the part of the American publishers as they failed to anticipate their needs—all of them more than moderately beyond the control of Prescott. Nevertheless, it pained the historian even as he used the fact, noted in a letter of July 2, 1851, to Bentley, that "the book is selling without any portrait at all" to prod his source of supply.

Because a reader's willingness, even desire, to explore the inner substance of a book is conditioned by his reaction to its outer appearance, Prescott logically gave the bindings of his books his close attention. Against the drab, plain black cloth of his day, he found himself in continuous rebellion. With the first edition of *Ferdinand and Isabella* garbed in tan floriated cloth, Prescott struck a blow against the prevailing pattern of binding design. Although he failed on occasion to keep his works in colored bindings, his preference for them never left him. His displeasure over the first Harper edition of the *Conquest of Mexico* he never attempted to conceal. "I suppose," he wrote his New York publisher on December 5, 1843, "all copies are in black cloth—as this is got to be a pretty common sort of covering, perhaps you will bye & by vary it with more fanciful colors."

That Prescott often encountered stubborn publisher resistance is seen in his letter, two years later, December 8, 1845, to the same house: "I see the Miscel, are out, got up in very neat & pretty style; . . . I think it would have a pretty effect to bind them in dif. colors beside the universal black." Prescott's persistence matched their resistance. Two years later, April 24, 1847, with the *Conquest of Peru* about to appear, Prescott delivered his plea in pre-publication suggestion rather than post-publication lament: "Do you not think that dark green or maroon color, for the bindings, would make an agreeable variety with the everlasting black?" On June 21, 1847, too late to affect the outcome of the book, Prescott added: "In the binding it will be an improvement if you had some variety of colors—rich maroons, mazarine blues or other delicate colors such as are used by Bentley & Murray. But if you are not provided with handsome materials, black, I suppose, wd be safer, & it will certainly look as respectable as a parson's cloak.'' Expressing arguments that referred to the superiority of English tastes, Prescott was rewarded with such colors as green and purple among the array of bindings in which the *Conquest of Peru* made its bow in America. Perhaps, at last, Prescott's complaint about earlier bindings had borne fruit.

Unlike the stereotype plates and the engravings behind his illustrations and maps, the binding of his books represented an area in which the historian never could and never did exercise the degree of control he desired. Yet he did his best to do so. In any gentleman's library, fine books normally stood like soldiers in neat rows, shelved in their proper places. This truth impressed upon Prescott the realization that the spines of his books deserved special attention, and he came to want to give the spines of his books something extra. In addition to the gold-stamped statement of the title of the book and of the names of the author and publisher, Prescott's works commonly carried a gold-stamped device, usually a coat of arms. As he awaited the appearance of his first book, he wrote Bancroft on December 20, 1837:

> I wish you would cast your eyes upon a rare little device, stamped on the back, & printed on the title page, being the arms of Castile and Aragon, emblazoned on a common shield by an English artist cunning in heraldry, here (of which you will find no other example the Spanish arms elsewhere having

> either the Austrian or the Bourbon quartered on them
> or the Aragonese omitted) surmounted by the crown
> of that day:—which, as it is a most appropriate, and
> purely historical device, will, I hope, give no offence
> to your republican eye.

At an early moment he commended the device to Bentley.[19]

In due course, the coat of arms of Cortés served as the device on the spine of the *Conquest of Mexico*. As with the stereotype and engraving plates, Prescott quickly established the habit of providing his publishers with the brass dies for this important decorative work. To Bentley he wrote: "I sent a stamp for you to Col. Aspinwall . . . a beautiful and appropriate ornament for the back of the book."[20] The Harpers, producing their first book for him, heard in greater detail in a letter dated September 17, 1843: "You will not forget to have the brass stamp of the arms sharply cut on the back of the book; and I will thank you to let me pay for it, as I should like to own all the gear myself." Here, too, the author insisted that the style established for *Ferdinand and Isabella* be that for the later works.

So different from his other works, the *Miscellanies* had no material that could inspire a device for the spine, but Prescott remedied that out of his insistence that the volume match his histories. "The caduceus of Mercury, surrounded by the palm and the laurel leaf, very suitable for a collection of literary essays," became the author's answer.[21]

The *Conquest of Peru* permitted a return to his historical theme, and that work accordingly bore the arms of Pizarro on its spine. As he thanked his indefatigable Spanish aide Pascual de Gayangos, who had supplied him with the arms of Pizarro, Prescott so expressed himself as to indicate the love of beauty and symmetry that had prompted his request. "It may seem a little matter," he wrote, "but I like to have books got up in a thorough manner and to have those that I may hereafter write ornamented on the back so as to be in keeping with the others, with a gilt stamp which is not merely an ornament but means something. The arms of Pizarro will be an appropriate embellishment of this work, and will match well with the arms of Cortés on the 'Mexico.'" [22] Similarly, *Philip the Second* bore its appropriate arms, as, too, in time, did *Charles the Fifth*. Amid the notes describing his illustrations and maps, Prescott commonly offered brief descriptions of the devices on the spines of his books.

Among the numerous ideas Prescott brought into his endless battle for elegantly styled books was a deep-seated affection for the octavo, which he considered manly and dignified. He held other opinions of the likely alternative to it, duodecimo. Long before his first publishing arrangements were made, the historian informed Aspinwall, "I should not like to fall into a duodecimo." [23] What began as a simple expression of preference soon became fiat as he stipulated that "the book should be handsomely executed, and not in duodecimo." [24] He wanted his first book to appear "in a handsome octavo form." [25]

With his first American contract calling for octavo and his English publisher willing to comply with the author's desire, Prescott saw his *Ferdinand and Isabella* emerge in that size. The switch to Little, Brown & Company found the stipulation in favor of octavo written into the new contract.

Lacking the equivalent tight control over the product of his English publisher, Prescott, with the prospect of each new London edition, feared that the octavo might yield to some other size. Rumor of a second edition by Bentley led Prescott to tell that publisher in a letter dated March 27, 1839, that he did not want it "in those plethonic little volumes, as thick as they are long, which seem begotten by quartos on octavos—being neither the one nor the other—now so unaccountably in vogue." Bentley's practice of using different typesettings for different issues repeatedly subjected Prescott to agonies of uncertainty. Prescott's preference, expensive as well as elegant, stood in England for many years, until the pressure of pirated editions forced change of outlook upon both author and publisher.

Contract after contract provided for the octavo form, and so it was the form for the *Conquest of Mexico,* the *Miscellanies,* and the *Conquest of Peru* in the 1840's. Yet the fear that his English publisher might degrade one of his titles in some baser form never left Prescott. He greeted the London edition of the *Conquest of Peru* with relief, noting in a letter to Bentley of June 30, 1847, that it was "in the usual style . . . the only form which can do justice to works of that nature, which are always injured by diminutive type and duodecimo form." Prescott strongly believed that certain types of writing automatically deserved certain form; and with so much of the cheap, ephemeral literature of the day in duodecimo, he automatically opposed it for his histories.

However, the day came when declining sales inspired Bentley to stimulate public interest in *Ferdi-*

nand and Isabella by the issuance of a duodecimo version. Disturbed at the prospect when it was first proposed, Prescott soon gave ground, protesting in a letter to Bentley, October 22, 1849: "I had hoped never to have seen myself brought down to the small type. But you are equally interested with me and can best judge of the expediency; so I acquiesce in your decision, whatever it may be." Once more Prescott the economic man confronted the aesthetically inclined historian. Nevertheless, even in this trying moment, a dozen years after the initial issuance of the book, Prescott consoled himself with the knowledge that the octavo version would also be maintained in the English market.

Though his preference for the octavo and his dislike of the duodecimo continued, Prescott altered his thinking somewhat. With a copy of the duodecimo before him, he informed Bentley on November 12, 1849: "I am agreeably disappointed in its aspect. The print, though small, is sharp and clear, and the mechanical execution of the work is very neat." Bentley quickly converted other titles into the same form. Approving its appearance, the author, with a 50 per cent interest in the net income from *Ferdinand and Isabella,* added, in a letter dated February 4, 1850, "I shall be very glad to hear from you that the reduced size of the 'Ferdinand' and other works puts money into your pocket." What he once had repudiated completely, he now positively enthused about on occasion. With the *Miscellanies,* the second title in which he shared profits with Bentley, selling very slowly in England, Prescott hazarded the suggestion in the same letter to Bentley, "Would an edition in this smaller size not pay?"

Meanwhile, the impressions of his works offered the American public by the Harpers continued in such strong demand that the preferred octavo remained the only form in the United States. Here, too, however, transition was evident in the phrasing of the contract with Phillips, Sampson, and Company in 1854, because, even as it pledged the issuance of octavo editions of every Prescott title, it also anticipated publishing them later in duodecimo.[26] The octavos appeared, but before the duodecimos could emerge Prescott had died and the company had collapsed.

With the middle 1850's, the piracy that had long threatened materialized in England, forcing even greater adherence to the duodecimo form by both Prescott and Bentley.

From the very beginning of their relationship, Routledge and Prescott accepted and operated upon the principle that multi-priced editions of his works were required simultaneously in an English market rendered chaotic by furor and court decisions related to international copyright. "I see," Prescott wrote Routledge on November 17, 1856, "you have taken the field strong with *four separate edns.*"

The historian's aesthetic inclination also repeatedly focussed his special attention on title pages, as when he wrote printer Nichols on August 4, 1853:

On Wednesday I shall take out my copy-right, and it will be necessary to leave a copy of the title-page at the clerk's office. I enclose a sheet containing it, and have underscored the words to give some idea of the comparative size in which they should be printed. It will be well to have it got out handsomely, and when

you have the draught before you your eye can judge
better than mine how it should be done. Perhaps
some well executed English work might guide you.
I wish you would have one or two copies struck off
and sent me as samples.

At the other end of his books, the index never drew
quite such a show of personal attention from Prescott. With more money than time for such eye-
straining, pedestrian activity, the historian regularly
hired someone to execute his indexes. Their fullness,
constant aid to the serious student, bespeaks the ex-
pansiveness that characterizes his books generally.
Though it outraged Prescott to pay indexer Sibley,
whom Jared Sparks had found for him, the sum of
one hundred dollars, the drudgery involved in the
construction of the thirty-five printed pages of index
for the three-volume *Ferdinand and Isabella* suggests Sibley earned every penny of it.[27]

Satisfied with Sibley's first index, Prescott employed him again in 1843. The historian never so
completely assigned something to someone as to
divorce himself from it. Witness his reaction to Sibley's original copy for the index to the *Conquest of
Mexico.* "The Index is now completed," he informed
printers Metcalf, Keith & Nichols on August 19,
1843, "which I return to Mr. Sibley. It now makes
between forty and fifty pages. You would oblige me
by asking him to sweat it down to thirty by dashing
in the scissors." Sibley, who lived in Union, Maine,
apparently did nothing to the index, for in its published form it embraced full forty-two pages. From
cover to cover for all subsequent books, the standard
represented by *Ferdinand and Isabella* stood before

printer and publisher alike. The author was in character, accordingly, when he wrote to Metcalf, Keith & Nichols on August 19, 1843, "The Index might be printed like this in Ferd. & Isabel. I know no other better model."

The interest in attaining beauty and perfection that pervaded his identification with every aspect of the book manufacturing art and industry clung to Prescott after the issuance of his titles and drove him in a relentless campaign to eradicate errors. From early 1838 to the day of his death, he unceasingly planned new and better editions. His stereotype plates knew constant revision in minor matters. To English publishers, generally operating from distinct typesettings in every instance, he sent letter after letter accompanied by lists of errata. And, needless to say, when a publisher misplaced a gathering in one of his books, the author informed him of it.

With Prescott, a sophisticated gentleman of financial means and a cultivated love for things beautiful insisting that his books reflect his tastes, the question emerges: were his book design ideas mere personal whims, or did they coincide with publisher and public interest? To answer the latter is to answer the former as well. Since an overwhelming percentage of the author's ideas were adopted by the publishers and since all of them posed additional expense, many of them in areas in which contract terms were not specific, it is plain that the worth of the ideas commended publisher acceptance. Accepting suggestions without pressures that forced them to accede to them, the publishers did so because they sensed value in Prescott's book manufacturing ideas. In like fashion, more than one reviewer of the works commented favorably upon Prescott-inspired features. *Ferdinand and Isabella* drew most reviewer comment on matters of mechanical execution. F. W. P. Greenwood, writing in *The Christian Examiner and General Review* for March, 1838, declared: "The external appearance of these volumes corresponds with their literary value. They take precedence in this respect over all the books of the day, of home manufacture." John Pickering spread the same sentiment in *The New-York Review* for April, 1838, saying: "We ought not to omit noticing the extraordinary beauty and finish of the mechanical execution of these volumes; they are, we believe, superior, on the whole, to any work that has ever issued from the American press." At any moment in the history of publishing an ordinary book merits no special attention for its unspecial quality; and similarly a book possessed of markedly superior mechanical execution surely receives the plaudits it deserves. At its moment in American publishing history, *Ferdinand and Isabella* deserved and received special praise for book design ideas which were Prescott's in large measure.

Relentless in his quest for historical manuscripts out of which he compounded his histories, Prescott was equally so in his insistence upon books published in a style in harmony with the dignity of his subject matter and his own personal tastes. At the dawn of his identification with book manufacturing it was his aim, noted in a letter of December 20, 1837, to George Bancroft, to offer a product that "cannot fail to have

some effect in raising the standard in the country.''
Remaining true to that noble aim, Prescott was a
party to the publication of some of the best executed
volumes produced by American publishers in mid-
nineteenth-century years.

A contemporary portrait of William H. Prescott at his noctograph, the wired device designed to guide the handwriting of the blind, which he used throughout his life.

Memorandum of an AGREEMENT, made this *Seventh*

day of *January* 18 *45*, between *Colonel Aspinwall*
acting on behalf of W. H. Prescott Esq of Boston,
United States
on the one Part, and RICHARD BENTLEY, of New Burlington Street, Publisher, on
the other Part.

It is agreed that the said RICHARD BENTLEY shall Publish at his own

Expense and Risk, *A Collection of Papers written by the*
said W. H. Prescott Esq

the same to be printed in demy 8vo similar in style
to the Editions published by the said Richard Bentley of
"Ferdinand & Isabella" & "The Conquest of Mexico"
and, after deducting from the produce of the Sale thereof, the Charges for Printing,
Paper, Advertisements, Embellishments, if any, and other Incidental Expenses, including the Allowance of Ten per Cent. on the gross amount of the Sale, for Commission and risk of Bad Debts, the Profits remaining of every Edition that shall be
Printed of the Work, are to be divided into two equal Parts, one Moiety to be paid

to the said *W. H. Prescott Esq*

and the other Moiety to belong to the said RICHARD BENTLEY.

The Books Sold to be accounted for at the Trade Sale Price, reckoning 25
Copies as 24, unless it be thought advisable to dispose of any Copies, or of the
Remainder, at a lower Price, which is left to the Judgment and Discretion of
the said RICHARD BENTLEY.

In Witness whereof, the said Parties have hereunto set their hands this day.
It is further agreed that an engraved Portrait of Mr Prescott is to be
published with the above work, the expence of which is to be defrayed
by the said Richard Bentley & is to be charged by him in the general account
of the work — but the said engraved plate is to be considered the
property of the said W. H. Prescott Esq.

Thos Aspinwall

The Prescott-Bentley contract for the *Miscellanies*, providing for the inclusion of the author's portrait.

RICHARD BENTLEY

Prescott's English publishers. Bentley was Prescott's principal publisher. Routledge pirated Prescott's early works.

GEORGE ROUTLEDGE

An American edition of *Ferdinand and Isabella,* printed from Prescott's stereotype plates. The book set the typographical style for subsequent works, except for the marginal notes.

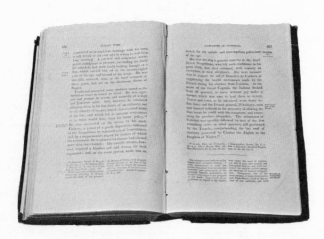

Elegant format of the first history.

HISTORY

OF THE

CONQUEST OF PERU,

WITH A PRELIMINARY VIEW

OF

THE CIVILIZATION OF THE INCAS.

BY

WILLIAM H. PRESCOTT,

CORRESPONDING MEMBER OF THE FRENCH INSTITUTE ; OF THE ROYAL ACADEMY
OF BERLIN ; OF NAPLES ; OF HISTORY AT MADRID, ETC.

"Congestæ cumulantur opes, orbisque rapinas
Accipit."
CLAUDIAN, In Ruf., lib. i., v. 194.

"So color de religion
Van a buscar plata y oro
Del encubierto tesoro."
LOPE DE VEGA, El Nuevo Mundo, Jorn. 1.

IN TWO VOLUMES.
VOL. I.

LONDON:
RICHARD BENTLEY, NEW BURLINGTON STREET,
Publisher in Ordinary to Her Majesty.
1847.

Title page for the first English edition of *Peru*, with Prescott's academic honors. Facing text pages of American edition of *Mexico* illustrate usual format after *Ferdinand and Isabella*.

Page format of all except first work.

CHARLES C. LITTLE

JAMES BROWN

Prescott's American publishers. Little, Brown was
Prescott's second American publisher. The first, American Stationers' Co., went bankrupt shortly after bringing
out Prescott's first book.

MOSES DRESSER PHILLIPS

FLETCHER HARPER

Phillips, of Phillips, Sampson & Co., was the member of the firm Prescott knew best. Likewise, Fletcher Harper was the Harper of Harper and Brothers with whom Prescott principally dealt.

Messrs Harper & Brothers

Boston. June 2 /47

Dear Sirs,

I wrote you last week advising you that the three last boxes of the stereotype plates of Peru had gone on to you by Harnden's express. I asked you to advise me of its safe arrival & also, to inform me at what date the book would probably appear. Not having heard from you, I fear there have been some miscarriage, & I shall be obliged by a reply now.

When your book is published, would it not be well to advertise my other volumes, as not putting my Miscellanies, with the portrait, as the first volume? I think you might get rid of the complete lot occasionally in this way.

I shall draw on you for $5000 of the copyright on the date of publication. The balance I will defer, unless you prefer to pay the whole at once.

A draft of a Prescott letter to the Harpers, concerned
with stereotype plates, promotion, and royalties.

CHAPTER SIX

PROMOTION AND DISTRIBUTION

THE VANITY OF AUTHORSHIP, so frequently and fully appeased by mere publication, was peculiarly complex in the career of William Hickling Prescott. As in so many other areas of his career as historian, Prescott's relation to the promotion and distribution of his works exceeded that of the average author. The practices initiated for the promotion and distribution of his works quickly became systematized, but the initiation of his and his publisher's approaches to the problems smacked of unrehearsed opportunism.

Prescott's recourse to a new, small Boston publishing house, the American Stationers' Company, and his local pride combined to guarantee a limited approach to the marketing of the first book, *Ferdinand and Isabella*. It was so restricted that the marketing area was in large measure synonymous with Boston. On Christmas Day, 1837, the following announcement in the *Boston Courier* launched the book.

Ferdinand and Isabella. Will be published this day, by the American Stationers' Company—History of the reign of Ferdinand and Isabella, the Catholic, by

William H. Prescott, in 3 vols. 8vo, with portraits of
Ferdinand, Isabella, and Cardinal Ximenes.

The day following its publication, booksellers C. C.
Little & James Brown and James Munroe & Company advertised copies of Prescott's work. Quickly
joining them were Perkins & Marvin, J. H. Francis,
Crocker & Brewster, O. C. Greenleaf, and Ticknor's.
Apparently every shop on Washington Street
stocked the latest work by a Boston author.

The booksellers' advertisements appeared regularly, with one pattern of advertising often serving
for several weeks in such papers as the *Courier,
Daily Advertiser, Mercantile Journal, Evening Mercantile Journal, Daily Evening Transcript, Boston
Recorder,* and *American Traveller.* A single advertisement by a bookseller often appeared simultaneously in several papers; and numerous issues of the
papers carried multiple advertisements of the Prescott title. At times the book was featured alone; on
other occasions it was listed with other titles.

The phrasing of the publisher's announcement and
the fact it was not followed by a barrage of publisher
advertising invites speculation concerning the company behind it. The absence of follow-up advertising
and the omission of the publisher's address from the
original announcement strongly suggest that the
publisher never intended to specialize in over-the-
counter sales of the history. Under the circumstances, the publisher apparently distributed the
book to any and all interested booksellers of the
community, and then left them to their own promotional devices. The advertisements varied greatly in
size and frequency of publication. One suspects that

the expense for the advertising, as well as its phrasing, was entirely the business of the individual bookseller. The American Stationers' Company seems to
have played a minimal managerial role in the publication of the book, the printing being executed by
Folsom, Wells, and Thurston and promotion and
sale by the individual Boston booksellers. Lacking
any evidence that the new publisher used the older
selling methods of subscription (hard hit by the
panic of 1837) and the traveling agent (never too
popular with Boston houses), one concludes from
the welter of advertising by individual booksellers
that the American Stationers' Company relied solely
on established booksellers for the retailing of *Ferdinand and Isabella*.[1]

From the earliest moments, the advertising of the
booksellers was supplemented by the published reviews with which the author was more than casually
acquainted. Ten days before the release of the book
Prescott discussed the review problem at length with
George Bancroft. After commenting on the unduly
lengthy review his close friend William H. Gardiner
had written for the *North American Review,* Prescott asserted in his December 16, 1837, letter to Bancroft, "If the book does not go well before the wind,
it will not be from want of a favorable breath from
my friends." The author appreciated Bancroft's
willingness to write briefly about the work "to four
or five of the principal editors at New York and the
South."

It was not only a moment in the history of American criticism in which one turned to one's friends,
one thoroughly exploited them—it being not uncommon for one individual to write a series of short re-

views for different publications, or even resorting to the use of the same item in different papers. Bancroft's aid was all the more welcome, because outside Boston Prescott considered himself ''in a land of strangers.'' In the general region of New York City, Philadelphia, and Washington, Bancroft's assistance would be supplemented by the pens of Pickering and Sparks. As for his home town, the author stated with assurance in his December 16 letter to Bancroft, ''Here I am well cared for—I come out under very friendly auspices.'' Concluding his communication about his forthcoming book, Prescott said, ''My object now in writing is to ask you what newspaper gentry you would recommend me to send a copy of the book to.''

When Bancroft supplied Prescott with the desired list, the neophyte author conveyed it to his publisher. A week before the appearance of the book, author and publisher put heads together to establish the list of out-of-town recipients of review copies.

Meanwhile, a second experienced author, Jared Sparks, counseled the Bedford Street author. Sparks had promised to provide the American Stationers' Company with a list of editors between New York and Charleston to whom review copies should be sent. Prescott's dependence on Sparks was complete and freely admitted. ''Your opinion, with these people will do more for me than any thing else,'' he confided in a letter on December 25.

In newspaper and magazine alike the early American reviews of *Ferdinand and Isabella,* penned by close friends and acquaintances of the author in most instances, were uniformly filled with extravagant praise for both the history and the historian. A leading Boston newspaper, the *Courier,* published an anonymous reviewer's opinions on January 4, 1838, which stated, "that the book will take a permanent rank, as a classic, in the language, may be predicted with perfect confidence." In *The American Monthly,* May, 1838, another critic asserted, "Less stately than that of Gibbon, and less ornate than that of Robertson, we think it a style which will wear better than either of them." For a time, at least, with friends reviewing and buying the work, it would have been difficult to establish objectively the real worth and popularity of the new multi-volume history had it not been for English criticism.

From the very beginning the estimates of the English critics parroted the friendly American voices. A London weekly, *The Athenaeum,* January 20, 1838, stamped the work, published in that city on Wednesday, January 17, 1838, "one of the most pleasing as well as most valuable contributions that have been made to modern history." A powerful British organ, the *Quarterly Review* of June, 1839, voicing the ultra-British opinion of Richard Ford, declared: "Mr. Prescott's is by much the first historical work which British America has as yet produced, and one that need hardly fear a comparison with any that has issued from the European press since this century began."

Time quickly demonstrated that this mushrooming promotional program outstripped distribution. On Christmas Day the publisher had only twenty-five copies available, and they were disposed of during the morning hours, according to a letter from Prescott to Bancroft, December 25, 1837. Despite the shipment of four review copies to Bancroft in New

York "to be disposed of wherever you think they will do me a service," as Prescott noted in his December 20 letter to Bancroft, none of the first impression of five-hundred copies went to any New York bookseller. Two weeks after the appearance of *Ferdinand and Isabella* in Boston and its promotion in many other places as well, Prescott asserted to Bentley in a letter dated January 9, 1838, "not a volume has been sent South as yet." The unmet demand outside Boston forced the American Stationers' Company, Prescott added in the same letter to Bentley, "to apologize in the newspapers for not forwarding the work to New York."

So great was the response, and so generous the reception, during those earliest months that Folsom, Wells, and Thurston, the printers of the book, published early in March, 1838, a ten-page prospectus crowded with extracts from reviews which had appeared in newspapers and journals in Boston, New York, Philadelphia, Baltimore, Washington, and London.[2]

The rapid acceptance of Prescott's book stood in marked contrast to the dull record of its distribution by the American Stationers' Company. Admittedly, the three-volume work on an old and far-removed theme knew a success which even the most experienced bookseller could not have anticipated for a book priced at $7.50 in the economically depressed days of late 1837 and early 1838. At the same time, the lack of experience and the limited outlook of the publisher were obvious barriers to even greater success. For Prescott's book and the breadth of promotional outlook envisioned by the author and his friends, a vigorously dynamic publisher was needed.

The American Stationers' Company was not such an organization, and its flimsy foundation and inadequate organization doomed it to dissolution amid the economic instability and intense competition of early 1838.

That spring, with remnants of the second impression by the defunct American Stationers' Company still in stock, Prescott, ready to "make any arrangement for the actual sale of as many as they could of these," as he wrote to Sparks on June 30, intended to have recourse to the trade sale in Boston.

No record details the final disposition of the volumes concerned, but Prescott thus became acquainted with another significant channel of distribution. In Boston the trade sales, held annually for a few days of fluctuating auction activity, served to bring publishers and booksellers together in transactions which permitted the former to sell sizable stocks for ready cash. The last-named objectives, peculiarly conducive to the liquidation of the stock of a defunct company, might have involved Prescott's work.[3]

Although the hit-and-miss approach to promotion and distribution by a poor publishing house and an unknown author had known unusual success, it left much to be desired. Accordingly, a more systematic approach to promotion and distribution was needed once Prescott found a second publisher—a system compounded of publisher's and author's ideas.

In that day publisher promotion included such devices as direct advertising in newspapers and other general publications, the issuance of house catalogues, the inclusion of publisher advertisements in their published books, the use of review copies, and the provision of the author with some copies of his work, copies which in their ultimate use often served the conscious ends of advertising.[4] Incidentally, the unknown quantity of review copies sent out by Prescott's first publisher is matched by the equally uncertain number of copies received by the author.

With most publishers doubling as booksellers, the house catalogues between the late 1830's and the death of Prescott were generally of sizable proportions, with varying amounts of attention accorded the individual entries. For example, the Little, Brown & Company catalogue, an annual item, exceeded one hundred pages in its 1839 edition. In addition to a routine, brief announcement of the then current edition of *Ferdinand and Isabella,* with a statement of its number of volumes, size, and price, the catalogue reproduced the coat of arms which embellished the title page and spine of the book, and quoted excerpts from English and American reviews of it. A later catalogue of the same house, issued after Prescott had moved to another publisher, found Little, Brown & Company carrying American, English, and French editions of titles by Prescott.

Firm in his belief that "advertising is the breeze that carries an edition off," a note carried in a letter of November 26, 1849, to Bentley, Prescott, from an early moment, wanted and expected his books to be advertised. And in the course of his persistent interest in the techniques related to promotion and distribution he came to voice many ideas of his own to his American publishers.

In relation to his English publishers, Prescott's normal interest in promoting the sale of his books was complemented and complicated by his distance

from the scene of activity, the high charges against
his books for advertising in England, and certain
suspicions he early entertained about Richard Bentley. Prescott's concern about promotion, evident in
his correspondence, was based on information derived from many sources, including his own regular
perusal of the literary notices in leading English
newspapers and journals. Even a tardy correspondent, such as Bentley was in the earliest period of
their relationship, could not keep the author in the
dark. "I see by your advertisement," Prescott told
Bentley in a letter dated June 11, 1839, "that the second edition of Ferdinand and Isabella is nearly
ready." Sometimes his London agent brought the
English advertising to Prescott's attention. Indeed,
one publisher even supplied him with copies of a
competitor's advertising.

On occasion Prescott did his best personally to
influence the pattern of advertising employed in
England. On the eve of the appearance of the *Conquest of Mexico* he wrote Bentley, "That you may
have a succinct notice of the work for advertisement, if you please, I enclose a copy of the advertisement used here."[5] Given to standardizing the histories themselves in their English and American
editions, Prescott extended that practice to include
advertising too. He not only contributed to the appearance of advertising; he also commented on its
absence. Disquieted, yet possibly not certain of his
ground, he relayed his displeasure via Aspinwall,
when he wrote, "I do not find any new edition of
Ferdinand and Isabella advertised by Mr. Bentley."[6]

In the absence of any record of Prescott's reaction

to the American advertising of his books, it appears
he was satisfied with it. Of course, his nearness to
the American scene made him more completely
aware of that advertising, and the terms of his American contracts—with straight royalty provisions—
never invited his concern about such profit-reducing
charges as advertising expenses. Needless to say,
Prescott's first history and his volume of essays, the
only works that he did not sell outright to his English publisher, were the historian's chief concern by
virtue of his continuing financial stake.

With the passage of time, Prescott resigned himself concerning his English editions to a degree
never equalled in his American experience. Indeed,
in his progress from affiliations with a poor publishing house, American Stationers' Company, and
with an establishment which then was more bookseller than national publisher, Little, Brown & Company, Prescott first reacted to and supplemented the
ideas of a promotion-conscious publisher when he
joined forces with Harper and Brothers. His awareness that Harper and Brothers possessed the best
publisher apparatus for promotion and distribution
in America had constituted an irresistible attrac-
tion when the author switched his publishing contract from Boston to New York in 1843. When John
Lloyd Stephens first approached Prescott about contracting with the New York firm for his *Conquest of
Mexico,* he emphasized the fact "that with their
capital and business connexions they have the means
of making larger sales than any other publishing
house in the country."[7] The production capacity
that permitted the Harpers to issue an initial edition
of that work of such size that it rivaled the total

number of copies in the first ten editions of *Ferdinand and Isabella* plainly called for methods of promotion and distribution superior to those Prescott had known from a pair of Boston houses. With the prospect of bigger sales and bigger income prompting the move to New York, Prescott saw his hopes converted into reality. The sale of three thousand copies of one title during the first two months eloquently recommended the Harpers' operation.

Prescott communicated his satisfaction to Harpers on July 10, 1845: "I have seen your advertising puffs of the 'Conquest' and 'Ferdinand' in your latest publications." But with the insistence of his intellectual breed, Prescott, as he negotiated with the Harpers regarding the *Conquest of Peru,* wrote the publisher on December 12, 1846, "Would it not be well for me to furnish you an advertisement of the book?" The sales and the promotion methods of the publisher were never so overwhelmingly successful that they eliminated the historian's continuing concern. Four months in advance of the *Conquest of Peru,* Prescott nudged the Harpers with the query, dated February 26, 1847, "Why do you not advertise the work?" Months later with the book launched on a sea of advertising that pleased him—and selling five thousand copies in less than five months— Prescott nonetheless prodded his publisher with the suggestion that they exploit foreign opinion of the work, adding, in a letter to Saunders on August 14, that such opinion carried "double the weight of one of our own country since the reader will acquit it of all suspicions."

Relentless in his efforts to promote his books, Prescott freely bestowed credit where it was due.

"I am much pleased with the success of the 'Peru,' "
he informed the Harpers on November 22, "it has
gone off in a dashing style—for which I think we are
much indebted to your liberal advertisement and distribution of copies." A half-year later, with new editions of *Ferdinand and Isabella* and the *Conquest of
Mexico* also issuing from the Harper presses, Prescott wrote on May 27, 1848, "I am glad to see them
walk off so briskly. I think we see in it the fruits of
your thorough advertising system."

Without exception, Prescott's publishers distributed review copies of his works. Indeed, in a period
characterized by an unsystematic approach to book
promotion, review copies represented the major expense in the publisher's advertising program. Review copies often involved 10 per cent of the first
printing, and it was not unusual for 150 to 250 copies
to be so employed.[8] The American Stationers' Company assigned an unspecified number of copies of the
first book for review purposes, with the author doing
more than the publisher to establish the list of recipients. Aided by Bancroft and Sparks, Prescott
spread review copies from Boston to Charleston,
South Carolina. Although they were divided between
journals and newspapers, the latter easily received
the greater number.

Despite the fact that the contract with Little,
Brown & Company concerned an already published
book, it nonetheless provided for the distribution of
additional review copies. In addition to the indeter-
minate number given gratis to publications approved by the publisher, other copies, requested by
Prescott for journals or papers which had not won
publisher approbation, were furnished at the price

of $2.50 per copy, a figure representing but a token
charge against the usual wholesale price of $6.00.
Logic would dictate that Prescott paid for such sup-
plementary review copies. In similar fashion, in the
case of the abridgment that never materialized, Little, Brown & Company were to supply, according to
the publishing agreement, such additional copies at
a charge approximating 75 per cent of the established wholesale price. Little, Brown & Company
employed a more businesslike ultimate control over
the distribution of review copies than had the historian's first publisher.

   In their assault on the reading public, the Harpers
paved the way for the *Conquest of Mexico* with 150
review copies. When Prescott switched the *Ferdinand and Isabella* plates to their custody, a third
series of review copies, issued by three publishers,
American Stationers' Company, Little, Brown, and
now Harpers, made their way to the desks of eligible
editors. Such arrangements were not stated in the
contracts, and gave rise, with the related issue of
whether or not the author received royalty on them,
to some discussion between author and publisher. Of
the 150 review copies of the *Conquest of Mexico,*
Prescott relinquished royalties on 70. When the same
issue arose concerning *Ferdinand and Isabella,* the
author promised in his letter of November 23, 1844,
to surrender his royalty on 50 per cent of the review
copies up to a total of 100. A later adjustment of
Prescott's part up to 60 copies, according to a letter
from Prescott to Harpers, March 16, 1846, suggests
that as many as 120 review copies of his book of 1837
were issued by its new publisher seven years later.
Behind their spectacular sales of Prescott's books

was a promotional program by Harper and Brothers embracing heavy use of review copies.

The uses to which the copies given the author by the publisher were put often were so frankly promotional that it is almost impossible to separate them from the normal review copies. Like the review copies set aside by that publisher, the number of copies received by Prescott from the American Stationers' Company cannot be determined precisely. The contract with Little, Brown & Company promised the historian 1 per cent of their output, in consequence of which he was due 45 copies of *Ferdinand and Isabella* between 1838 and 1844. For the abortive abridgment, the author's share fell to one-half of 1 per cent of the output, which would have meant 20 copies from the first printing. In his search for equal treatment from his London publisher, Prescott emphasized the 1 per cent provision of his American contract, but accepted Bentley's offer of 6 copies, which in terms of an edition of 750 copies represented eight-tenths of 1 per cent of production. With the appearance of a second edition the issue was reopened and then resolved in the same fashion. A half-dozen copies for the author, it appears, was standard practice with the English publishers.

However, time and reputation altered the number of copies allotted Prescott by the publishers. The London publisher, Bentley, provided the historian with 12 copies of the *Conquest of Mexico*. From the first Harper edition of the same work, which numbered 5,000 copies, Prescott received 25 copies. The same figure held for the edition of 7,500 copies for the *Conquest of Peru*. With the increased size of the editions of his books, Prescott, though likewise in-

creasing the number of his own copies, did not do so
on any fixed formula. However, he apparently sought
as many as he could expect from the publisher, and
trusted thereby to serve his own purposes as completely as possible. Of the *Miscellanies,* quite properly considered by their author an insignificant
work, Prescott received 12 copies from Harper and
Brothers. The contraction of the author's quota was
a response to the reduced size of the edition—2,500
copies—as well as an indication of the author's estimate of the volume.[9]

As time and reputation served to increase the
number of copies assigned the historian, Prescott's
desire for them grew and exceeded the number he
received gratis. Accordingly, he often bought additional copies at reduced prices. At the time the contract for the *Conquest of Peru* was being negotiated
with the Harpers, Prescott expressed the hope that
they would sell him additional copies at $1.40 each.
Occasionally, as with Bentley in 1847, the publisher
gladly increased the number of copies given to the
author. Out of repeated experiences in England and
America, the following pattern emerged: from Bentley he generally received twelve copies, plus irregu-
lar supplements which came as gestures of the publisher's friendship for Prescott; from Harper and
Brothers he normally received twenty-five copies, a
number he often supplemented by purchases at a
specially low price.

In the course of giving away untold hundreds of
copies of his works, a number which, however uncertain, established Prescott as his publishers' best
customer, the historian did much to promote their
sale in England and America and their translation

into other languages. As in other matters, the pattern of use made of the presentation copies of *Ferdinand and Isabella,* opportunistic and unplanned, became the foundation of what later had more than a semblance of system to it.

Three months prior to the release of Bentley's first edition of the first book, the New Burlington Street publisher received a promotion-conscious letter from Prescott, dated October 4, 1837.

> My friend, Mr. Ticknor, now in France will be in London in the winter, and will take eighteen or twenty copies to distribute among persons whose good opinions would be desirable. And as this will be a mutual benefit, I hope you will not think it unreasonable to let him have them at a moderate price.

Ticknor took only six copies, but they were distributed with a judiciousness that produced marvellous results. One copy went to Nicolaus Heinrich Julius, a German literary figure, who, after visiting Prescott in Boston, had tried to ease the historian's way in English publishing circles. Another copy went to Friedrich von Raumer with a request that he review it. Von Raumer did more than was expected of him: he facilitated its translation into German, in which form he then reviewed it. A third copy went to François Guizot, whose friendship greatly facilitated Prescott's subsequent researches. A fourth copy went to Count Adolphe de Circourt, whose response resulted in the lengthiest review ever written of any Prescott work.[10] The fifth copy went to Charles Fauriel, termed the finest scholar in Spanish literature and history in his day, with the request that he review it. The last copy, which Ticknor intended to keep himself, he promptly loaned to Robert Walsh, who in his enthusiasm for Prescott's history quickly began to hunt for a translator capable of converting it into French.[11] Time soon proved that Ticknor, American though he was, did more than any other individual to establish the friendly climate of reviewer opinion which quickly spanned the literary sky of Europe like a rainbow in the wake of the three-volume shower he judiciously rained here and there upon influential persons. Thus the story of only six of Prescott's presentation copies of his first work is compounded of friendships which served him for many years, reviews in continental languages, and translations that widened his acceptance and likewise promoted the sale of his book.

In addition to the presentation copies distributed for him by friends, Prescott applied himself to the matter, and in so doing demonstrated real capacity for honoring people who in turn could and often did assist him. One of the earliest copies, with a letter dated December 25, 1837, was sent to historian George Bancroft, who, doubling as Democratic politician, had entrée to numerous powerful editors. Prescott sent a copy to the successful traveler-writer Captain Basil Hall, one of the many English literati who in the course of American travels crossed the path of the socialite-historian of Bedford Street. To Tomás González, a complete stranger to the author but one whose favor was required if research in the Spanish archives of Simancas was contemplated, went an early copy. The book in hand paved the way for others in the making, and bluntly so, because Prescott accompanied the present to González with the expressed hope that he might "obtain . . . permission to copy such manuscripts in the archives as would further the objects I have in view."[12] The same day the archivist's gift started toward Spain, Prescott also shipped a copy to Martín Fernández de Navarrete, Spain's senior historian and a man who could open other doors for the American. Forthrightly, the Bostonian asked Navarrete for permission to have copies of "such manuscripts in your possession as relate to the Discovery and Conquest of Mexico and Peru."[13] In similar fashion a warm friendship and important support in English critical circles stemmed initially from the presentation copy sent Henry Hallam by Prescott. When the Italian Marquis Gino Capponi informed a touring acquaintance of Prescott that he would like to see the book with a view toward translating it, the historian sent a copy to him. The presentation to Henri Ternaux-Compans, holder of one of the finest personal collections of manuscripts of interest to Prescott, was accompanied by a request that the American's copyists be given access to them. The generous French scholar acceded to Prescott's request, and went beyond it with a warm personal invitation to him to come to Paris. In still another strategic quarter, Mexico, a presentation copy helped to inaugurate the generous assistance accorded Prescott by Lucas Alamán. Requests for aid also accompanied presentation copies to the Prince Andrea Corsini and the Vatican Library.[14]

Such names are but illustrative of the pattern of generosity with his presentation copies which saw Prescott put *Ferdinand and Isabella* into the hands of royalty, nobility, literati, leading historians, manuscript collectors, and archivists. Although commonly portending future books, the significance of such contacts in the promotion of Prescott's first book cannot be overlooked. The presentation copies that led to translations and the enlargement of Prescott's reputation also produced "puffs" that served to swell the popular acceptance of the historian's labors in America, because, as Prescott well knew, there was a measure of American intellectual dependence upon European criticism that made the winning of favor in European circles particularly meaningful at home. The author, whose naturally generous disposition was reinforced by desire for general acceptance, early realized that the widespread bestowal of presentation copies redounded to one's benefit, in the area of book-promotion, in such measure that it defied complete assessment.

With time and other titles, the lists of the recipients of the presentation copies lengthened, for copies had to go to social acquaintances, to reviewers of previous works, to translators who might be interested in translating still another title, to men who controlled access to rich manuscript collections. Such copies for social acquaintances carried with them, in the mid-nineteenth-century years, a measure of promotional value easily forgotten now, for those were years in which the arts of reading and conversation often focused on a common theme, and the word-of-mouth promotion of new books assumed considerable significance. Quite possibly, with his employment of his presentation copies as but one aspect thereof, it may be hazarded that Prescott, his publishers' best customer, was also their best advertising medium.

Review copies and presentation copies united to produce a barrage of publicity for Prescott's works. In America, where he was primarily concerned with the promotional role of the newspapers, Prescott gave attention to two journals he considered more significant than others—the *North American Review* and the *New-York Review*—but he looked to them under circumstances which stamped his interest as frankly promotional. Coupled strangely to his own increasingly dim view of reviewing, an activity which he himself had dropped, was Prescott's pre-publication knowledge of the contents of the reviews written by men he counted among his warmest friends and admirers. In this connection it could be that the rushed publication of the first book was not without relation to the long review article which appeared one week later in the *North American Review*. The timing seems more than coincidental, for the combination of holiday book sales and immediate commendation by the nation's leading literary journal represented a one-two punch promotionally that could not be overlooked.

The willingness of newspapers to publish "puffs" as well as advertising about new books enabled many of Prescott's friends to render him yeoman service. Within forty-eight hours of the release of *Ferdinand and Isabella,* Boston newspapers began to carry anonymously-written review articles. Sometimes the very same review appeared more than once, in different newspapers. Summarizing the contents of the latest issue of the *North American Review,* a Boston newspaper, the *Courier* for January 3, 1838, extolled Prescott's history anew with copious quotations from Gardiner's friendly review. The newspaper reader was told that *Ferdinand and Isabella* would

"place its author's name—an American name too—
on a level with Gibbon, as a classic historian."

In England, Prescott was aided by word-of-mouth
advertising, also, and through judicious distribution
of presentation copies. Here, he was assisted by
Ticknor. Prescott sought his help when he wrote:
"But, after all, my market and my reputation rest
principally with England, and if your influence can
secure me, not a friendly, but a fair notice there, in
any of the three or four leading journals, it would
be the best thing you ever did for me." [15] Sharing
with Prescott and most sophisticated Americans of
the day a concern for approbation from the English
and Scottish literary giants that almost approached
worshipful respect, Ticknor set to work. His greatest
contribution Ticknor recorded in these words: "I
made, through the ready kindness of Lord Holland,
arrangements with Mr. McVey Napier, the editor
of the 'Edinburgh Review,' for the article in that
journal by Don Pascual de Gayangos." [16] Among
many other kind words of approbation, Gayangos'
review in the January, 1839, issue stated: "The in-
habitant of another world, he seems to have shaken
off all the prejudices of ours; he has written a history without party-spirit, and without bias of any
sort. In a word, he has, in every respect, made a most
valuable addition to our historical literature."

Although Prescott never attempted to assemble
full files of the reviews and "puffs" of his books, he
gave English critics his special attention. To bookseller James Rich, of London, he wrote concerning
the *Conquest of Mexico:*

I wish you would be good enough to send me two
copies of each of the respectable periodicals and
papers which shall happen to contain any criticism on

the work. I wish them for my publishers here, as the opinions of the British press have considerable influence on the sale of a work.[17]

The attention bestowed upon reviews of his books sprang primarily from his desire to promote sales and only secondarily from any wish to re-evaluate his historical method in the light of such criticism.

In any appraisal of the promotional techniques applied to Prescott's works, the author's own special ideas must be added to the routine and unusual approaches employed by his publishers. Always, as he wrote new books, followed the sales of the last one, and hoped that the sales of the earliest one might be jogged, the historian persistently dedicated some of his activities to promotional ideas. Early in his association with Harper and Brothers, he accompanied some of his proposals with this statement on December 11, 1843:

> You may smile at the idea of my pretending to give you any assistance in your own business, which you must understand so much better than I can. But . . . I shall be most glad if I can do anything in my small way to facilitate your success.

We do not know if they smiled, but we do know that they, and other publishers, too, used the historian's ideas.

The idea that his books should be advertised by means of generous extracts, while not original with his titles, did originate in this specific instance with the author rather than the publishers. With the appearance of *Ferdinand and Isabella,* a joyous Christmas letter to Sparks, December 25, 1837, found Prescott asking:

Would it not be well to secure room from the editors of the newspapers for a few extracts, at times, which might recommend the book to purchasers? If you think so, Andrews has one or two unstitched copies in his possession, from which he could easily forward such extracts occasionally, to the printers. It seems to me that a judicious use of the scissors is, after one or two good notices, an effectual way to recommend the book.

Concerning the forthcoming *Conquest of Mexico,* the historian wrote his New York publisher, Harpers, on December 11, 1843:

I shall furnish the Courier & Advertiser [Boston dailies] with proof sheets containing extracts from various parts of the work. As the most showy & striking passages are selected, it seems to me this must be one of the most efficient means for advertising the book. The newspaper editors do not like to spoil their own copies & have not time to copy off extracts themselves; but if you will furnish them with the proofs containing the precise extract they would I am sure be glad to transfer them to their columns.

Though enthused over this means of selling his books, Prescott viewed it not in isolation but in relation to promotion in general. His concept of the relationship between review and extract, he set before the Harpers in a letter dated December 19, 1843: "The extracts . . . I consider quite as effective a way of introducing a book to notice as criticism . . . both may serve to support each other." No record exists of either the degree of use or the success of the "extract" idea.

Another promotional idea dating from a very early moment was Prescott's suggestion, in a letter

to Bentley, dated January 9, 1838, that "an advertisement of the contents, as briefly exhibited in the
Preface, would furnish such a bill of fare, as would
convince the public that it must be the writer's fault,
if it is not rich in important and interesting matter."
This bill-of-fare-advertising, often supplied by Prescott, was used frequently by his publishers.

The scissors-and-paste approach to advertising
employed by Prescott in regard to extracts from his
works was repeated in the use he made of many of
the choicest words of domestic and foreign commendation. As he requested copies of "friendly"
English notices, he plainly announced his intention
of generating advertising copy out of them for his
American publishers. Concerning one of the earliest
significant English reviews of the *Conquest of
Mexico,* Prescott commented to the Harpers on January 23, 1844: "You will see the London Quarterly
contains a long favorable notice of the Conq. It is
fr. the pen of Milman the historian of the Jews. The
last paragraph might furnish a good extract, as coming from the highest foreign authority." Months
later, on November 23, 1844, the historian wrote the
same publisher: "I find a few puffs selected by me
. . . for Little & Brown & put in their advertising
sheets, which I enclose. If you want any more puffs,
I can send them to you to your hearts content from
English & Continental Journals, only let me know."
Successful initiation of the technique in his dealings
with Harper and Brothers inclined Prescott to make
a habit of it.

When French words of praise for the *Miscellanies*
came into his hands, Prescott sifted out the best and
sent a part of the review to New York with a letter

of October 10, 1846, to the Harpers: "As I think that a good notice from a foreign source would help the work, at any rate bring it by way of advertisement before the public, I have had part of it translated, which I now enclose to you." When the Harpers failed to incorporate it speedily into their advertising the historian repeated his suggestion in a letter on December 12.

Whenever a new work appeared, it was the practice of Harper and Brothers to jog the sales of the older titles with another wave of advertising. Preparing for the advent of the *Conquest of Peru,* Prescott accordingly sent copious extracts from old American and English reviews. The modesty he knew in other areas of his life was put aside in those dedicated moments. One batch of review extracts included such unblushing sentiments as these sent in a letter to the Harpers, May 24, 1847: "Perhaps the ablest work which has yet issued from an American pen" [*Conquest of Mexico*]; and "Mr. Prescott will be ranked among the very few American writers who have taken a high and permanent station in English literature" [*Miscellanies*].

Sometimes, too, Prescott borrowed advertising material used by his English publisher and sent it to his American house, as when he wrote the Harpers on June 21, 1847: "I enclose you also a few notices relating to my Miscellanies, (which seems to require bolstering the most), which I find in one of Bentley's late publications." With a sharp eye on sales reports, Prescott tended to plug the lagging title.

Six months after the release of the *Conquest of Peru,* Prescott was unrelenting in his promotion of it. "I should think," he wrote the Harpers on De-

cember 27, 1847, "some good English notices of the
Peru short and pithy, might be now got by Mr.
Saunders from the London Quarterly, Blackwood,
the London Eclectic &c. some of which I sent him
last summer." Difficult though it is to imagine, there
came a moment of supersaturation even for the author, as in the spring of 1849. "When I saw you in
New York the other day," he wrote Fletcher Harper,
"you mentioned that if I would select any new extracts from the reviews of my works, they would be
printed in the advertising sheets of Hildreth's forthcoming work. On looking over your late advertisements, I do not think they can be materially improved." [18]

Persistent in putting advertising extracts into the
hands of his American publisher, Prescott was
equally faithful to his English publisher, Bentley,
whom he prodded intermittently across almost two
decades. In a letter of March 27, 1839, he sent a translation of selected portions of the first of five review
articles written by Count Adolphe de Circourt on
Ferdinand and Isabella. On occasion he even called
the London publisher's attention to prominent British reviews, as when he wrote on May 30, 1845: "I
think the last 'Edinburgh' will furnish you with a
puff—if you want one—of your 'Conquest.' It is
written in a hearty tone—not dealing out commendation drop by drop—as if it went hard like the critics
own life blood." Similarly, a decade later, on March
9, 1857, he asked Bentley: "Have you seen a notice
of 'Philip II' in the London Times of January 12th?
The Times may furnish you with good extract for
a puff."

Another promotional technique inspired by Pres-

cott was the garnishing of his title pages with brief
statements of his academic honors. A gratifying
number of learned societies conferred honorary
membership upon him in the months following the
release of his first book. Writing to Middleton in
Spain, he expressed his desire, though he dismissed
many other honors, to win one distinction. He said,
"There is one academic honour . . . I do covet . . .
that of being a member of the Royal Academy of
History of Madrid." It was a logical longing in view
of Prescott's assertion that "it now seems probable
that my future life is to be consecrated to the illustration in one form or another of Spanish history."
He soon attained that honored membership, and
quickly weakened in the resolve that had found him
saying, "I certainly shall never display their titles
on my banner, or in other words associate their
initials with my name on the title page of any work
of mine." [19]

Immediately upon receipt of word of the Spanish
honor, he wrote his London publisher, Bentley, on
August 15, 1840:

> It has occurred to me, that the membership of the
> Spanish Academy may be of some use in England
> where I am less known, as a voucher for the faithful-
> ness of my work, from the most eminent literary body
> in Spain, and the one particularly entrusted with care
> of its annals. But, unless you think it will be of
> real use in recommending the work to purchasers I
> had rather not have it inserted; as I show by not do-
> ing it here.

To clinch his inclination favoring its use by Bentley,
the historian penned the copy, saying, "It should be

'*Cor. Member of the Royal Academy of History at Madrid &c. &c.*'' Initially at least, the English publisher ignored his author's recommendation, because his 1842 edition of *Ferdinand and Isabella* did not so identify the author on its title page. With persistence a basic ingredient in the Bostonian's nature as promoter as well as historian, Prescott soon recurred to the idea. Again he emphasized solely the Spanish honor. ''If it would help the sale of the book, you can stick in on my name. Otherwise not,'' he wrote to Bentley, November 15, 1841.

Prescott momentarily repudiated the idea of titles with the appearance of his third book. ''My literary titles, you will recollect,'' he wrote to Bentley on July 15, 1845, ''are not to be prefixed to the volume 'Miscellanies,' but to the next edition of my *Historicals.*'' But even as he distinguished between his historical writings, for which he received the honors, and his volume of reissued literary essays, Prescott weakened to the point of including much more than the Spanish honor alone. ''For fear of mistake in the titles,'' he informed Bentley on November 29, ''I repeat those now which I should prefer to specify —'Corresponding Member of the French Institute, of the Royal Academy of Sciences at Berlin, of the Royal Academy of History at Madrid, &c &c.'' With the prestige of the French group possibly the highest, and the Germans distinctly ahead of the Spaniards in the matter of translating Prescott, the sequence of the statement of the honors suggests author awareness of their comparative promotional value.

By the late 1840's and the appearance of the *Conquest of Peru,* the practice of associating academic

honors with the name of the author on the title page
was commonplace in America as well as England.
That work's first American edition identified its
author as "Corresponding Member of the French
Institute; of the Royal Academy of History at Madrid, etc." The honors which Prescott had once considered too alien and aristocratic to fall sympa-
thetically upon the gaze of his own countrymen drew
no condemnation. Henceforth they commonly re-
placed the earlier pattern of promotion which had
coupled short titles of his early works with his name
on the title page. The list of honors lengthened with
the years, and included his election as fellow of the
Royal Society of Literature and his receipt of a di-
ploma from the English Society of Antiquaries.
However, Prescott satisfied himself with a modestly
brief list, which, though varying on occasion, always
found his title pages focusing exclusive attention on
European honors. In terms of his own knowledge of
the groups, American and European, that honored
him, as well as his firm belief that favorable European reception was the touchstone for author success, the choices were logical ones.

Prescott's dislike of the prospect of ocean travel,
which may be thought strange for a person who
flavored his correspondence with phrases related to
the sea, makes his trip to and triumphal tour of England in 1850 take on some of the coloring of promotion. A poor traveler who in his love of Boston was
seldom long or far from it in his adult years, Prescott required years before he summoned the courage
to visit England at the peak of his popularity. Illness,
delay, uncomfortable quarters, homesickness, and
memories of his experiences afloat in 1815 bore in

upon him and reinforced his natural inclination to stay on the American side of the Atlantic. However, early in 1841 he tried to overcome his lethargy, hinting in a letter to Bentley February 28, 1841, that "I have some thoughts of paying a visit to London myself—this Spring." Bentley warmed to the idea so quickly that one suspects the publisher, rather than the author, first consciously tied the idea of such a trip into book promotion.

In 1850 a happy combination of circumstances finally got Prescott aboard ship bound for England. The imminent return of his son, still in Europe, helped to prod him, as did Bentley's urgings and his own indisposition to buckle down to further work following the completion of the *Conquest of Peru*. However incidentally, if such be true, the trip was conceived as a promotional idea, it nonetheless served that purpose admirably. British sales, evidenced by the appearance of new editions of various Prescott titles, soared after his three-month triumphal tour of England. In society and press alike, he was lionized as no previous American literary figure ever had been. However, though he was a social being all his life, Prescott knew limits to his economic outlook, and despite insistent pleas from his English publishers in the mid-fifties, when the turmoil attending copyright suggested that Prescott could greatly increase his English income by going abroad at the time of the publication of his books, he never made another transatlantic crossing.

Little things as well as big ones took their place in Prescott's identification with the campaign to widen public acceptance of his books. Noting that Bancroft's English publisher, Murray, employed an edition number which suggested that he was adding American and English impressions to arrive at an imposing figure which connoted popularity and value, Prescott suggested a similar course to Bentley. At a moment when only two English editions of *Ferdinand and Isabella* had appeared, Prescott wrote to Bentley on November 15, 1841, ''As I have had eight . . . here, would it help you to put it in your advertisements?'' Bentley's lack of enthusiasm for the idea explains his failure to adopt it. Quite often Prescott's ideas, facing initial publisher disinterestedness, reappeared. This one did so.

On December 21, 1846, Prescott urged Harper and Brothers ''to put [a] new edition on the title page of Ferdinand and Mexico'' to let the public know that the editions were not endless. At that time the New York house was labeling its *Ferdinand and Isabella* as the tenth edition, which number, incidentally, had already been used by Little, Brown & Company in Boston. With this title the Harpers saw fit to ignore Prescott, and kept numbering their new impressions, at least one of which emerged annually between 1848 and 1854, as the tenth edition. Indeed, it took the transfer of the contract to Phillips, Sampson, and Company to produce the desired eleventh edition in 1856. However, with the *Conquest of Mexico* the Harpers reacted differently. Their early impressions, between 1843 and 1846, bore no mention of the edition, but suddenly in 1847 they numbered the new impression eighth edition, a number used regularly with successive impressions through 1851. Then suddenly the title page bore the legend twenty-second edition. In the case of *Ferdinand and Isabella* the publisher rejected Prescott's suggestion and never confused impressions with editions; but with the *Conquest of Mexico* they adopted the suggestion, let it die, and then renewed their use of it. They ended up equating impression with edition. At no time in his career did Prescott monopolize what might be termed erratic behavior.

Another minor matter, but one that received Prescott's repeated attention, was his insistence, expressed in a letter to Harpers on September 17, 1843, "I must request you not to cut the leaves of the copies sent to Boston." Lest his request be ascribed to his own picayunish whim, the historian explained that in Boston cut leaves were considered a sign of cheap publication. When early copies of the first volume of the *Conquest of Mexico* complied with his request, Prescott expressed his appreciation in a letter dated December 5.

In the course of having his portrait executed to please relatives and friends, Prescott embraced another opportunity to promote his books. His preference for English engravers logically led to alerting Bentley to his need. Suddenly in a communication to the publisher the new idea cropped up in a letter dated May 30, 1844. "Although I am not willing to have an engraved portrait prefixed to my volumes here, should you think it expedient to have it in the English copies of 'Ferdinand and Isabel,' I can furnish you with a painting . . . for a model." Of interest is the fact that Prescott proposed using the portrait only in the older of his histories, the one whose lagging sales he desired to bolster.

And, of course, what he said about never using his portrait in America went the same way as his insistence that he would never flaunt his academic honors on American title pages. In pre-publication days, as they readied his *Miscellanies,* the Harpers scuttled Prescott's reluctance to put his likeness before his readers. Concluding a convincing argument in favor of including the portrait, the publisher insisted in a letter to Prescott dated July 15, 1845, that the Americans had "more cause to feel interest in you than the 'beef-eaters' of England have. If you would gratify the public, by all means give the Portrait." Having originated the idea for England, Prescott adopted it for American use.

In the late 1840's Prescott initially suggested the advertising that found the individual titles all grouped as "works," an idea which after the author's death meant much to many editors and publishers. Apparently it began with Prescott searching for yet another means of bolstering the sale of lagging titles. In a frank discussion with his English publisher about the varying successes of the three-volume *Ferdinand and Isabella,* the three-volume *Conquest of Mexico,* and the volume of *Miscellanies,* as well as the soon-to-emerge two-volume *Conquest of Peru,* he concluded a letter to Bentley dated May 13, 1847: "I should think you might sell all the nine volumes together in a batch, as my 'Works,'—and 'For the money, quite a heap!' "

The idea he shared with his English publisher also winged its way to the Harpers. "Would it not be well," he wrote on June 2, 1847, "to advertise my nine volumes as Works, putting my Miscellanies, with the portrait, as the first volume? I think you might get rid of the complete batch occasionally in this way." Between the lines one senses sale by subscription, with the first work to be received by the subscriber the one gathering the most dust on warehouse shelves, not the work representing the brightest jewel in the diadem of the author's reputation. In England as well as in America, the question was, how best could the publisher dump a slow-moving commodity? He soon wrote Bentley on February 11, 1848: ''Could you not, by selling the whole as my 'Works,' get rid of the 'Miscellanies' in the lump?''

Even when publishers ignored the idea, Prescott proceeded in his own way. For a wedding present to an English friend, he directed Bentley in a letter dated July 20, 1852, to have a richly bound complete set of his writings stamped ''Prescott's Works.'' Although he also explored the idea with his last English publisher, Routledge, Prescott found publishers uniformly difficult to convince until his return to Boston with his contract with Phillips, Sampson, and Company, and even then the practice, though adopted, was not provided for in their contract.

Perhaps the best evidence supporting the fact that when he wanted to help the sales of one title he had them all in mind exists in the periodic jogging of the older items. As the publication date for his second book neared, Prescott wrote Bentley on September 14, 1843: ''I heartily hope this work will help off its *Elder* brother who seems to have been struck with a paralysis of late.'' In similar vein he wrote the Harpers years later, on December 21, 1846: ''I hope the 'Peru' will give the whole string a jog.'' Indeed, Prescott's idea of marketing his wares as a unit under the label ''works'' became one specific recommendation intended to jog the sales of the laggard titles. Perhaps, however, the very reluctance of the publishers to adopt the proposal lay in the fact that the emergence of a new book did stimulate the sales of earlier volumes, a truth to which Prescott's publishers attested on several occasions.[20]

Doing all he could on many fronts, Prescott even policed availability of supply, and promptly let his publisher know if local booksellers had empty shelves. In the autumn of 1844 the Harpers read in a letter from Prescott dated October 28: "They tell me here they were unprovided with books for some weeks at the Bookstores." Years later, on December 27, 1847, they received the terse report, "Your Peru is out in some of our shops." The aristocrat who wrote of Spanish history and promoted its sale to literate men the world over pensively walked the streets of his home town knowing that both the writing and the promotion came to naught if the book itself was not within reach of the reader-purchaser.

Quite probably William Hickling Prescott the man was Prescott the historian's best and most persistent promoter. The record of his adroit use of the author's copies and additional ones, too, for presentation purposes, his systematic use of extracts from his books and from the reviews of his works, his citation of his academic honors, his visit to England, his ideas about edition numbers and uncut leaves and colored bindings, his willingness to incorporate his portrait in his books, and his approach to selling his writings as a unit support that claim.

Paralleling his lengthening list of new works and his lively concern about the promotion and distribution of all his writings was the interesting and complex financial side to Prescott's relations with his publishers.

CHAPTER SEVEN

THE FINANCIAL SHEET

INVOLVING AS IT DOES two decades, six publishers, and an even greater number of contracts, the financial side of the book publishing career of William Hickling Prescott is exceedingly complex. The record gives a general pattern of income and expense, but defies the final precision of a statement that would please an accountant. Complicating the problem is the incompleteness of the records which involve a half-dozen publishers, several agents, artists, engravers, countless postage and freight bills, expenses for indexing, proofreading, and stereotyping, charges for the copying of manuscripts, books purchased, and commissions for the service of bookdealers, among other expenses. Indeed, the other expenses include such considerations as the following: Should the cost of the special collections behind certain of his histories be charged off as expenses? Should the services of his reader-secretaries, stemming almost strictly from his needs as historian, be assessed against the works produced? To this list of such factors, must be added others, such as the difficulty of ascertaining the exact size of every printing of his works and the complexities attending the accounting for three or four different, yet simultaneous, versions of a single work by a single publisher. Facing, then, a question for which Prescott himself never could have formulated a clear, crisp answer, this assessment of the financial side of the historian's career estimates his gross income during his lifetime and establishes the nature though not the exact range of expenses he incurred.

The money market was tightening, the book-buying public was shrinking, and the Panic of 1837 was coloring the thinking of Prescott as he approached his first contract arrangements in America. For 1,250 copies of *Ferdinand and Isabella,* the American Stationers' Company promised to pay the author $1,000. This sum amounted to 80 cents per copy (26⅔ cents per volume), or 10.67 per cent of the retail price of $7.50 for the three-volume work. Since the publisher promised the $1,000 as a flat sum without reference to any such per volume calculation it is difficult to compare this contract with later agreements paying royalty on the basis of volumes. There were additional factors in this agreement with Prescott's first publisher: the second printing, planned to be 750 copies to complete the 1,250 provided for, actually ran to 800, making a total of 1,300 copies under the imprint of the American Stationers' Company. This, incidentally, reduced the author's income to 77 cents per copy, or 10.27 per cent of the retail price. Prescott apparently pocketed his $1,000 before his first publisher collapsed, a victim of the Panic.[1] Considering the fact that he not only received his money but salvaged his stereotype plates as well, Prescott emerged unscathed from this financial debacle.

Prescott's expenses for his first book greatly exceeded his income. To the Cambridge printers he paid $2,143.90 for the stereotype plates. Two engravers received a total of $560, and the indexer $100. To serve as inspiration to one engraver, he paid $40 for a portrait. These direct expenses amounted to $2,843.90 Facilitating the sale of the manuscript to American Stationers' Company was a pre-publication printing of four copies, which cost an additional $456.10. The books and manuscripts purchased in the course of his research represented an expenditure of $1,200. Total expenses were $4,499.90. Prescott plainly spent four and one-half times as much as he received under his first American contract.[2]

Tempering this approach to scholarly publication, which indeed called for the wealth, as well as the leisure, of an aristocrat, are several more factors: A simultaneous publication in England would afford, Prescott hoped, considerable additional income, with minimum expenditure; and secondly, the existence of the stereotype plates, in addition to controlling quality of product, promised a high ratio of profit for the author if and when the work had subsequent printings in America.

Prescott has left a fine record of the relationship of the scholar to the economic man in his thinking at that time.

> I never regarded the cost of the affair, for I should not have selected such a topic with the idea of making money. But, as I have gained some experience . . . I shall note a few hints for my future government. . . . One cost I shall never count—i.e., reasonably

speaking—the cost of original and authentic materials. . . .

But, after all, although I note down these estimates
that, in my future calculations and bargains I may
have something to guide me with the slippery "trade,"
yet I trust I shall never make the profit the main object; and never put my name to a work which I have
not made as good as I can make it, *coûte que coûte.*[3]

Scholarship and quality of product would come
first, but at the same time Prescott, suspicious of
publishers, would be increasingly the economic man.
The latter tendency he speedily demonstrated in the
financial terms of his second American contract.

For the right to publish 1,700 copies of *Ferdinand
and Isabella,* Charles C. Little and James Brown,
Prescott's second American publishers, agreed to
pay Prescott $2,975, or, put on a per-copy basis, as
it was in the contract, $1.75 per copy of the three-
volume work. His second American contract thus
gave Prescott a royalty of 23.33 per cent. The historian's ability to more than double his income
clearly stemmed from public acceptance of his work
as well as from his sharper business outlook. Should
demand render 1,700 copies an inadequate supply
in the allotted five-year period, according to the
contract the publisher could exceed that number indefinitely by paying Prescott at the rate of $1.75 per
copy. In a maze of practices that confuse the issue
of Prescott's income, one issue serves to clarify it
somewhat, namely the practice of paying royalty on
copies manufactured, not sold. This simplifies and
unifies information which otherwise might be spread
at random over the publisher's ledgers. Incidentally,

this practice of paying an author out of current assets rather than expected income possibly contributed to limit the size of the operation of many publishing houses.

Nine consecutive printings of 500 copies each of *Ferdinand and Isabella* were issued by Little, Brown & Company between August, 1838, and March, 1844. However, Prescott's income from the work was not a simple matter of multiplying 4,500 by $1.75. That total was reduced by the agreement that the author would pay two-thirds of any sums between 90 and 112½ press tokens. Charges for presswork in New England were then reckoned at so much per token, meaning 500 impressions per form. With any fraction of a token counted as a whole, the 500-copy printings cut token charges to an absolute minimum.[4] On three successive occasions this reduced his expected income of $875.00 to $844.25.

Definitely applying in three of eight instances, this reduction of income quite likely obtained for other impressions as well. One printing of five hundred copies destined for Paris in a transaction about which too little is known found Prescott accepting payment in the amount of three hundred dollars, a sum so small that one concludes the author's concern in France was prestige rather than income. However, Prescott had a potential maximum income of $6,959.75 from Little, Brown, as shown in the following table.[5]

When Prescott turned his back on Boston publishers, he did so not out of dissatisfaction with the quality of the home-town book manufacturing but out of economic consideration. The Little, Brown connection, however profitable, had been characterized by a monotony of small impressions that suggested that the author was associated with a small publisher. The continued sale of his first work, buttressed now by the completion of his second history, prompted a connection with a bigger house.

Prescott's Income from Little, Brown & Company *

DATE	NUMBER OF COPIES	PRESCOTT'S EARNINGS
Aug., 1838	500	$ *844.25*
Nov., 1838	500	*844.25*
Feb., 1839	500	*844.25*
Sept.–Oct., 1839	500	844.25
Sept., 1840	500	844.25
Sept., 1841	500	844.25
Jan., 1842	500 (to Paris)	300.00
April, 1843	500	*844.25*
March, 1844	500	*750.00*
Total	4,500	$6,959.75

* Figures in italics are estimated.

For the initial 5,000 copies of the *Conquest of Mexico* printed in 1843, Harper and Brothers paid Prescott, immediately upon publication, $7,500. Indeed, even before the last of the three volumes appeared, Prescott could write, as he did on November 4, 1844, to the Harpers, "I take this occasion to acknowledge the receipt last week of the whole sum due on the copyright [the contemporary term for royalty] of 5000 copies." It was almost as much as he had received from two previous American publishers over a five-year period, and the historian understandably termed it "an enormous price which I should not have had the courage to ask of any publisher." [6]

Dedicated to the volume-producing promotional program of his New York publisher, Prescott willingly saw his royalty per copy cut in his agreement with Harpers from the previous $1.75 to $1.50. Percentage-wise, however, he actually increased his royalty from 23.33 per cent to 25 per cent, because the new work retailed for $6.00 instead of $7.50. At the same time, the author, who had refused an offer of $15,000 for his copyright, looked forward to other Harper impressions at the rate of $1.50 per copy for the author.

With this second work similar to the first one in size and style, the stereotype plates for the *Conquest of Mexico,* according to the historian's entry of November 17, 1843, in his literary memoranda, cost Prescott $1,773. This lower figure is explained, in part, by the omission of the expensive marginal notes.

A phenomenal sale in the holiday season of 1843 and early 1844 of *Conquest of Mexico* under the Harpers' imprint paved the way for a second printing, in 1844, of 500 copies, which meant, and which was duly noted in a letter of November 4, 1844, from the Harpers to Prescott, $750 royalties for Prescott. One-tenth the size of the edition of 1843, the small printing was explained by the publisher in a letter to Prescott of June 2, 1845, as follows: "Our principal object in printing small editions is to save *space.* Our buildings are already crammed with stock.''

The expiration of his contract with Little, Brown & Company for his work and the great success of the *Conquest of Mexico* led Prescott to shift the plates for *Ferdinand and Isabella* to the Harpers under an agreement modeled on the contract for the *Conquest of Mexico.* It provided a royalty of $1.50 per copy for a $6.00 book and an initial printing of 1,500 copies. Early 1845 thus brought $2,250 additional income to Prescott. By early June of that same year, the Harpers, with two profit-producers from the Prescott pen, also prepared to publish the *Miscellanies.*

Without the sales prospects of the histories, Prescott's volume of essays elicited a kind of secondary interest from both his American and English publishers. To both, the rehash of previously published essays represented a question mark. The magnetism of Prescott's name, already a significant factor in publishers' calculations, led them to believe it would sell, and so their normal reticence to handle such a book yielded to cautious, half-profits agreements. The first Harper printing, as indicated in their June 30, 1845, letter to the author, called for 2,500 copies, with 500 of them left in sheets.

While time alone could tell whether the author would realize income from the *Miscellanies,* his *Conquest of Mexico* was printed again in another impression of 500 copies, for which Prescott presented his draft for $750. Harper and Brothers accompanied word of this printing in a letter to Prescott dated September 25, 1845, with the assertion: ''We hope to repeat the dose before the year expires. Your works are selling grandly. Good books cannot be too extensively advertised.'' That next printing, in January, 1846, rose to 750 copies, meaning $1,125 for the author. At that time the New York publisher insisted, in a letter of January 17, ''Business prospects are good, if the *war* question can be dropped.''

All the financial records moving between author and publisher were not simple statements of books printed and royalties paid. Three titles alone would have complicated the issue, but in addition Prescott was providing illustrations, at cost, off engravings made in England, yielding royalties on certain numbers of review copies, and buying personal copies at reduced rates. Confusion was rampant when the author penned the following long letter to the Harpers on March 16, 1846.

> I have examined your acct of the ''Conquest of Mexico'' & ''Ferd and I'' & I must say I never had the fortune to see one so inaccurate in all my life. Indeed it cd not be well more so, as I do not think there is one item stated correctly; as I believe I can easily satisfy you. I recommend that wh. another acct be made out I should recom. the clerk sh. 1st see the contract. You charge me 4.50 a copy for the 25 copies which were to be delivered to me gratis by *Contract*. You charge me 4.50 upon all other copies wh. should only have been charged at 2 doll. a copy & the copyright or $3.50 pr. copy by *contract*.
>
> The number of copies delivered to me by your account falls 2 short of the number according to my accts.
>
> I agree to allow you (in conversation w. Mr. Fletcher Harper in N.Y.) copyright on 70 copies of the Con-

quest for your liberal advertising of same. This you have omitted.

I agreed to allow you also I think copyright on 50 copies of F & I for the same object. You call it 60 & I will not dispute it, for I may be mistaken, as contrary to my usage I omitted to make a memorandum of it at the time.

Lastly I have to charge you w. the cost of the engravings wh. I furnish you both for the ''Conq' '' & ''F & I.'' This was also provided in our *Contract* and I charge you no expense but the price I pd for them in London.

You have charged me w. 12 sets of the Miscellanies wh. I shd have gratis by my *Contract*. But as we have just begun upon the Miscellanies, it is not worth while to bring you into this account at all.

As you may not have another copy made out of the account wh. your clerk has drawn up for me I send a copy of it enclosed & on the following page I state my own acct, as I understand it w. you. If you are satisfied w. the correctness of the last, I will thank you to send me a statement of the amount for wh. I am to draw for the last edition expressed so as to show that it is the balance of all our accts relating to the histories up to present date.

The accompanying summary of the account by the author, in addition to claiming $1,125 for the last printing of the *Conquest of Mexico,* sought reimbursement for $133.50 for engraved illustrations furnished the publisher, as noted in a Prescott memorandum dated March, 1846.

The August printing of *Ferdinand and Isabella,* in an impression of 500 copies, netted Prescott $750. The war dreaded by the publishers earlier that year was a reality, but optimism attended their book-selling prospects, at least as far as Prescott's titles were concerned. A national endeavor which ordinarily might drive even the most literate elements from books to newspapers might actually promote the sale of such a title as his *Conquest of Mexico*. At the Christmas season of that year, just as Prescott and the house of Harper were initiating negotiations leading to the publication of the *Conquest of Peru* on similar terms, the publisher announced that another printing of the *Conquest of Mexico* was being rushed. Appearing early in 1847, it ran to 797 copies, representing a royalty of $1,195.50 for Prescott, according to a Harpers' letter of February 27, 1847.

The spring of 1847 found Prescott shipping, at his expense, the stereotype plates and engravings for the forthcoming *Conquest of Peru* to Harpers. The illustrations, of which he did not yet have a full supply for the initial printing, "for which you are to reimburse me," he wrote to the Harpers on April 24, 1847, "cost me twenty pounds in London, or ninety-six dollars eighty cents; and the duties on the prints of twenty per cwt, cost me nineteen dollars thirty six cents, making a total of 116 dollars 16 cents, for which you are to account to me."

Another factor complicating the account of Prescott's earnings was the manner in which the publisher consigned shipments of books to dealers. With it possible that books might be returned unsold six months later, some statements of inventories rose on occasion, to Prescott's dismay. "In the accounts you gave me, when in New York," he wrote the Harpers on April 24, 1847, "of the sales of my work, you state that I have 996 copies of the 'Miscellanies' on hand. In the account which you rendered me on the 19th of June last, you state there were on hand 614 copies in sheets, and 140 bound, making 754 in all. At this rate, we shall have the whole edition back again. Pray explain it.'' The publisher detailed the system of distribution to the author, and the historian realized that his volume of warmed-over essays was so unlike his histories in its appeal that it might be considered a dud. However, the histories satisfied Harper and Brothers that the Prescott name could defy the age-old fears of bad business in wartime and the doldrums of summertime. On the second day of summer of the second year of the war with Mexico, Prescott's *Conquest of Peru* was published by Harpers.

Just prior to the appearance of his third history, Prescott summarized his financial position as follows.

> The Harpers give me good accounts of my works. They consider my copyrights as worth no less than $25,000 apiece. If I allow only half that sum, which I should be very loath to take for them, the amount, with about $30,000 I have already received on the two histories, will swell up to a very pretty little *honorarium* for my literary lumber.[7]

Three-fourths of that statement of his total gross earnings, Prescott might have added, had been earned in America.

The publication of *Conquest of Peru,* scheduled in an edition of 7,500 copies, found the author expecting as many dollars for the new two-volume work as for its three-volume predecessor. With his terms basically the same as for the

Conquest of Mexico, that is, 50 cents per volume, it required a 50 per cent increase in the size of the edition to net the author the same amount, $7,500. Three weeks before publication, on June 2, 1847, Prescott wrote the Harpers: "I shall draw on you for $5000 of the copyright [i.e., royalty] on the date of publication. The balance [$2,500] I will defer, unless you prefer to pay the whole at once."

The stereotyping alone of this new work probably cost the historian about $1,200.

Sometimes, with the exception of the addition of illustration charges, for which he regularly sought reimbursement, the statements from publisher to author were satisfactorily complete, as was one sent Prescott in the autumn of 1847. "It appears to be all correct with one exception," Prescott wrote the Harpers on November 22, following receipt of the statement. "There remains some charges for the portraits of Pizarro and Gasca and also for my own portrait for the Miscellanies. The separate charges I herewith add to the balance due me." And so Prescott presented a bill for $132.66.

The big, busy Franklin Square publishing house, with records of its own based on the bookkeeping system administered by Frederick Saunders, sent many communications to the man on Beacon Street which expressed their differences of opinion, their agreement, and their publishing plans. On one occasion, November 24, 1847, illustrative of the multi-faceted nature of their letters to Prescott, went small-minded quibbling over the number of copies gratis for the author, a request for more illustrations for one work, and the announcement, "We find that our workmen have wet down paper for the

new edition of *Peru*." This last was an invitation
to the author to rush to New York any corrections
that he cared to make.

Both Prescott and the Harpers had hoped to ex-
haust the big initial printing of the *Conquest of Peru*
in short order; consequently some disappointment
attended the Harpers' statement of February 6,
1849, 20 months after publication, that they had
about 800 copies on hand. Six months later, with
that inventory down to about 300 copies and the
demand for *Ferdinand and Isabella* and the *Conquest of Mexico* also continuing, a new impression
of 295 copies of *Ferdinand* was released in April,
1849, and a new impression of *Mexico* was scheduled
for September. The 295 copies of his 12-year-old
history, *Ferdinand,* meant $442.50 royalty, as Har-
pers indicated in their letter to the historian on July
12, 1849.

With business prospects darkest just before the
dawn of a new season, Harpers complained on
August 2, 1849, that "at present business of every
kind is very much depressed." Six weeks later, on
September 15, it was a different story. "We have
now on the press an edition of 500 copies of your
Ferdinand and Isabella," they wrote Prescott.
"Business is just beginning to look up." Plodding
along slowly and steadily in the assured manner of
a masterwork, the first history added $750 more to
its author's income. Four weeks later, on October
11, with the new publishing season at full tilt, Harpers reported, "We have ordered another edition
of *Peru* to be printed forthwith. Business is good."

The full picture of Prescott's American sales during the early 1850's is not available, but Prescott,

gleefully reporting them to his English publisher, Bentley, on January 30, 1853, said, "My account of sales of the several works by the Harpers for the eleven months preceding April last, when I had my last settlement with them, showed a profit to me . . . of $6025."

Sales slowly declined year after year when no new title jogged the string of earlier works. However, activity was strong in the spring of 1853, when a new printing of 783 copies of the *Conquest of Mexico* netted the author $1,174.50. Accompanying that good word was a promise in a letter from the Harpers on May 3 that the author soon would hear of both *Ferdinand and Isabella* and the *Conquest of Peru,* "new editions of which are printing or about to be printed." The projected printings quickly materialized, with the 771 copies of the *Conquest of Peru* produced in May worth as many dollars in royalties, and the 750 copies of *Ferdinand and Isabella* worth $1,125 to the author. With the American printings bringing him $3,070.50 during the year 1853, in which Prescott had a total income from his writings of $3,505.00, the historian was deriving more than 85 per cent of his literary income from his fellow-countrymen.

When mid-1854 brought Prescott's willingness to contract for the first two volumes of *Philip the Second,* attended by his desire for more favorable terms than he had received during his eleven years with Harper and Brothers, it presaged the end of his relationship with the New York house and the need for a final accounting between them. New printings, which unfortunately are not broken down by titles and numbers of copies, meant a balance of

$2,624.83 for the author, some small part of which surely represented reimbursement for engravings supplied by Prescott. At what appeared to be the parting of their ways, Prescott could write the Harpers on August 7, "I am glad to see that the books continue to do so well."

Depressed business conditions, plus the desire of Phillips, Sampson, and Company to launch their publication of Prescott through his new work, delayed the transfer of the plates to Boston. Accordingly, Prescott and the Harpers agreed that the New York publisher should use them to keep the market supplied. At this time, the Harpers held 549 copies of *Ferdinand and Isabella,* 388 copies of the *Conquest of Mexico,* 24 copies of the *Miscellanies,* and 456 copies of the *Conquest of Peru,* according to the stock inventory the Harpers supplied Prescott in a letter of August 10, 1854.

In November, 1854, with the supply of the *Conquest of Mexico* exhausted, and orders on hand, the Harpers asked for and received permission to print a small quantity. When Prescott indicated that the Boston house, Phillips, Sampson, would not be in the market until August, 1855, that information helped the Harpers determine the sizes of the printings needed. In time, word of the depressed state of the book business in England during the Crimean War brought a request for deferment of the publication date for *Philip the Second* until November, 1855. Prescott's compliance meant that the market was open to Harpers throughout that year.

Consequently, on July 24, 1855, Prescott wrote: "Nearly a year has elapsed since the last account of sales from you of my books, and I should be glad to

receive one . . . which I trust will be our final settlement.'' Requesting shipment of the plates to him,
Prescott guaranteed that it would be the last accounting. Indicating that Prescott's draft, at one
day's sight, would be honored, Harper and Brothers
stated the balance in favor of the author as $1,153.60
—another sum for which details are lacking. However, it involved several works and also minor sums
related to illustrations supplied by Prescott. ''The
sales of your works during the past year,'' the publishers continued in their letter of August 16, ''as
you will perceive, have been unusually small. This
has arisen from the fact that both the Trade and the
Public have been waiting for new and cheaper editions.'' Quite possibly, some of the terms of the
contract with Phillips, Sampson, and Company,
which included the prospect, though not the immediate promise, of duodecimo editions had leaked
to the market. If so, dealers and readers were destined to disappointment, because the anticipated
cheaper American editions never appeared in Prescott's lifetime.

The puny income from this final settlement with
Harpers disturbed Prescott so much that his first reaction was to request a re-examination of the records
by the publishers' bookkeeper. When that was done,
and his findings suggested that the account was correct as rendered, Harper and Brothers added in a
letter to Prescott dated August 27, 1855: ''Business
generally, during the past year, has been unusually
dull—and we have never known so poor a year for
books.''

Incidentally, in the midst of this dismal final accounting for the twelve-year relationship with the

New York firm, Prescott, optimistically looking forward to a profitable relationship in Boston, closed out the Harper period by buying, for $224.80, the publisher's half-interest in the plates for the *Miscellanies,* as well as offering to buy back any unused illustrations.

The arrangement terminated with the Harpers had grossed more than $35,800 for Prescott. Occasional thinness of the record, especially in the 1850–52 interval, suggests that the true figure may exceed that sum by thousands of dollars. However, on the basis of definitely known earnings, the con-

Prescott's Income from Harper and Brothers

Books

YEAR	FERDINAND	MEXICO	MISCEL-LANIES	PERU	ANNUAL INCOME
1843		$7,500.00			$7,500.00
1844		750.00			750.00
1845	$2,250.00	750.00	_____		3,000.00
1846	750.00	1,125.00			1,875.00
1847		1,195.50		$7,500.00	8,695.50
1848	1,066.50	1,500.00			2,566.50
1849	1,192.50				1,192.50
1850					
1851					6,025.00
1852					
1853	1,125.00	1,174.50		771.00	3,070.50
1854					
1855					1,153.60
Total	$6,384.00	$13,995.00	_____	$8,271.00	$35,828.60

tracts with the Harpers yielded four times as much income for the historian as his combined earnings through the first two Boston publishers. Admittedly, some of this was a tribute to the larger operation and more skillful promotion and distribution program afforded by the New York house. Some of it, too, was the direct product of twelve years of publication versus six, and four titles versus one. Far from making Prescott, the Harper years did, nevertheless, enhance his reputation and enlarge his purse. When he left them, he looked to a home-town house to do better for him in both regards.

At once the most complex and potentially rewarding of Prescott's American contracts, the agreement with Phillips, Sampson, and Company of August 5, 1854, was doomed to limited operation. Pre-publication delay came from the depressed state of the national economy. Subsequently, the withdrawal of one partner, the death of another, the death of Prescott, and the collapse of the business combined to prevent numerous provisions of the agreement, including those calling for cheaper duodecimo editions, from ever coming into operation. Therefore, this last publishing arrangement offers a wide margin between the prospect and the fulfillment of the contract. Nonetheless, it was, in three short years, Prescott's most lucrative publishing arrangement.

Although pledged to a first printing of 12,000 copies of the first 2 volumes of *Philip the Second*, Phillips, Sampson, and Company initially printed 7,000 copies, in what was probably a mutually agreed upon cautious approach to the dollar-pinched public. With considerable publicity before the work was available, *Philip the Second* enjoyed a heavy early sale. Rejoicing on the day of publication, Prescott declared in a letter to Richard Bentley of December 10, 1855: "It has made a promising debut . . . 7000 copies having been struck off—5000 of which have already been disposed of." The author's satisfaction was tempered by the thought expressed in another letter to Bentley on December 16: "But after all, that is 'small deer' compared to the great miracle-worker Macaulay."

Nine months after the issuance of *Philip the Second* in Boston, Prescott wrote Bentley on September 15, 1856: "At my last settlement of six months' sales, my publisher paid me 17,000 dollars (leaving them 2000 copies of the Philip still to sell on their own account)." Such, of course, means that the initial printing was speedily supplemented, though not immediately, to the full 12,000 copies contracted for over a three-year period. In less than a year, 10,000 copies of *Philip the Second* were printed in Boston. And as soon as the historian's latest work was launched, the plates for the earlier histories were put to work.

Along with *Philip the Second,* December, 1855, witnessed the release by Phillips, Sampson, and Company, of printings of the *Conquest of Mexico,* the *Conquest of Peru,* and the *Miscellanies.* The new year not only brought further printing of the newest work and a printing of the oldest history by the Boston house, it also provided additional printings of all the recently released older works. Informing an English publisher, George Routledge, of his American sales, Prescott reported on November 17, 1856, just eleven months after the initiation of the arrangement with Phillips, Sampson, and Company:

"My Boston publishers have paid me about $20,000 for the actual sales of all the works, about half of which was earned by the Philip. These are larger sales than I have ever made before and I am inclined to let well alone." Although it explains author and publisher willingness to stick with the octavo editions and forgo for the time the idea of releasing cheaper duodecimo editions, this statement does not afford a clear understanding of the components of that income.

Of the $20,000 earned by late 1856 through the new Boston connection, Prescott's word that half of it was from *Philip the Second* corresponds with the fact that the tenth 1,000-copy printing of the work, indicated as such on its title page, was released that year. The 10,000 copies represented $10,000 to the author. With a predilection for printings of 1,000 copies each clearly in evidence in the handling of *Philip the Second,* Phillips, Sampson, and Company possibly applied that pattern to all the older titles as well. If so, the following prospect develops: *Ferdinand and Isabella,* with both the eleventh and twelfth editions issued in 1856, represents 2,000 copies and $3,000 income; the *Conquest of Mexico,* with the twenty-third edition in 1855 and the twenty-fourth, twenty-fifth and twenty-sixth editions in 1856, involves 4,000 copies and $6,000 income; the *Miscellanies,* with printings in both 1855 and 1856, suggests 2,000 copies and $1,000 earnings; and the *Conquest of Peru,* with one printing in 1855 and a second printing in 1856, suggests 2,000 copies and $2,000 income. Thus, the maximum income from all of the older works through the *entire* year of 1856 would be $12,000, which sum, added to the $10,000 earned by *Philip*, would exceed the total of $20,000 noted by Prescott in his letter to Bentley by $2,000. This discrepancy can be explained, in part, by smaller-than-average printings of the *Miscellanies* and in terms of the fact that Prescott's calculation was made in mid-November instead of for the entire year. With his report coming at the height of the publishing season, it follows logically that several thousand copies of the older works—possibly the twenty-sixth edition of the *Conquest of Mexico* and the twelfth edition of *Ferdinand and Isabella* (the most expensive items)—came after his calculation of November. Omitted from this calculation is *Charles the Fifth*, which the Boston house published on December 8, 1856, so late a date that it is presumed settlements related to it came during 1857 rather than 1856. At any rate, Prescott's accounting, released three weeks in advance of the publication of that title, did not include it.

In early March, 1857, Prescott, writing to England, recapitulated his recent American sales and his future prospects. "The sales of all my works here for the last year," he informed Bentley on March 9, "was not far from 40,000 *volumes,* which, as they are all of the expensive 8vo size, was not a bad year's work. The present year, so far also promises exceedingly well." With his royalties of 50 cents per volume on every title in the octavo form, this again substantiates the $20,000 income for 1856.

The historian was quite right, too, about the promise of 1857. That year witnessed one printing of every one of the six titles, from the twenty-year-old *Ferdinand and Isabella* to the infant *Charles the Fifth.* All was rosy with this prospect of $1,500 from

Ferdinand and Isabella, another $1,500 from the *Conquest of Mexico,* $500 from the *Miscellanies,* $1,000 from the *Conquest of Peru,* and $1,000 from *Philip the Second.* With *Charles the Fifth* published on a half-profits basis, it quite possibly was not yet producing income. However, the year that opened with sunny prospects quickly turned bleak and disappointing.

With his health failing, William Lee, long considered the active businessman of the house, retired from the firm, selling his entire interest to his partners Phillips and Sampson "for the sum of $65,000, the largest portion of which was in promissory notes." [8] The impact on the company of the depression which set in that year was all the more severe because of the double blow of loss of capable leadership and the attendant indebtedness of the remaining partners. What the worsening circumstance meant to Prescott is evident in the following letter penned to his publisher on December 10, 1857.

> The account you present is on the whole a pretty fair one considering the horrid times. It is a pity to see a book that opened so brilliantly as Charles the Fifth thus nipped in the bud. But sunshine will come sooner or later.
>
> You have omitted one important item in the account —that is the account due to me on your guaranty of $4000 per annum for the sales of the old books. Last June you paid me on their account $2195. This December you are to pay me $1508.50 on the same account. The two sums make $3703.50, leaving $296.50 due to me on account of the guaranty. This last sum added to that which you state to be your indebtedness to me, namely $1945.47, will make $2241.97 the real sum now due to me.

With respect to the payment of the money, I am sorry that it is not convenient for you to make it now, inasmuch as I am borrowing money myself for my own expenses, and had reckoned confidently on this payment. But the pressure has been too hard, I know, for one to be confident of anything. I shall be glad to accommodate you, and shall be content if you will pay me $1000 in cash and your note for the remainder at 4 months, adding as you propose, the interest at 6 per cent, as I shall get the note discounted at my bank. Perhaps it may be more convenient for you, and it will answer my purpose, if you pay *one third cash,* and leave the remaining *two thirds* to be covered by the notes.

I shall be obliged by your having the account made up today by the bookkeeper and sent to me.

Quite probably it was in this troubled moment of late 1857 that Prescott voluntarily went to his publishers and so amended the contract as to release them from the necessity of paying him for the unsold portion of the twelve-thousand copies of *Philip the Second* for which they had contracted. In a memo dated December 11, 1857, Prescott summarized the matter in these words: "Told Mr. Phillips that if these times continued I should be perfectly willing to do whatever was reasonable in regard to the guaranty of $4000 a year on the sales of the old books." Knowing the appearance of more of his unfinished *Philip the Second* might stimulate sales and help his publisher, the historian confided to him that he hoped to conclude the third volume by June, 1858, adding, "But told him he must not understand this as in a respect a promise on my part, as I could never consent to be a bookseller's hack." Prescott's warmly generous action evoked friendly expression of thankfulness from Phillips in a letter of December 30.

Six months later, with business still distressingly bad, Phillips wrote Prescott on June 12, 1858: "I have filled a check for one half the balance of the account and added the interest to the other half." He continued as follows: "Do not trouble yourself about any acknowledgement of them. We can adjust that and the contract matter together. For these repeated concessions and accommodations on your part, I have no parallel in my business relations."

Even as it fell apart, the publishing house optimistically issued more printings of Prescott's works. The year 1858 saw new impressions of unknown sizes, but quite possibly in the usual thousands, of every title except *Charles the Fifth*. It suggests the following income earned by Prescott: $1,500 for *Ferdinand and Isabella*, $1,500 for the *Conquest of Mexico*, $500 for the *Miscellanies*, $1,000 for the *Conquest of Peru*, $1,000 for the first two volumes of *Philip the Second*, and an indeterminate sum for the third volume of that work. Receipts against these earnings cannot be determined, with further chaos introduced by the death of the partner Sampson.[9] In the failure and attendant liquidation of the firm, Prescott's financial stake cannot be determined.

In a last gasp of publishing operations, printings of every Prescott title, except *Charles the Fifth*, were introduced into the market in 1859. However, that final Boston operation was beyond Prescott, with death coming to him on January 28, 1859. One author's business relations with four American publishers had ended. Despite the combination of uncertainties attending the last thirteen months of his final Boston publishing arrangement, it can be asserted that Phillips, Sampson, and Company produced greater earnings for Prescott than had any other American publisher.

Every time Prescott changed American publishers he bettered himself financially. From the American Stationers' Company he received $1,000; from Little, Brown & Company approximately $7,000; from Harper and Brothers more than $35,800; and from Phillips, Sampson, and Company he earned but most probably did not receive all of a sum that exceeded $40,000. (Prescott himself insisted that this last was his most lucrative contract.) In twenty-one years, from the first settlement in early 1838 to the last in late 1858, his gross American earnings were in excess of $83,000. With the historian's death the copyrights and the all-important plates went to his heirs, as did the continuing American income from his six books. Meanwhile, during his lifetime, a remarkably dissimilar financial record was compiled through his arrangements with English publishers.

The agreement of 1837 with Richard Bentley, calling as it did for publication on half-profits, inspired endless accounting, author-publisher wrangling, and a final picture which is clearer in general outline than in specific detail. Deducted from the Bentley payments were two continuing categories of expense: a flat 10 per cent commission for Prescott's agent Aspinwall, plus reimbursement of his agent's postage expense.

The first prospect of English income from *Ferdinand and Isabella* appeared on August 17, 1839, when Bentley presented a promissory note to Aspinwall for £100 at six months, as Aspinwall duly informed Prescott in a letter dated September 2. Falling due on February 17, 1840, it was duly paid. This practice of Bentley's payment with promissory notes, unlike the American practice in the same period, was routine across the years. Deducting his commission of £10 and postage expenses of £3 2s 9d (covering thirty-four communications between late 1836 and early 1840), Aspinwall instructed Prescott in a letter of February 29, 1840, that he could draw the balance of £86 17s 3d. Needless to say, even this sizable bite into the Bentley payment did not represent all Prescott's expenses, because he had paid charges for illustrations and postage and freight related to his correspondence with and shipments of proof sheets to his London publisher.

The small first English earnings, coupled with his Little, Brown & Company income in a period of adverse business conditions, whetted Prescott's desire for more transatlantic accountings. Closing a letter to Bentley in mid-summer 1840, he wrote: "I shall be very glad to hear from you through Col. Aspinwall, whom you will be good enough to furnish with the statement of your sales." [10]

In early November Aspinwall reported receipt of a second promissory note for £100 at six months, with payment due May 3, 1841. "I am sorry," Aspinwall continued in his letter of November 3, "that he has so mixed up the account for the two editions [1838 and 1839] that it would be difficult to ascertain the result of either separately." To fantastically high charges for advertising—judged so by Prescott—the publisher added an accounting system of his own invention which endlessly confused and irritated both Prescott and his agent. Compounding the historian's doubts about the honesty of Bentley was his realization that during the same three full years of 1838, 1839, and 1840, for which his English income approximated $500, his American earnings had surpassed $5,000. Never willing to admit it, Prescott, early in his career might have realized that America would provide dollars and England prestige, two different but mutually desirable forms of author income. At least it did not displease the historian to hear, in early 1841, that his book was selling in England in the steady way of a classic.

By August of that year, with only 70 copies of the second printing of 750 copies on hand, Bentley spoke of a third edition of the same size. Not long after the promised impression was released, the London publisher, complaining of stagnant business conditions and dreary prospects, asked the historian when his second history would be ready for the market. Bentley not only wanted to secure that work for his firm, but he hoped that its publication would stimulate sale of the earlier title. With the second edition a matter of history, the publisher presented Aspinwall with a final accounting for it. Both the agent and the author were astounded that the historian's share was a meager £17 6s 6d. When Bentley in a letter of April 19, 1842, to Prescott, suggested, possibly because of the smallness of the sum involved, that settlement be postponed until such occasion arose for the new third edition, Aspinwall, backed by Prescott, insisted upon an immediate settlement. Their disappointment was enough without the prospect of tolerating the publisher's violation of the contract by deferring payment and complicating the accounts by merging the records of different editions. Bentley's natural desire to minimize bookkeeping prompted proposals which made him increasingly suspect in the minds of both Aspinwall and Prescott.[11]

When the settlement for the second edition was effected, Prescott, in January, 1843, could say, "I have received from Bentley for the 'Ferdinand and Isabel' rather over £350 in five years." [12] Deducting his agent's commission and expenses, Prescott had a personal gross income of £321 from the first 1,500 copies of *Ferdinand and Isabella* published in London.[13]

Prescott's dissatisfaction with his English income was plainly a relative thing. With his gross income for 1,500 copies approximating $1,750 (prior to deductions for his agent, and converting the pound sterling at the rate of $5.00 for ease of calculation), Prescott averaged $1.17 per English copy. In America, with the first 1,500 copies grossing him $1,337.70 ($1,000 for 1,300 copies by his first publisher and $337.70 as the prorated income for 200 copies of the first 500 published by Little, Brown & Company), his average income was $.89 per American copy. With no dissatisfaction possible with the English record in terms of dollars and cents per volume, Prescott's concern arose from the difference in the retail prices of the American and English editions. Whereas in his own country the price was $7.50, it was $10.50 (42*s*) in England, almost 50 per cent more expensive. In view of the price differential, the percentage yield for Prescott was much lower in England than in America.

Illustrative of the kind of accounting periodically

sent to Aspinwall for Prescott by Bentley is the following, the fifth Bentley account of May 19, 1843, which concerns the third English edition of *Ferdinand and Isabella.*

Dr.	*1842*	Cr.	*1842*
Feby 24 To printing 3rd edition 94¼ sheets No. 750	£234,18,6	Feb. By 750 copies printed, less 8 presented— 742	
" " Paper for do. 14½ Reams @ 17/6	123,16,3		
			1843
		May 16 175 sold as 168 @ 30/6 567 (copies)	£256, 4,0
	1843	*Deficit to debit next Acct.*	£222,13,0
May 17 Advertising 3d edition to this date	46, –,–		

	1841
Feb. Illustrations Paid Freebairn for engraving medallion portrait of Gonzalvo for 3d. Edition (substituted for former portrait) of Gonzalvo	12,12,0
To writing to do.	0, 5,0

1842

Feb. Printing & Paper 768 sets of 5 plates for 3d Edit. @ 6/	11, 9,9
Lithograph drawing of fac- similes for 3d edition	2, 2,0
Printing & pa- per 765 @ 7/6	2,17,6

1843

May To Binding 200 sets in cloth 3 vols 2/–25 as 24	19, 4,0
" To 1 op lt. Commr. & risk of bad debts on amt. of copies sold (£256,4,0)	25,12,0
	478,17,0

1843

May 16 To deficit
brot.   forward
£222.13—1843
May 16. By 567
copies on Hand.

Complete enough to reveal many of the inner aspects of his business operation, Bentley's accounts
invited Prescott's doubts. Did the £46 assigned to

advertising, without benefit of details, actually serve that purpose? If so, was it not likely that Bentley, often advertising his books in magazines published by his own firm, merely transferred funds from one of his accounts to another? For such questions no answer was ever forthcoming.

Accountings, doubts, and questions continued routinely in connection with the English production of the first title on a half-profits arrangement, but not so for Prescott's second history. His willingness to sell it outright to Bentley for £650 surely stemmed, in part, from the irritations and annoyances suffered over the first book. In retrospect it can be said that Prescott was the loser financially, because his eventual English income from *Ferdinand and Isabella* was greater than that from the *Conquest of Mexico*.

With the publication of the second history, Bentley executed notes at six, nine, and twelve months, each in the amount of £216 13s 4d, dated from October 24, 1843. Whether for half-profits agreements or outright purchases, Bentley regularly paid Prescott with promissory notes. When Bentley paid the first note on April 27, 1844, Aspinwall notified Prescott on May 2 that a balance of £208 10s 3d awaited him. The difference of £8 3s 1d, the agent's commission presumably, is noticeably less on an outright sale of a manuscript than had been the case with a half-profits agreement. However, when Bentley paid the second note on July 27, Aspinwall only forwarded Prescott £194 18s on August 2. The difference, almost exactly 10 per cent of the face of the note, suggests that something else had influenced Aspinwall's earlier transfer of funds and that his commission was still 10 per cent of Prescott's gross earnings, with the sum in excess of 10 per cent, in this instance 2 shillings, representing the agent's postage charges. This inference concerning the second note is borne out when on October 26, with the payment of the third note by Bentley, Aspinwall indicated in a letter of November 4 that Prescott had £194 16*s* available, the remainder representing his commission of £21 13*s* 4*d* and postage charges of four shillings.

The dreary business prospects which Bentley had mentioned several years earlier found him still marketing the third edition of *Ferdinand and Isabella*. On February 3, 1845, Bentley's accounting to the historian, forwarded to Prescott by Aspinwall, indicated the following changes from the previous inventory: 6 of the 567 copies had been presented by Bentley; 226 of the remaining 561 copies were on hand, making a total of 335 sold since the previous settlement. With that sale the book had moved into the profit column, with Prescott's half amounting to £74 4*s*. Not liking it, the historian wrote Aspinwall on February 27:

> *I have had no account nor remittance for this third edition* till now.—He now allows by this 6th account £74.4.0. as due, (his note it seems is for £100) from sales of the third edition, leaving 226 copies on hand Feb. 3, 1845.—The other two editions gave me £321.14.0 in all. *Why is this to fall so short* when the expences, as the engravings are already paid for, must have been necessarily less? And where is the 5th account of sales? *Was not this 3d edition also 750 copies?*

The author's dissatisfaction was well grounded, and his turning to Aspinwall was the more logical, because the agent, retaining the original Bentley reports in London, customarily only forwarded copies to Prescott.

Proof that Prescott's expenses attendant upon historical writing consumed much of his earnings is dramatically demonstrated in a settlement of mid-1845. When Bentley paid off a £100 note, Aspinwall deducted the following: his commission of £10, his postage expense of 13s 7d, and £60 for bookseller Rich, leaving the historian the rather trifling sum of £29 6s 5d.

Publishing a fourth 750-copy edition of *Ferdinand and Isabella* in February, 1846, Bentley submitted, by the following summer, another accounting, the first to deal with two half-profits undertakings. With 466 copies of the *Miscellanies* edition of 1,000 on hand, that work showed a deficit of £32 17s 8d. Despite the fact that only 125 of the 750-copy new edition of *Ferdinand and Isabella* had been sold, Bentley owed Prescott £100 on the previous edition of that title. This time his promissory note was given at four months, due October 14. When Aspinwall collected that sum in the autumn, he deducted £10 commission, 12s 9d postage, and £6 10s 3d for artist Greatbatch for the engraving of Prescott for the plate in the *Miscellanies*. Forwarded to Prescott was the sum of £82 17s.

Before another accounting on the two half-profits ventures, Bentley bought Prescott's *Conquest of Peru* outright for £800. Differing from his purchase of the *Conquest of Mexico* only in amount paid, this work, costing him an added £150, found Bentley issuing three notes for £266 13s 4d each, due six, nine, and twelve months from the day of publication, which was duly reported to Prescott by Aspinwall in a letter of February 3, 1847.

On November 30, 1847, six months after the publication of the *Conquest of Peru,* Bentley paid his initial note. Deducting his commission of £26 13*s* 4*d* and £1 4*d* for postage, Aspinwall credited £238 19*s* 8*d* to Prescott's account, and so reported to Prescott in a letter dated December 2, 1847.

Four weeks later, on the last day of the year, Bentley gave the historian a clear general picture of his books in the English market: *Ferdinand and Isabella* was moving slowly; the *Conquest of Mexico* had perked up, the *Miscellanies* was a continuing disappointment, with the publisher holding half of his original edition of 1,000 copies; and the new work, the *Conquest of Peru,* was "a general favorite." The last title had jogged the sale of the earlier ones. Less than two months later Bentley made an accounting and signed a promissory note for £125 at four months. With Bentley insisting in a letter of February 24 to Prescott that the *Miscellanies,* down to 389 copies on hand, were "yet without profit," the note covered the earnings of *Ferdinand and Isabella.* Less than one week later, on March 1, 1848, Bentley paid his second note on the *Conquest of Peru.* Aspinwall deducted his commission of £26 13*s* 4*d* and postage charges of 3 shillings and sent a credit for £239 17*s* to Prescott. On June 1, 1848, Bentley paid the third and last note on that title, and Prescott's agent sent him £239 18*s* after deducting his commission of £26 13*s* 4*d* and 2 shillings for postage. On June 20, Aspinwall reported Bentley's payment of the £125 note at four months, £112 8*s* of which he credited to Prescott, with the remainder divided between his own commission of £12 10*s* and postage charges of 2 shillings.

Such reports mistakenly suggest that business was good for Bentley in 1848 when, in truth, it was dull all that year. The reports actually covered sales prior to the outbreak of the French Revolution of February, 1848. With public interest in current events and reader interest focused on newspapers, the disquieting scene on the continent of Europe depressed book sales. A stock of 120 copies of the previously popular *Conquest of Peru* sufficed more than a year. However, at last, four years following publication, the sale of the *Miscellanies* had just about covered expenses, according to a letter from Bentley on March 23, 1849. At this moment the threat of a cheap competing edition of *Ferdinand and Isabella* was forcing Bentley's initial move from the octavo to the smaller sizes. Although Prescott had no continuing financial stake in the English publication of the *Conquest of Peru,* the news from Bentley grieved him. "I am sorry," he wrote Bentley on April 30, "for what you say of 'Peru.' It was no wonder, however, that the hurricane which overthrew monarchies should have upset our little cockboat too. Yet it was a pity, when you were running on so merrily before the wind."

In late May, 1849, Aspinwall forwarded an accounting to Prescott which indicated the author's profits were £75 15*s* 8*d,* for which the publisher executed his note at four months for £75. With the *Miscellanies* still showing the small deficit of £12 19*s* 4*d,* these earnings once more came from *Ferdinand and Isabella.* Due on September 20, the note was paid to Aspinwall, who deducted his own £7 12*s* and credited Prescott with £67 8s. Despite these profits, Bentley insisted that the French Revolution still had the book trade in a paralyzed state. After two dreary years for publishers, business began to brighten at mid-century.

On December 11, 1850, Bentley paid off a note he had given Prescott in the amount of £105. Retaining £10 12s commission, Aspinwall, in a letter to Prescott dated December 12, credited Prescott's account with the remainder, £94 8s. The continuing success of *Ferdinand and Isabella* pleased Prescott greatly, and in the early 1850's, when no new title was immediately forthcoming, the historian particularly relished the reports from Bentley on his first work. On August 19, 1851, he wrote to Bentley: "Shall I not before long receive your annual account through Col. Aspinwall, with a prosperous balance on account of the 'Ferdinand'?"

When Bentley sent the anticipated accounting for the publishing year 1850–51, he prefaced it with the dismal word that it had been the dullest year that he had ever experienced. But with hope springing eternal in the mind of the New Burlington Street publisher, he added in his September 26 letter to Prescott, "The Crystal Palace is about to close, and I trust people will begin to think of reading." The cheap edition of *Ferdinand and Isabella* which had been issued to counter Bohn's printing of it had so disturbed the sale of the octavo edition that the last such impression still showed a deficit of nearly £250. It was not the kind of report that Prescott had anticipated.

However, in a rare instance of a mistake on Prescott's part, the author, studying his files, had somehow concluded that Bentley owed him £60, and had so informed Aspinwall. Rectifications were speedily in order, and the historian wrote Bentley on January 22, 1852: "I am truly ashamed of the blunder which I have made in advising Col. Aspinwall that £60 were due me from you on account of sales. I cannot explain it in any way. I have your letters as well as my own all on file; but I find nothing to afford a clue to my blunder."

A year later, in response to Aspinwall's request for an accounting, Bentley indicated that *Ferdinand and Isabella* had earned £9 1s 4d for Prescott. Preparing to pay that sum, the publisher restated his desire to buy up the half-profits arrangements with Prescott for the *Miscellanies* as well as the first history. His offer of £400 was refused by the historian, who, in turn, asked for £600, which Bentley refused. From the accounting given by Bentley, Aspinwall deducted his commission of £9 8s 1d and postage charges of 2s 4d and credited Prescott with £89 11d in a letter to the Boston author dated February 4, 1853.

More than a year passed, and with Aspinwall, who was preparing to leave London, no longer available to serve Prescott's purposes, the historian was himself negotiating the sale of the first pair of volumes of *Philip the Second*. In a letter to Bentley of June 20, 1854, he noted: "My last account of sales of 'Ferdinand' & the Miscellanies was to Nov. '52. At your convenience, I should like to have another from you." The ensuing report by Bentley, given to Prescott in a letter of August 11, illustrates the added complexities in accounting posed by the concurrent issuance of octavo and duodecimo editions.

The 4th account of the cheap Edition of 'Ferdinand
& Isabella' gives a profit to you of . . . £87,   6, 6
and the 8th Acct of 'Miscellanies' 8vo . . .   4, 18, 8
                                             £92,   5, 2

on the other hand
I am still a loser by the cheap Edition of Miscellanies,
the deficit on the 3rd account being . . . £25, 19, 0
and by the 8vo Edition of Ferd & Isab the
14th acct showing a loss of   97,   7, 0

On the basis of editions, Bentley owed Prescott
money; but on the basis of titles, which would permit the unification of octavo and duodecimo editions
of a work, Bentley could point out that both works
showed deficits.

However, the summer of 1854, with a House of
Lords' decision denying copyright in England for
the works of American authors, speedily took on an
even bleaker aspect. It was particularly so for Bentley, because he of all London publishers was, and
had long been, the leading promoter of American
works in England. Indeed, many of the vaguely de-
fined but nevertheless real financial difficulties immediately ahead for his firm must have stemmed
from the strong trust he had previously entertained
that an American work could enjoy English copyright.

Compounding the dull prospects before Bentley
—and all the rest of the English publishing world—
was the harsh reality that the mid-summer 1854
plans for invading the Crimea foretold a reduced
English interest in books. Making the bad situation
still worse, Routledge challenged Bentley, on the
basis of the recent Lords' decision, and put cheap

editions of titles by Prescott into the English market.

Bentley's lament to Prescott was real and repeated. "I trust this cruel war will soon be terminated," he wrote to Prescott on December 14, "and the public may have time for something else besides newspapers, which now literally absorb the attention of everybody." Referring to the Crimean War, Bentley, writing to Prescott six weeks later, on February 9, 1855, said, "It has for the time generally affected commerce very seriously, and particularly the trade of bookselling, books being a luxury which people with a double income tax feel disposed to dispense with."

While England fought a war abroad, Prescott campaigned vigorously in England against odds for a remunerative contract for the first two volumes of his *Philip the Second*. A victim of the state of copyright confusion, he received only £250 from Bentley in his fifth agreement with, and third outright sale to, that publisher.

When the truth of Bentley's assertion that Prescott was one of the few names that could sell a book in those times in England demonstrated itself, the author thanked him in a letter dated December 16, 1855, and added: "I am glad to hear that the book is doing so well. It rejoices my heart, and gives me a stimulus for new efforts." While the new title thus held forth bright promise for author and publisher, the latter in his accounting for the two half-profits ventures through the end of 1855 reported in a letter of February 21, 1856, "The 8vo edition of 'Ferdinand' still exhibits a deficiency, I am sorry to say." Prescott voiced the best possible reply on April 18:

"I trust the peace will show some good results in the bookselling business." Sharing that hope, Bentley could add on May 7: "I am sure you will feel pleasure in hearing that the temporary cloud under which I suffered, is fast passing away."

Having long since come to consider Prescott his author, Bentley had some of his optimism dashed when, in September, 1856, he learned that the despised Routledge had won the Robertson-Prescott *Charles the Fifth* with his bid of £110. However, Bentley bore up, and in the course of extending New Year's greetings to Prescott on January 8, 1857, said, "Russia wants peace *at present;* and so I trust the world will turn its swords into ploughshares; and literature may claim an audience."

In early 1858, anticipating more of Prescott's *Philip the Second,* Bentley enlarged upon his improved financial condition. He had re-established himself fully by paying off every creditor with interest at 5 per cent. "My position," he informed Prescott on April 8, "is considered by all who have dealings with me higher than it stood before, and second to no London publisher."

With September, 1858, Bentley experienced a repetition of the bitter blow of September, 1856; he lost the bidding for the third volume of *Philip the Second* to Routledge. The latter's offer of 260 guineas (£273), paid Prescott in January, 1859, covered the last work penned by the historian.

Prescott's short-term income from Routledge, easily arrived at, totaled £383. That which he received from Bentley, not so easily nor so completely established, can be summarized as shown in the following table.[14]

Again converting the pound sterling at $5.00, the historian's English income of at least $13,673.60 from Bentley and $1,915 from Routledge gives a lifetime minimum total of $15,588.60 from his English editions.

Prescott's Income from Bentley

TITLE	PAYMENT PERIODS	TOTAL		
Ferdinand and Isabella	1838–	£1,000	0s	0d *
Conquest of Mexico	1844	650	0	0
Miscellanies	1845–	34	14	5
Conquest of Peru	1847–48	800	0	0
Philip the Second	1856	250	0	0
Total		£2,734	14s	5d

* For this work the figure is a minimum.

With American earnings of at least $83,000 and English earnings of more than $15,588.60, Prescott's gross income from his books approximated $100,-000.[15] In no other country in which his books were published did the historian have any financial stake in the undertaking.

In terms of publisher Putnam's often-quoted insistence that any royalty in excess of 10 per cent is immoral, Prescott's earnings on his American editions were excessively so. To be remembered, however, is the fact that he maneuvered himself, as did other authors, into higher income through recourse to and control of stereotype plates for his books.[16]

Never in more than two decades did Prescott's titles appear in the United States in any form other

than octavo. This is to say that the aristocratic historian wrote for aristocratic readers, that his books
were generally beyond the reach of the common folk
of his times. When *Ferdinand and Isabella* first appeared, it cost $7.50 for the three volumes, a figure
that exceeded the weekly earnings of the average
American worker. In the spring of 1838, according
to contemporary newspaper market quotations, ham
cost 10 cents and coffee between 13 and 15 cents per
pound, and the farmer sold his oats at less than 30
cents and his potatoes at less than 60 cents per
bushel. Such prices scarcely admitted of interest in
the luxury item that was a Prescott book. And similar patterns of prices and worker income persisted
throughout the years that Prescott offered his books
to the American reader. Keeping his prices high,
never lower than $2.00 per volume, Prescott neither
reached as large an audience nor reaped as large an
income as he might have.[17] For more than a decade
the gap between the prices of his books in their
English editions and the average English worker's
income was even greater than in the United States.
And then, after the first decade of expensive books
—Bentley never had more expensive items in his annual lists—the lower price was an accident of copyright confusion and pirated editions, not author and
publisher desire.

From beginning to end, Prescott sought reputation above income. Although he did not disdain the
idea of earning money with his books, Prescott's
heavy expenses surely reduced his gross earnings
to a very modest net income. Meanwhile, the man
whose scholarly tastes and intellectual desires and

financial well-being led him to desire something above monetary reward was such a warm personality that his relations with his publishers were far from completely given over to business, for they also knew a personal side.

———•◆•———

CHAPTER EIGHT

THE PERSONAL SIDE

WHEREAS Prescott the historian was a man apart— introspective and aloof—immersed in problems of his favored sixteenth century and removed from those of his own day, Prescott the social being was a totally different kind of person. A gregarious extrovert, he was constantly in or on the fringes of the whirl of polite society in Boston. Against a background of experience as American minister to the Court of St. James, Boston-bred Edward Everett, writing to English nobility, termed Prescott "one of the brightest ornaments of our social circle." The historian, he further insisted, was "not less distinguished for his amiable manners and excellent character than for his literary merit." [1]

On the social side of his personality, Prescott delighted in giving small dinner parties, sometimes for couples but often restricted to a masculine contingent that included George Ticknor, William Amory, William H. Gardiner, Jared Sparks, George Bancroft, Henry W. Longfellow, and a few others. Over fine wine and tasteful food, conversation ranged widely but returned ever again to their common concern, the problems of authorship. Holiday

seasons brought carefree social scenes, especially
the Thanksgiving dinners and the vacations that
found streams of visitors interrupting scholarly
labors at the summer houses at Nahant and Lynn.
For Prescott, the infrequent junkets to such places
as New York City and Washington were synonymous
with almost endless rounds of festivity. In the grow-
ing city on Manhattan his friendship with the Rev.
Jonathan M. Wainwright ushered him into a select
social circle. In the national capital Prescott moved
in the society of cabinet members and ranking diplo-
mats. In Boston he entertained many of the British
literary figures who toured, lectured, and then wrote
of America. To Prescott's home and table came Lady
Emmeline Stuart Wortley, who remembered her
host in her book, Thackeray, who, first entertained in
America by Prescott, honored him in the opening
sentences of *The Virginians,* and Charles Dickens, in
the full fury of his lonely American crusade in behalf of international copyright.

Prescott's triumphant tour of England in 1850,
devoid of any idea of lecturing or of gathering material for a travel account, was an uninterrupted social season that lasted all summer, with lords and
ladies, literati, politicians, and others. It may be
suggested that some real measure of Prescott's
capacity for delineating personality in his histories
came from his flesh-and-blood awareness of man as
a social being. One might similarly suggest that his
friendly disposition is seen in his relations with his
publishers, despite the fact that his was a day in
which the social worlds of the aristocratic intellectual and the money-grubbing publisher seldom
met.

With the early failure of the American Stationers' Company, his first American publisher, no evidence suggests the relationship between the author and his publisher was other than a business one. However, it was a close arrangement, for Prescott often crossed the sill of the establishment—to complete a list of publications to which review copies of his book should be sent, to learn if he could obtain a pre-publication copy for a friend, to check on the sale of the book. This pattern of professional contact is the only tie between Prescott and the Boston house to which, for business, not personal, reasons, he had initially turned. Accordingly, its failure found Prescott losing a partner, not a friend.

The second publishing house, that of Charles C. Little of Maine and Massachusetts-born James Brown, three and four years, respectively, Prescott's juniors, epitomized the current economic opportunities which permitted men of little formal education and similarly modest family background to rise rapidly in the business life of bookselling Boston. With no social tie between either of them and the historian, it was their business-world vigor that attracted Prescott to them, and the contract of 1838 was formulated solely as a business arrangement. As successive impressions of his book emerged bearing the Little, Brown & Company imprint, Prescott routinely endorsed the contract as he accepted note after note, obligations which seemingly were paid with such regularity that no strain occurred between author and publisher.

The nearest approach to a genuinely friendly gesture toward his publishers came after three years of business relations when Prescott penned a helpful letter of introduction. To his London publisher Richard Bentley he wrote on May 30, 1841: "This letter will be handed to you by Mr. Brown, one of the publishers of my history, and a principal publisher in the United States. He visits Europe to make some arrangements connected with his business, and any facilities or information that you can give him in this way will be a favour to me." The significance of this aid by Prescott is unknown, but it did help to pave the way for the first of five trips James Brown made to Europe.[2] The early 1840's marked the emergence of Little, Brown & Company as the first American house "to import the best English books at reasonable prices."[3]

Though no warm, personal tie ever developed between the author and his second Boston publisher, no ill will marked their parting. On the contrary, in the course of shuttling completed copy from his Bedford Street residence to the Cambridge establishment producing his stereotype plates, Prescott did not hesitate to drop off at Little, Brown & Company portions of the manuscript of the *Conquest of Mexico,* which the author had contracted with the Harpers in preference to the Boston house. At the start, and for many years thereafter, more prominent as booksellers than publishers, Little, Brown & Company, after the end of their publishing arrangement with Prescott, continued to feature his books in the bookselling end of their business.[4]

With the transfer of his publishing arrangement to Harper and Brothers, a new dimension of social prospect as well as business outlook emerged, for the volume of correspondence, plus occasional visits to New York on publishing matters, increased both the opportunity for and the record of personal ties between Prescott and members of the New York house.

For Prescott, the witty assertion that any one of the quartet was Harper and the remaining three were the brothers of Harper and Brothers was actually true because he knew Fletcher Harper better than all the rest combined. Customarily the one who examined manuscripts for the house, the creative and able Fletcher was the member of the clan who went to Boston and, after nervously pacing the neighborhood, summoned courage to call upon Prescott during the initial contract-making days.[5] The two men hit it off well together, and Prescott's approach to the firm, on any real problem, was thereafter through Fletcher, to whom he wrote on one occasion, September 4, 1845, "I always address my letters directly to you when I am in a quandary." In New York, too, it was with Fletcher Harper that Prescott held conversation on professional matters.

However, for all twelve years of his close business association with the New York house, Prescott regularly addressed them in the severely formal fashion of

Messrs. Harper & Brothers
Dear Sirs—

Considering his normal tendency to write long letters, Prescott addressed unusually brief ones to the Harpers. The publishers more than matched the formality and brevity of the historian, for it was an unusual communication from them that used both sides of a small sheet of paper. Like Prescott's, the letters from Harper and Brothers were direct and business-like, seldom closing with any other than the corporate signature.

Sometimes certain staff members so regularly handled specific matters that they appended their names to that of the company. One such person, bookkeeper William H. Demarest, the historian knew as the source of information on advertising, the size of the last printing, the inventory on hand, and related issues. On other occasions it was Frederick Saunders with whom the historian corresponded about such matters as the estimated cost of publishing a Spanish language edition of one of his works, the planning and placing of advertising—including the use of extracts from reviews—and the disposition of numerous presentation copies in compliance with the author's wishes. Most of Prescott's interests were attended to by the trio of William H. Demarest, Frederick Saunders, and Fletcher Harper. However, Prescott generally dealt with the corporate entity, a practice that promised little prospect of personal relationship.

The distribution of Prescott's presentation copies by the publisher, while just another chore for the person who ultimately performed the task, did entail some expression of company favor toward the historian, since it was not a routine service of publisher to author, especially when considerable numbers of volumes were involved. On occasion Prescott sent Harper and Brothers slips of paper which were to be inserted in the copies that were destined for acquaintances in Philadelphia, Washington, and Charleston, as well as New York City itself. For the *Miscellanies,* the author's imposition assumed even greater proportions, because then he merely listed the names of seven New Yorkers, adding in a letter of December 8, 1845, to the Harpers, "You know the addresses of these gents better than I do." When the *Conquest of Peru* appeared, Prescott wrote the Harpers on June 30, 1847, "I have a dozen copies, more or less, which I wish you would send to some of my friends in New York, writing in each of them 'From the Author.' " A list of fifteen names followed, among them those of leading citizens such as Dr. Wainwright, Robert Ray, Henry Brevoort, and Philip Hone. "Where I have not filled out the address," he continued, "you can do so, or correct it if wrong. Where I have put asterisks, I forget the address and you can supply it." Then, as an afterthought, came a list of five more names. Some affection for the author—which, of course, might spring from the realization that his was a leading name on the list of the publishing house—was called for to see such requests fulfilled.

On two occasions, at least, the punctilious decorum with which the house of Harper carried out the contract with Prescott was disturbed by ripples of interest born of something other than business alone. In a letter of August 2, 1849, the firm chided the historian for addressing a letter to them at Boston rather than New York. And on January 10, 1850, a son of Fletcher Harper, just returned from England, reported that the great Macaulay considered Prescott "the greatest living historian."

In New York, Prescott's social life always involved him with leaders of the community. Never did a hint arise of any close relationship with Harper and Brothers, no word that any of them dined with him at his hotel, the Clarendon, no word that he was ever their guest in their homes or otherwise. For Prescott, New York City represented two distinct and separate worlds: gay gatherings with Wainwright, Brevoort, and others, and business affairs in Franklin Square, down where the ten huge buildings of Harper and Brothers covered the block between Cliff and Pearl Streets.

In mid-1850, as the house of Harper prepared to launch *Harper's New Monthly Magazine,* they sought Prescott's co-operation. Conscious of the popularity of high-class periodical literature in Europe, the publishing house entered the field, so it announced in the first issue in June, 1850, to reach "the great mass of the American people." Fletcher Harper, prime founder and long-time conductor of the publication, also admitted, "It was a tender to our business." Just prior to the publication of the first issue, the Harpers wrote Prescott on May 7, 1850, "We are about starting a Monthly Magazine." Discussing the contents of the first number, in which they wished to carry a portrait and some commentary about the Boston historian, the communication continued, "We are also to have one [engraving] made of your Bust, and wish some reading matter, as with the others." As the lone American in the group of three literary figures honored in the initial issue, Prescott was in company with historians Archibald Alison and Thomas Babington Macaulay, both of whom he was soon to meet in England.

Prescott was busy, because, having finally summoned the courage to carry into reality his often-expressed intention of making a trip to England, he was packing and otherwise preparing for his departure. However, Prescott gave his publisher the desired assistance. Much of the commentary which accompanied the bust, much longer than that for either Alison or Macaulay, smacked of pride of heritage and the success of his histories at home and abroad, garnished with details such as few persons, if any one other than the historian himself, could have supplied. Helping his publisher plug his works was an old routine for Prescott; assisting Fletcher Harper inaugurate the new publication was a new, yet related, one. The historian's role in helping to launch the new publication was a mixture of business and friendship. Prescott's identification with the magazine was a one-time thing, there being no evidence of any other connection between him and it.

When fire, started by a careless plumber who dropped a match into a pan of camphene, left the entire Harper establishment in smoldering ruins on December 10, 1853, Prescott's expressions of sympathy were warmly sincere, above and beyond his justifiable concern about the safety of his own precious stereotype plates. Acknowledging his "kind and welcome expression of sympathy," the company indicated in a letter of December 28 that his plates, all of which were safe, would be put to work as soon as presses and paper could be found. Prescott's expression of sympathy went beyond mere words as he instructed his publisher to strike off, without payment of royalty, as many copies of his titles as had been lost. Indeed, his kind sentiments toward the Harpers led him to hope that other authors would be equally generous in the trying moment experienced by the publishing house.

Eighteen months later, when the lure of a Boston offer enticed the historian away from his New York connection, the prospect of separation produced the warmest expressions that passed between author and publisher, and yet even those were but mild-tempered business exchanges. Learning that their offer for *Philip the Second* had been unsuccessful, Harper and Brothers wrote Prescott on July 10, 1854, "We cannot ask you to make any sacrifice solely for our benefit," closing with the obvious truth, "we should greatly dislike to part Company with you." Prescott read the communication, as he wrote the Harpers,

> with sincere regret, as it announced to me the dissolution of the business relations that have so long subsisted between us. . . . And now allow me to say that this is one of the most unpleasant letters I ever wrote in my life, since it is to break off a long and pleasant intercourse with friends with whom I have never interchanged any words but those of kindness and regard. And the feelings will not be lessened, I am sure, between us.[6]

A year passed, and preparations for publication in Boston got under way, but the New York memory lingered on. Perhaps few publishers, in their dealings with literary geniuses, have had finer testimonials bequeathed them than that penned the Harpers by Prescott in mid-1855.

> I can not forget the long and pleasant relation I have had with you in which the good understanding which should subsist between author and publisher has not been interrupted for a moment. Every year of our connection has confirmed me in the opinion I had early formed of the high and honorable character of your house, for every member of which I beg to express sentiments of the most sincere regard.[7]

The Unitarian author and his Methodist publishers had jointly produced a decade of mid-nineteenth-century author-publisher relations so devoid of suspicions and recriminations as to indicate there was nothing slippery about the business that brought them together.

Preparing to ship to Prescott the many boxes of stereotype plates and thus sever their last tie with Prescott, Harper and Brothers wrote on July 28, 1855: "Trusting that nothing may ever occur to disturb the friendly relations so long and happily maintained between us—and wishing you every success in your new enterprises, we remain, with thanks and respects." The mutually advantageous business arrangement, punctuated throughout by consideration and gentlemanly behavior on both sides, thus ended.

The historian soon thought of his recent publisher when Thomas Motley, Jr., decided to seek a New York publisher for his brother John Lothrop's history. Prescott recommended the Harpers and gave Motley a letter of introduction to the firm. After extolling John Lothrop Motley's attractive style and his business-like approach to the writing of history, Prescott concluded, "I hope therefore that you will give it careful examination, and that he will be able to make an arrangement with you which will be satisfactory to both." [8] The Harpers liked what they saw and published the work. And so, even in parting, Prescott gave to Harper and Brothers another work that became a best seller for the New York house.

Among the partners composing his last American publishing house, Phillips, Sampson, and Company, Prescott knew best Moses Dresser Phillips, who, like

Fletcher Harper, was the member of the firm who first met and did business with the historian. Business was the heart of the arrangement from first to last, but the personal side was not completely absent.

Trying, on one occasion, to learn about the feasibility of his English publisher's marketing an autograph collection in America, Prescott turned to Phillips for aid. The publisher, in turn, sought and obtained the advice of a leading firm of auctioneers. As Prescott's willingness to aid his London publisher transcended normal author-publisher relations, so, too, did the generosity of Phillips.

By mid-summer, 1857, Phillips, ready to launch his magazine *The Atlantic Monthly,* sought a contribution to an early issue from Prescott in order to associate the historian's prestige with the fledgling publication. Conscious that every new publication needs to set sail under most favorable conditions, and willing to lend a friendly hand at the launching, Prescott agreed to write a few pages of material. In mid-August Phillips prodded him, and Prescott replied on August 21, "I am at this moment engaged in the bloody battle of Lepanto: and I think it would be hardly fair to my Spanish friends if I were to leave them in the lurch and go about some other business." To fulfill his promise to Phillips and to minimize the interruption to his own project, Prescott suggested that he provide "part of a chapter, equal perhaps to a dozen or fifteen or twenty pages, of my history—which I flatter myself would have more interest for the public than any hoozy-moozy nonsense which I could manufacture."

Prescott prevailed with his suggestion, and the article "The Battle of Lepanto" appeared in the

second issue, December, 1857, of the new magazine.
For the first and only time in his life, Prescott published in article form a portion of one of his histories. Though destined to pass quickly from the
hands of Phillips, Sampson, and Company, the journal he helped to found with an unsigned article
proved to be a rich addition to the American literary
scene. Himself a founder of a minor, short-term literary organ some thirty years earlier, Prescott probably rejoiced in his role of 1857.

The same month the battle of Lepanto was thus
spread before American periodical readers, the
deepening depression so embarrassed the Boston
firm as to evoke special consideration from Prescott. At a moment when the company owed him several thousand dollars, Prescott agreed in a letter of
December 10, 1857, to extend the terms of payment
required of Phillips, Sampson in their publishing
agreement. The worsening economic scene, threatening the very existence of the publishing house
with which his own economic well-being was en-
meshed, inspired still another friendly gesture by
the author. Walking into the Phillips, Sampson, and
Company office one day, Prescott asked to see the
contract they had signed, indicating he wanted to
make a change or two in it. When it came to hand,
he scanned and struck out those clauses compelling
the company to pay him certain royalties during a
stated time whether they sold the specified number
of copies or not.[9] Though the gesture was sincere, it
was insufficient, for the disquieting effects of the
withdrawal and death of partners, added to the depressed state of business, hastened the demise of the

firm, which, like Prescott, passed from the Boston scene in 1859.

Meanwhile, the personal side of the relationship between Prescott and his English publisher Richard Bentley was unlike anything written into the American record. The distance between Boston and London invited voluminous correspondence, as did Prescott's peculiar and persistent concern about British acceptance of his works. With the special attention and the mounting mass of letters came unusual opportunities for the development of personal as well as business relations between author and publisher. Prescott's willingness that such might be the case seems based somewhat on his estimate that English publishers, like English men of letters and English critics, generally surpassed their American counterparts. Bluntly put, the social gap between an American gentleman and an English publisher, who on the side might exhibit truly sophisticated tastes seldom seen in his American equivalent, was not an unbridgeable chasm.

At first, a discreet formality enveloped the business relationship, with Prescott, informed of the initial contract with Bentley, notifying that publisher, "It gives me much pleasure that the work is to come out under your auspices." [10] Seven months passed before Bentley replied, during which interval Prescott had fired a volley of communications at him. After the London publication of *Ferdinand and Isabella,* six more months passed before an English copy reached the author.

When Bentley, eager to illustrate the book, proposed a portrait of Loyola, Prescott induced him to omit it on the grounds of its irrelevance. "I have written him word," he informed Bancroft on July 24, 1838, "he might pass it off as the Author's portrait, should it come to a second edition. It would be something of a joke if he took me *à la lettre.*" Along with his joking nature went Prescott's forthrightness, as when he wrote to Bentley on June 11, 1839:

> My correspondence with you is rather of an Irish character, in which the correspondence is all on one side. This is the fourth letter I have written since I have had the favor of an answer. . . . I really think Lord Melbourne, with the nation on his shoulders, would have found time for a line or two, under these circumstances;—especially as he finds it for scribbling answers to maids of honor and their dowager mammas.

On another occasion, when Bentley was remiss about acknowledging receipt of copy and illustrative material, Prescott wrote: "You are a very bad Transatlantic correspondent, and fancy you are dealing with some North country squire whom you can answer by next post, if too late for this. But a thousand leagues of salt water is a damper in this way, as the chances only come around once a fortnight. So if you have not responded already, pray look over my last letter and reply to it and its several queries." [11]

In the early years, gathering suspicions about business matters so complicated the Prescott-Bentley relationship as to preclude any friendly tie emerging between them. Prescott and his London agent Colonel Thomas Aspinwall wondered if the English editions were not larger than Bentley indicated, wondered if the advertising charges against the books were not exaggerated, and wondered if Prescott's income was not unnaturally low. For example, on May 13, 1842, Aspinwall wrote the historian: "I am disappointed in the results of Bentley's sales. I have had surmises that the number of copies exceeded the stated amount of the two editions, and have endeavored in various ways to ascertain the truth of the matter."

However, Prescott presented to Bentley a façade of satisfaction, writing on September 14, 1843: "It is with much pleasure that I have learnt from Col. Aspinwall that he has made a Contract with you for the publication of my 'History of the Conquest of Mexico,' and that I have received a copy of the Contract from him. I feel much satisfaction at this continuance of our relations, which have been always so harmoniously conducted." The agreement providing for outright sale by Prescott obviated future concern on his part about sizes of editions, advertising charges, and the ultimate income to be derived from a half-profits arrangement. Thus, though the terms of the first contract hampered the establishment of friendly ties, the second arrangement reduced the areas of suspicion.

Even during the doubt-ridden early years, certain business matters gradually built up a measure of mutual dependence between author and publisher. Most conspicuous in this regard was the exchange of illustrations. Prescott sent Bentley copies of portraits by American engravers, and Bentley, introducing certain illustrations that the author admired, reciprocated. Prescott's admiration for the products

of English engravers quickly caused his American
editions to be markedly dependent upon the illustrations supplied by Bentley.

In one of his periodic inquiries about the next
book, Bentley discussed the need of illustrations for
it, concluding with the query of April 19, 1842, ''Can
I be of any service in getting these prepared?'' Such
an offer, at that moment, easily combined a disposition to help the author with his desire to help himself, for Prescott's acceptance of such aid would be
tantamount to promising Bentley that history.

In 1845 Prescott pushed a collection of his essays
into the English market, and was surprised and
pleased with Bentley's terms. Ready to contract it
without remuneration, if need be, the author must
have warmed toward the publisher who agreed to
produce the *Miscellanies* on a half-profits basis. Still
more warmth came into the author-publisher relationship when Aspinwall negotiated a contract
for the outright sale of the *Conquest of Peru* with a
minimum of trouble and at terms which led Prescott
to exclaim in a letter of February 22, 1847, to Aspinwall, ''The price you obtained for the book gives me
great satisfaction.'' The fourth contract foretold a
new day in the author-publisher relationship, but certain clauses stemming from Bentley's concern about
the size of the two-volume history evoked fears
which caused Prescott to admit in the same letter to
Aspinwall, ''I must confess it has a tricky look to
me.''

''Of all the works which I have yet been the hum-
ble medium of presenting to the world yours are
those which will live,'' Bentley wrote Prescott on
March 27, 1847, shortly before his release of the

Conquest of Peru. With this superlative praise, beyond the call of duty in a publisher's correspondence with his author, Bentley's admiration broke into the open. Ten years of co-operative and punctilious business relations were now reinforced by an elusive, but ever present, thread of friendship. That Prescott reciprocated it is evident in his letter expressing his satisfaction with the fourth contract between them. On that occasion he told Bentley: "I am glad that you are to be my publisher. Indeed our long and friendly relations led me to instruct Col. Aspinwall to deal with you on more favourable terms than with other publishers." [12] Bentley's gesture in placing six additional copies of the new work at Prescott's disposal pleased the historian, who wrote to thank Bentley for them on June 30, 1847.

In 1848, as William Gardiner Prescott, the historian's Harvard-trained eldest son prepared to tour Europe before entering upon his career, his father armed him with numerous letters of introduction, including the following to Richard Bentley dated August 5.

> As he first visits the Continent, he will probably not be in London till next summer. But whenever it may be, I was not willing that he should be there without becoming acquainted with one with whom I have been for so many years in such friendly and important relations.

More than anything else, it was the presence of his son in Europe that led the historian to England in 1850. In preparation for the trip Prescott turned to former ministers to the Court of St. James, Edward Everett and George Bancroft, for a sheaf of letters of introduction to leaders of fashionable society and politics.

Almost overnight in early June, Prescott was committed to a full month of days crowded with breakfasts, luncheons, teas, dinners, balls, tours, picnics, and other social activities. Sometimes it was a small, intimate group, as when he dined with Richard Ford, who, steeped in things Spanish, had reviewed *Ferdinand and Isabella* a dozen years earlier. On occasion the gatherings were large and formal, as when Prescott was presented to Queen Victoria as the "historian of Ferdinand and Isabella." The Bostonian recorded his enjoyment of it all in long letters written to his wife Susan from England, letters in which he shared tidbits of conversation, offered picturesque thumbnail sketches of prominent personages, discussed menus and winelists, commented on ladies' dresses and gentlemen's behavior, as well as other social trivia.

In the whirl that included literati such as Macaulay and Thackeray, statesmen such as Peele, Palmerston, and Disraeli, lords and ladies such as the Duke and Duchess of Northumberland, the Carlisles, the Lyells, the Argylls, and the Sutherlands, it was easy for the visitor, swept into highest circles of fashionable society and political life, to have but limited contacts with the world of London publishers. But he did meet publishers.

John Murray and the historian, destined never to conclude a publishing agreement between them, seized the occasion in London to underscore the personal admiration each held for the other. On Friday, July 5, Murray took Prescott and a select literary-minded company that included Hallam,

Lockhart, Ford, and Stirling to Greenwich for a whitebait party. The well-known fish delicacy, accompanied by generous quantities of wine and heady conversation, made the occasion one of the jolliest of the historian's English summer—topped off as it was by a cigar-puffing midnight return to London atop a coach, as Prescott reported to his wife in his letter of July 11.

Ten days later, on Monday, July 15, Prescott called upon Richard Bentley. To Susan, the traveler confided in a letter penned the next day, "You can't imagine how civil Bentley is." Chagrined that Murray had bested him in the matter of priority of entertaining Prescott, the New Burlington Street publisher, as though to make up for it, invited Prescott to two affairs, urging him to name his own company. Pressed by an exacting schedule which found him declining invitations from duchesses, Prescott concluded, as he reported to his wife on July 16, "I shall take the will for the deed." Although Prescott and Bentley had only limited contacts in England, their brief face-to-face encounter did introduce added warmth into their correspondence ever thereafter.

Bentley presented Prescott, while in England, with a handsome edition of the letters of Horace Walpole. Thanking his publisher for the gift, Prescott wrote on September 12, "I shall keep [it] as a lasting memorial of my personal acquaintance with one with whom I have known for so many years . . . the most friendly relations." Less than a week after his arrival home, Prescott wrote Bentley on September 30 about "the friends I have left in England and the kindnesses I have received there."

Increasingly, the correspondence of the early

1850's was compounded of friendly trivia—the "ungenial foggy wet weather" of London, issues under debate in parliament, and the like, as recorded, for example, in Bentley's October 26, 1852, letter to Prescott. This trend served to maintain the ties between author and publisher during the historian's overly long, nonproductive period following his *Conquest of Peru*. When a publisher could only hope for a word about the next book, and his author, reluctant to drive himself, refused to state a schedule of expectation, little else could pass between them. "Touching the contract of Philip the Second," Prescott wrote Bentley November 26, 1852, in reply to repeated inquiries,

> it seems to me there is no occasion at present to bother our brains about the matter. I am getting on in a comfortable way, and if I stimulate myself by a contract it will, I fear, only create a nervous sensation such as I used to feel when I came tardily with my exercises to school. Of one thing you may be sure, if you are alive—and I trust the period is not so far off as to give any ground for apprehension on that score—I shall much prefer, for the sake of "auld lang syne"—unless I feel very differently from what I now do—to deal with you to dealing with any other publisher.

With the same warm sincerity, Bentley replied on December 14, "To continue to possess your good opinion will always be my anxious desire: for it is from the lustre of your name as an author that I as your publisher derive an honorable position among the publishers of the Nineteenth Century." These were not idle words from the New Burlington Street publishing house intended to flatter the vanity of an author. Many years after both men were in their graves a later generation of Bentleys, busy compiling a list of the more prominent American writers published by the firm, so arranged the scores of names that Prescott's led all the rest.[13]

For twenty years Richard Bentley obligingly disposed of his American historian's presentation copies in such fashion he complied with Prescott's every wish. This kindness, with the passage of time that widened Prescott's English and continental contacts, assumed mounting proportions. Anticipating the early release of the *Conquest of Peru,* Prescott wrote Bentley on April 30, 1847, "As soon as the work is published, I shall trouble you to distribute a dozen copies for me to some of my friends in London, writing on the blank page of each copy, 'From the Author.' " After listing his friends in England, he added special instructions, such as: "the copy for Mr. Rogers I wish you would get handsomely full bound with gilt edges. He sent me two quarto volumes of his works of the largest size, superbly bound." Prescott knew that his requests were an imposition on Bentley. "It will, perhaps, please you," he continued, "that I don't send my bantlings oftener into the world, if I give you so much trouble at the christening."

When Bentley put additional copies of Prescott's books at his disposal, he paved the way for the historian's request that he also help to distribute them. Nor did Prescott limit himself to requesting such services only at the moment a work appeared. Irregularly, but continuously, the rivulet of presentation copies went out from Bentley's office to the author's friends, new and old. Needless to say, the flow of such gifts increased in the wake of Prescott's visit in England. Obligingly and faithfully fulfilling the author's every request, Bentley was the recipient of his deepening appreciation.

Another channel of the deepening affection Prescott felt for the New Burlington Street publisher related to Bentley's practice of raining copies of books newly off his press upon the historian. In time, the number of titles involved became a sizable segment of the Beacon Street library of Prescott. At first the titles were few and far between, but by the closing years of the 1840's the tempo had increased greatly.

Since the number of books Bentley gave him swelled, and since Prescott maintained the curiosity that led him to look into them, it might be said that Bentley, in thus distracting an author whose lethargy was already mounting, contributed to postpone the volumes of *Philip the Second* he longed to publish. For Bentley it was a simple matter of accompanying a query about the next book with a gift; for Prescott it was a simple matter of reading the gift volumes, thanking his friend, and postponing his own return to diligent creativeness. On at least three occasions in 1850 Bentley sent gift packages to Prescott. The next year the publisher sent the author at least six volumes. By mid-1852, by which time still more publications had reached Boston, the London publisher offered Prescott any volumes he might want from his entire forthcoming list. Amid the continuing flow of Bentley's selected gifts, Prescott occasionally availed himself of the opportunity to signify his personal preferences. "You desired me to suggest any work that you were publishing which would be acceptable to me," he wrote Bentley on February 1, 1853, "I avail myself of your kindness to mention Ranke's History of France, of which you advertise a translation, that no doubt contains matter germane to my present subject, as Ranke's book chiefly refers to the 16th century." Only in this manner did gifts from Bentley assist the historian.

The flow of books continued down into the last year of Prescott's life. In general, they fell into certain patterns, with greatest emphasis on travel, memoirs and correspondence, biography, and history. The first theme, the most heavily represented, found the armchair traveler in Boston trudging over all quarters of the earth. Although the works rarely served his purposes as historian, Prescott welcomed them as expressions of the kind regard in which Richard Bentley held him.

Prescott reciprocated Bentley's gifts and friendly acts in a number of ways, one of which found him directing American manuscripts toward Bentley. "My friend and townsman Mr. Samuel Eliot has been engaged for some time in the composition of an historical work of which he has now completed two volumes," Prescott wrote Bentley on February 9, 1849. "He wishes to have the book brought before the English public at the same time that it appears here and I have mentioned you to him." Prescott only placed an entering wedge for his friend, since he left it to Eliot to correspond with and send proof sheets of his work to Bentley. Bentley, liking the work, arranged through Aspinwall for its publication. Prescott's agent, reporting the matter, told the historian in a letter dated March 24, 1849, "Your opinion of the merits of Mr. Eliot's work had very justly great weight with Mr. Bentley.''

Given to encouraging the efforts of his country-men interested in invading English publishing cir-cles, and surely pleased by Bentley's reaction to his first such proposal, it was not long before Prescott was at it again. In the spring following his return from England, Prescott recommended a work by Bostonian Francis Parkman. Discussing the content of the work in a letter to Bentley dated May 20, 1851, Prescott indicated it dealt with ''the occupation of this country by the French, and their intercourse with the Indians. . . . it seems to me to be written with much spirit, with many picturesque descrip-tions and stirring incidents—told in a skilful man-ner, that I should think would engage the interest of the reader. . . . I hope you will be able to make some arrangement with Mr. Parkman for the pub-lication of it.'' Bentley liked the manuscript, thanked Prescott for his kindness in a letter of June 19, and rushed to complete the terms that permitted him to publish the *History of the Conspiracy of Pontiac* that same summer.

Neither Eliot's nor Parkman's book succeeded in England, but Prescott continued to bring his London publisher into contact with American authors. In the spring of 1852 he recommended that Bentley give Harriet Beecher Stowe's *Uncle Tom's Cabin* his attention. However, with the book previously published in America, and intensely popular, it at-tracted the English pirates in such fashion that Bentley never had a real chance to deal with the writer. He joined the rush to put the abolitionist novel in a very cheap edition before the English reading public and cast his eye on the possibility of getting the author's next work under more favorable conditions. Failing to get Mrs. Stowe's next book possibly contributed to the sour-grapes attitude in his comment to Prescott on December 14, 1852:

> The success of Uncle Tom has indeed been marvellous: but it is not cheering to sound literature to see immense successes follow productions, one of whose chief merits, in my very humble judgment, is that they strike a particular chord at a moment when the public mind is in a sort of furore. So it is with us in regard to Slavery, and the most extravagant stories are eagerly swallowed.

In a December 28, letter, Prescott addressed Bentley as follows:

> A friend of mine, Mr. Bulfinch, of this town, has now in the press a work relating to Ancient Mythology. . . . As Mr. Bulfinch is desirous of being put in communication with an English publisher, I have thought I could not do better than by introducing him to you, and I shall be most happy if when you have seen his work, you shall find it so well suited to the English market as to allow of your publication of it.

Thanking Prescott for the suggestion on January 20, 1854, Bentley promised to consider the work. Although *The Age of Fable,* the work in question, was not immediately published in England, it did prove to be a fine work, passing through numerous editions and establishing itself as a reference work in its field.

Again, reading Prescott's preface to the earliest volumes of his *Philip the Second,* Bentley pounced on the reference to Motley's forthcoming work. He asked his author in a letter of November 23, 1855: "Has that gentleman published his work? If not, may I ask whether he is at Boston? In that case probably he would do me the favor to negociate with me for it, if you would kindly ask him." Nothing came of Bentley's early rush of enthusiasm, and Motley experienced difficulties getting the *Rise of the Dutch Republic,* destined to become a best seller, into print in England. Prescott's American interest in that work and author, it will be recalled, found him successfully recommending it to Harper and Brothers.

Prescott's last known support of a Boston author searching for an English publisher again saw him turn to Bentley, in mid-1858, in support of a literary product of John Gorham Palfrey's pen. Of Palfrey, his close friend and editor-owner of the *North American Review* during the years of Prescott's heaviest contributions to that publication, the historian wrote to Bentley on May 3, 1858: "A friend of mine, Dr. Palfrey, . . . will publish this autumn the 1st vol. of a History of New England Puritans, in a couple of volumes, I believe. It will, I doubt not, be an able & learned book. Whether the theme will interest the English reader you can judge better than I." Later Prescott wrote a letter of introduction to Bentley, June 18, 1858, for Francis Bowen, former editor and critic, who in the course of travels abroad intended to recommend the Palfrey work in person to Richard Bentley. Nothing came of the combined American efforts. Bentley did not publish this last work recommended to him by Prescott.

In addition to offering Bentley the manuscripts

of his Boston literary acquaintances, Prescott gave
the London publisher some personal gifts. While
Prescott was in England, Lord Carlisle had com-
missioned his portrait by George Richmond. Several
years later, on February 22, 1853, the historian wrote
his publisher from Boston:

> The engraving of Richmond's portrait of me for Lord
> Carlisle, I understand from Lady Lyell, is completed,
> and the prints are to be disposed of on his own ac-
> count. I have requested Lady L. to send one of the
> prints to yourself, and you will oblige me by accept-
> ing it as a proof of my regard.

Bentley promptly acknowledged the gift, terming it
"a very pleasing but truthful portrait." And he
added in his March 10 reply: "I shall place it among
my treasures. Has any bust of you ever been published? I should like to get one, if there be one which
you approve." The query paved the way for still another gift from Prescott, but at the moment Bentley
returned present for present, for he signified that he
was sending copies of travel books on Canada and
Italy to the historian.

Giving the publisher's request his early attention,
Prescott wrote Bentley on April 26:

> You ask if there has been a good bust of [me]. A few
> years since a bust was made of me by Richard Green-
> ough, an American artist, now in Florence. He is a
> man of real genius, and this bust is executed with
> great delicacy. I have the original in marble, from
> which casts have been taken; and I have had the pleas-
> ure to order one to be put up for you. It will go by
> the steamer that takes this, and I trust will reach you
> in good condition. I have directed that all charges be

paid. Should there be any blunder in this particular, you will please let me know it, as I would not have the outside of my head put you out of pocket, any more than I would the inside. It is the only cast of me, I believe, that has been sent to England.

The uniqueness of this gift, in a land in which the historian had many friends, emphasizes in real measure his esteem for his publisher.

As soon as the bust came into his hands, Bentley penned his appreciation to Prescott. ''This morning [May 13] I received safely the valuable present you have sent to me. Nothing could have been more gratifying to me than such a mark of your kindness—the present itself, and the manner in which you have done the honor to present it to me. . . . Indeed I greatly prize this present, and it will be a chief ornament of my library.''

This warm, friendly, ever-deepening personal relationship between author and publisher, it must be added, flowered during strife-torn years in their business relations—while Bentley was refusing to meet Prescott's terms for the purchase of the author's interest in *Ferdinand and Isabella* and the *Miscellanies;* while Bentley, in days of adverse copyright decisions in England, was offering the historian a niggardly pittance for the first volumes of *Philip the Second;* while, indeed, Prescott's dissatisfaction with Bentley's offers for *Charles the Fifth* and the third volume of *Philip the Second* was causing him to turn to another English publisher.

In the last half-decade of the historian's life he and Bentley frequently exchanged special holiday greetings. Quite commonly they came in the general period rather than upon any exact day, as when

Bentley, on February 3, 1853, closed a communication "wishing most heartily to you and all yours, health and happiness during the new Year on which we have just entered." The following year, 1854, on January 20, Bentley wished Prescott "every blessing" for the new year. By the close of 1855, the Christmas season also drew Bentley's attention, with his Thanksgiving-time letter of November 23 wishing Prescott "the compliments of the approaching festive season." The following year the Englishman honored Prescott as he wrote on January 1, "My first letter of the new Year I write to you, and beg to wish you every blessing during its continuance!" At Christmas-time that year Bentley wrote on December 27: "Permit me to offer you the compliments of this festive season and to wish you the continuance of health and other blessings, that you may be able to continue your valuable labours, and add new laurels to a brow, which has already won such just renown."

Although Bentley exceeded the historian in the matter of recognizing the seasonal side of their healthy exchanges of good wishes, Prescott did not ignore it. Thanking Bentley for a recent shipment of books, he added in a letter dated January 25, 1857, "I beg you will accept my best wishes in return for a Merry Xmas and a Happy New Year tho' they come—like an Irish greeting, the day after the fair." The American, it might be added, never was overly Christmas-conscious; to him, Thanksgiving, always a memorable occasion, was followed by a general holiday season in the Christmas-New Year's Day interval.

In 1857, Bentley sought Prescott's advice and aid

as he undertook to dispose of his collection of autograph letters related to the Civil War period of
English history. Explaining that he was getting on
in years—scarcely as good an excuse as the wobbly
financial condition of his business, since he was
Prescott's junior by several years—Bentley sent
the historian a copy of a catalogue of the letters, asking for Prescott's suggestions regarding sale, in the
wake of his failure to sell the collection to the British
Museum. Bentley wrote to Prescott, June 26, 1857:
"Next to our National Collection possessing them,
the most fitting place for them will be the United
States; many of the descendants of the men who
fought the Great fight of liberty—political and re-
ligious—still being . . . found there."

Appreciative of Prescott's efforts in his behalf,
Bentley informed the historian on August 11, "I
shall now make up my mind either to dispose of them
to some individual purchaser here, or to sell them by
public auction in the ensuing season."

More than one episode testifies to the fact that
author-publisher friendship complicated the continuing business relations between them. Prescott's
frank statement that he had instructed his agent to
give Bentley a considerable preference, even mon-
etarily so, reduced the agent's bargaining capacity
in certain contract negotiations. Similarly, Bentley
demonstrated the personal factor in the business relationship, writing to Prescott on February 16, 1853,
while in the midst of one such negotiation: "I have
approached the matter in that spirit which I desire
to do in regard to all matters in which I have the
honor to be connected with you, feeling unfeignedly
that that connection has reflected upon your Pub-

lishers increased reputation, and in some measure connected me with your world wide fame.''

When Prescott, in the mid-fifties, heard rumors of the distressed financial state of Bentley's publishing house, he instructed his agent to make discreet inquiries in London. Hearing of this round-about approach, Bentley was hurt, and so informed Prescott. ''I think it would have been more in accordance with the long-continued friendly terms of our correspondence,'' he wrote in a letter of June 22, 1855, ''if, when any injurious reports about me reached you you had addressed yourself to me direct.'' However, Prescott would not let claims of friendship transcend all else, because he bluntly informed Bentley that he had done so only after repeated failures to get replies from the publisher himself.

Perhaps, however, the proof that friendship did challenge business considerations is best seen in Bentley's statement in a letter to Prescott of October 27, 1856, after losing the contract for the Robertson-Prescott *Charles the Fifth* to Routledge, that he would not pirate the work.

While Prescott's last two English contracts went to Routledge rather than Bentley, the latter, still issuing titles by the historian, continued the transatlantic friendship. The last months, even as Bentley hoped for another contract, were punctuated by gifts of books, exchanges of views about the autograph collection, and the publisher's increasing concern about the health of his author. Letter after letter closed with sentiments such as, for example, the letter of August 11, 1857: ''Now wishing you health to continue your important labours.'' Following the author's apoplectic stroke of 1858, the health theme, dominant, opened the correspondence. "With very sincere regret," Bentley wrote Prescott on April 8, 1858, "I heard a little time ago of your illness, and have hesitated to write to you until now, when I was gratified to learn that you were recovering. Earnestly do I hope your health will soon be reestablished!" Yet the time was not far distant when death would terminate the friendly relations which had transcended earlier suspicions, pirated editions, adverse business conditions, copyright chaos, and other pressures born of economic considerations. In a day during which no editor stood between author and publisher and the author's agent served as a catalyst rather than barrier to author-publisher relationship, Prescott knew his most intimate personal ties with his longest and most distant publisher, Richard Bentley.

From Prescott's side of the record there is no indication that his high regard for Bentley, as a person, ever diminished. However, with Bentley, business considerations competed with and overruled social sentiment, and when the full impact of his loss of the third volume of *Philip the Second*—synonymous with his loss of Prescott as author—struck him, he was bitter. His blistering last letter, received by the historian just two months before his death, pulled no punches: Prescott was discourteous; Prescott was no gentleman; Prescott was no friend of his. Surely it upset the friendly, weary man in Boston in the closing moments of his life. The only friendship with a publisher that he ever lost was, in part, a price he paid for his own essential indifference to the copyright struggle.

All was denouement in the short period of his contracts with the firm of Routledge. Aside from the fact that Routledge also shuttled Prescott's presentation copies straight from publisher to recipients, the ties between them were all business, with the exception of Prescott's unsuccessful effort to interest his second English publisher in Palfrey's still unpublished manuscript. Queried about the next volume or volumes of *Philip the Second,* Prescott wrote to George Routledge on January 11, 1859, in his last letter to a publisher, "I have not broken ground on it yet." Death intervened, terminating not only his *Philip the Second,* but also the prospect of further relations with his publishers.

During the twenty-two years of his relations with publishers, at home and abroad, William Hickling Prescott knew a variety of experiences. Tempering his below-average concern about earnings was his above-average interest in the beauty and promotion of his books. In one respect the result was the same —close ties between author and publisher; in another, since his books and their earnings were above average, his relations with his publishers were unique. Prescott lived and wrote in a period in which, it has been said, "the relation of author and publisher is generally regarded as that of the cat and the dog, both greedy of the bone, and inherently jealous of each other." [14] But the gentlemanly scholar of Boston, in long experience that involved him with the American Stationers' Company, Little, Brown & Company, Harper and Brothers, and Phillips, Sampson, and Company in the United States and with Richard Bentley and George Routledge in England, contributed to a record of author-publisher relations which were relatively free of suspicions and fighting and recriminations. As the stamp of genius was upon his histories, so in his relations with those he once had termed "the slippery trade," Prescott was a party to something to be remembered.

APPENDICES

REFERENCES AND NOTES

INDEX

AGREEMENT WITH BENTLEY,
March 20, 1837

MEMORANDUM OF AN AGREEMENT made this twentieth day of March, 1837, between Colonel Aspinwall, acting on the part of W. H. Prescott Esqr. of Boston, United States on the one part, & Richard Bentley of New Burlington Street, London, publisher, on the other part.

It is agreed that the said Richard Bentley shall publish at his own risk & expense, a work written by the said W. H. Prescott, Esqr. entitled The Life & Times of Ferdinand and Isabella, and after deducting from the produce of the sale thereof, the charges for printing, paper, embellishments if any, advertisements, and other incidental expenses, including the allowance of Ten per Cent. on the gross amount of the sale for commissions & risk of bad debts, the profits remaining of every edition that shall be printed of the Work are to be divided into two equal parts, one moiety to be paid to the said Colonel Aspinwall acting on the part of the said Prescott Esqr., and the other moiety to belong to the said Richard Bentley.

The Books sold to be accounted for at the Trade Sale price, reckoning 25 as 24 copies, unless it be thought advisable to dispose of any copies, or of the remainder at a lower price, which is left to the judgment and discretion of the said Richard Bentley.

IN WITNESS WHEREOF, the said parties have unto set their hands this day

Thos. Aspinwall

[*Jacket notation reads: Colonel Aspinwall acting for Mr. Prescott   Life of Ferdinand & Isabella   ½ profit*]

AGREEMENT WITH LITTLE, BROWN & CO.,

May 14, 1838

AN AGREEMENT made this fourteenth day of May, in
the year of our Lord eighteen hundred and thirty eight, by
and between William H. Prescott, of Boston, of the first
part, and Charles C. Little and James Brown, both of said
Boston, Booksellers, of the second part.

Whereas the said Prescott, on the tenth day of April,
in the year eighteen hundred and thirty seven, sold to the
American Stationers' Company a right to print and publish twelve hundred and fifty copies of a work of which he
is the author, entitled "The History of the Reign of Ferdinand and Isabella, the Catholic," within the United States,
in five years from that date, the greater part of which
copies have already been disposed of, and the said Prescott
has sold to the said Little and Brown the right to print and
publish seventeen hundred copies of said work after the
sale of said twelve hundred and fifty copies shall be completed, for the sum of Two thousand, nine hundred, and
seventy five Dollars, to be paid in manner and at the times
hereinafter provided:

Now it is hereby granted and agreed by and between the
parties aforesaid, as follows.

First. The said Prescott grants to said Little and Brown
a right to print and publish within the United States seventeen hundred copies of the work aforesaid, the publication
to commence when the said twelve hundred and fifty copies
of said work shall be all sold, and that they shall have the
exclusive right to print and publish the same within the
United States, from and after the sale of the said twelve

hundred and fifty copies shall be completed, until the first day of November in the year eighteen hundred and forty three; and that the said Prescott will furnish said Little and Brown the use of his stereotype plates to print said seventeen hundred copies of said work, and also the use of an engraved plate for a portraiture for each volume, the same that were used in the first edition.

Second. The said Little and Brown agree with said Prescott that they will print and publish at their own expense seventeen hundred copies of said history, in three volumes octavo, not less than two hundred and fifty copies at any one impression, before the said first day of November, eighteen hundred and forty three; that the paper shall be as good in sizing and quality as the paper of the first edition, and worth six dollars a ream; and that the binding and execution shall be in every way equal to the first edition of said History, said Prescott to be the judge; that they will pay him for the use of his plates aforesaid, and the exclusive right to publish said History within the United States, at the rate of one dollar and seventy five cents a copy, amounting to Two thousand, nine hundred and seventy five Dollars in the whole, in manner following, viz: by their promissory note for the amount of each impression, at the rate aforesaid per copy, to be made at the time such impression is struck off, payable in six months; and if the printing of the whole seventeen hundred copies shall not be completed six months before said first day of November, eighteen hundred and forty three, the payment of the whole Two thousand, nine hundred and seventy five Dollars, notwithstanding, is to be completed on that day. And it is also agreed that if said Little and Brown shall neglect to give their notes at the times above agreed, or if any one of their said notes shall not be paid when due, or within thirty days after the same is payable, the said Prescott shall have a right, if he think proper, to avoid the contract for the future, and their right to print or publish further copies shall thereupon be determined and cease.

Third. The parties further agree that the said stereotype plates shall remain in the possession of Messrs. Folsom, Wells, and Thurston, at Cambridge, and shall never be taken from them without an order in writing from said Prescott: that all the presswork on the stereotype plates shall be done by said Folsom, Wells, and Thurston, or such other persons as the said Prescott shall approve; that no power press shall ever be used, nor any press by Little & Brown's orders but what said Prescott shall approve; that all risk of destruction or damage by fire or other accident to the stereotype plates, after the same shall be taken from said Folsom, Wells, and Thurston, by said Little and Brown, or their agent, until they are returned, shall be borne by said Little and Brown.

Fourth. The work shall be printed by said Folsom, Wells, and Thurston, and said Prescott shall be chargeable with five cents a token, being considered half the extra expense of employing them, and the printing shall not be transferred to any other person not approved of by him. This agreement, nor the right of publishing the said History, shall never be assigned by said Little and Brown to any other person, without said Prescott's consent. The wholesale price of the book for a large number of copies is to be six dollars a copy, and during the six months next preceding the first of November, eighteen hundred and forty three, they are not to sell the work for less than the average prices of the preceding years, without first giving notice to said Prescott, and offering him the copies remaining, at four dollars and twenty five cents a copy. The said Little and Brown are to furnish copies, at two dollars and fifty cents apiece, to any editor of a journal or paper, or writer of a notice, that said Prescott desires, and that they shall not think worth while to give one to on their own account.

Fifth. The said Little and Brown are to have any engravings of portraits that said Prescott may obtain from England, at the prices they shall cost him. The said Prescott

shall have one copy of the History of every hundred printed,
and said Little and Brown will allow him four dollars and
twenty five cents apiece for any copies he does not take. The
said Prescott is to have the exclusive right of publishing
the work in Europe. He also reserves to himself the right to
abridge the History within the said term, and agrees to
give said Little and Brown the preference as to publishing
such abridgment, provided they will pay him as much
therefor as any other person.

Lastly. The said parties further agree, that if any dispute
or difference shall arise between them respecting any matter or thing under this contract, the same shall be submitted to arbitrators, one to be chosen by each party, and
the third by those two. That said Little and Brown are to
give said Prescott notice when F. Andrews returns to Boston from his present journey, and if he, said Prescott, shall
then prefer to print and publish his said History on his
own account and employ agents to dispose of it, and shall
notify said Little and Brown thereof within seven days,
he shall be at liberty to do it, paying said Little and Brown
one hundred dollars, and this contract shall thereupon become null and void. And it is further understood and
agreed, that said Little and Brown shall have the right of
purchasing, at any time previous to said first day of November, eighteen hundred and forty three, any further
number of copies beyond the seventeen hundred aforesaid,
not less than two hundred and fifty at a time, at the same
rate per copy, payable in the same manner, and subject
to all the same conditions and regulations, as are above
expressed of and concerning the said seventeen hundred
copies. Provided, however, that if at any time the copies
shall be all disposed of, or said Prescott shall be ready to
take what remains at the wholesale price, and said Little
and Brown shall not then and at that time avail themselves
of their right to purchase a further number of copies, the
said right shall thereupon cease, and said Prescott shall
thereafter have the exclusive right to print and publish

the said History, notwithstanding any thing herein contained.

IN WITNESS WHEREOF, the parties aforesaid have hereunto set their hands respectively, the day and year first above written.

IN PRESENCE OF: *J. Reed*
                    W. St. Dennett

                              Wm. H. Prescott
                              C. C. Little & Co.

[The words "by Little & Brown's orders" on third page interlined before signing.]

[The following serves as cover for the document.]

Wm. H. Prescott

Contract

"Ferdinand & Isabella"
1838

1.75 p copy   Note at 6 mos
entitled to 1 copy for every 100 printed
previous Ed. by Stat. Co.

1st Ed. by C. C. L. & Co	Printed	Augt.	1838	500	Copies
2d "	"	"	Nov.	"	500	"
3d "	"	"	Feb.	1839	500	"
4th "	"	"	Oct.	1839	500	"
5 "	"	"	Sep.	1840	500	"
6 "	"	"	"	1841	500	"
" sent to Paris			Jan.	1842	500	"

Mr. P pays ⅔ between 90 & 112½ press token
Recd. of C. C. Little & Co. their Note for the first Edition of five Hundred Copies printed by F. W. & Thurston Augt 1838 for C C L & Co.

                              Wm. H. Prescott

Recd. of C. C. Little & Co their Note for the 2d Ed. of 500 Cops printed for them by Folsom & Co Nov. 1838
Wm. H. Prescott

Recd. of C. C. Little & Co. their Note for the 3d Ed. of 500 Cops printed for them by F. Wells & Thurston Feby 1839
Wm. H. Prescott

Recd. of C. C. Little & Co their Note for the 4th Ed printed for them of 500 Copies, printed by Folsom & Co Sept. 6 Oct (binder) 1839
$844.25
Wm. H. Prescott

Recd. of C. C. Little & J. Brown their Note for 5th Ed. 500 Cops. printed for them by Folsom & Co Sept. 1840 (9 mos from 26 Sept) $844.25
Wm. H. Prescott

Recd. of C. C. Little & Brown their notes for 6th Edit. 500 Cop. printed for them by Folsom & Co. Sep. 1841. 9 mos. $844.25
Wm. H. Prescott

Recd. of C. C. Little & Brown their note for 300 dolls for edition of 500 copies sent to Paris and printed by Folsom & Co. Jan. 1842.
Wm. H. Prescott

Recd. of Little & Brown their Notes for the Edition of 500 Cops printed by Metcalf Keith & Nichols (recd from bindery Apl 3d 1843)
Wm. H. Prescott

Recd. of Little & Brown their Note dated 25 Mch 1844 at Six mo. for Copy right of Five Hundred Copy Ferd. & Isabella.
Wm. H. Prescott

AGREEMENT WITH LITTLE, BROWN & CO.,
May 27, 1841

THIS AGREEMENT made this twenty seventh day of May
in the year of our Lord one thousand eight hundred & forty
one by & between William H. Prescott of the city of Boston Esq. of the first part, and Charles C. Little and James
Brown both of the same Boston, booksellers

WITNESSETH. That the said Prescott agrees to make
an *Abridgment of the History of Ferdinand & Isabella,* in
one volume to contain not less than 400 pages of the size
of the abridgment of the history of the United States by
George Bancroft, and that said Little & Brown shall have
the exclusive right and privilege of publishing four thousand copies of the same within the United States, within
five years after the stereotype plates for printing the same
are completed and delivered to them for use, and that said
Prescott will at his own expense procure stereotype plates
for printing the said Abridgment to be made, and furnish
the said Little & Brown therewith to print said four thousand copies of said work, and with an engraved plate for a
portraiture and, also, with two engraved plates for small
maps for the volume.

Second. The said Little & Brown agree with said Prescott
that they will print & publish, at their own expense, four
thousand copies of said Abridgment in one volume of the
size of said Bancroft's history aforesaid not less than 1000
copies at any one impression; that the paper shall be as
good in size & quality as the paper used in said Bancroft's
said Abridgment, and that the binding & execution shall be

equal to that of said abridgment, said Prescott to be the judge; that they will pay him for the use of his said plates, and the exclusive right of publishing 4000 copies of his said Abridgment within the United States as aforesaid, at the rate of twenty cents a volume, amounting to eight hundred dollars in the whole, in manner following viz: by their promissory note for the amount of each impression at the rate of aforesaid per copy, to be made at the time such impression is struck off, payable in nine months, and if the printing of the whole four thousand copies shall not be completed six months before the expiration of said five years from the time said stereotype plates are completed & delivered to said Little & Brown, the payment of the whole of said $800, notwithstanding, is to be completed on that day. *Third.* And it is agreed by said parties that if said Little & Brown shall neglect to give their notes, or any of them, at the times above specified, or if any one of their said notes shall not be paid when due, or within thirty days after it becomes payable, the said Prescott shall have a right, if he thinks proper, to avoid the contract for the future, and their right to print or publish further copies shall thereupon be determined and cease. And it is further agreed that neither this agreement, nor the right of publishing the said Abridgment, shall ever be assigned by said Little & Brown to any other person without said Prescott's consent & that the wholesale price for an hundred copies or more shall be eighty cents a copy, and that said L.&B. shall furnish copies at 60 cents a copy to any Editor or a journal or paper that said Prescott shall desire, and that they shall not think it worth while to give one to on their own account and that said Prescott shall be entitled to one copy of the said Abridgment for every 200 copies printed. *Fourth.* It is further understood and agreed by and between the parties aforesaid, that said Little & Brown shall have the right of purchasing, at any time before the expiration of said five years, any further number of copies beyond said 4000, not less than 1000 at a time, at the rate aforesaid per copy, payable in the same manner, and subject to the same conditions and regulations as are before expressed herein concerning said 4000 copies; provided, however, if said copies shall all be disposed of, or said Prescott shall be ready to take what remain at the whole sale prices, and the said Little & Brown shall not then choose to avail themselves of their right to purchase a further number of copies, the said right shall thereupon cease, and said Prescott shall thereafter have the exclusive right to print & publish the said history, notwithstanding any thing herein contained.

Lastly. The parties aforesaid further agree, that if any difference or dispute shall arise between them respecting any matter or thing under this contract, the same shall be submitted to Arbitrators, one to be chosen by each party, and the third by those two: provided always that if said Prescott shall be prevented by want of health or death from completing the aforesaid Abridgment, then the aforegoing agreement is to be void.

IN WITNESS WHEREOF we hereunto set our hands—in duplicate agreements.

Witness. *John Reed*　　　　　*Wm. H. Prescott*
　　　　　　　　　　　　　　　Little & Brown

[The last page which now serves as cover reads:]
W. H. Prescott
agreed to cancel
this contract
27 Mch of 43
Dupl
the same

AGREEMENT WITH BENTLEY,
July 3, 1841

MEMORANDUM OF AN AGREEMENT, made this third day of July 1841, between Colonel Aspinwall, acting on the part of W. H. Prescott Esq. of Boston United States of America on the one Part, and Richard Bentley, of New Burlington Street, Publisher, on the other Part.

It is agreed that the said Richard Bentley shall Publish at his own Expense and Risk, a work entitled "The Life and Times of Ferdinand & Isabella, abridged from the original work by the author W. H. Prescott Esq. and, after deducting from the Produce of the Sale thereof, the Charges for Printing, Paper, Advertisements, Embellishments, if any, and other Incidental Expenses, including the Allowance of Ten per Cent. on the gross amount of the Sale, for Commission and risk of Bad Debts, the Profits remaining of every Edition that shall be Printed of the Work, are to be divided into two equal Parts, one Moiety to be paid to the said Colonel Aspinwall acting on the part of the Said W. H. Prescott and the other Moiety to belong to the said Richard Bentley.

The Books Sold to be accounted for at the Trade Sale Price, reckoning 25 Copies as 24, unless it be thought advisable to dispose of any Copies, or of the Remainder, at a lower Price, which is left to the Judgment and Discretion of the said Richard Bentley.

IN WITNESS WHEREOF, the said Parties have hereunto set their hands this day.

Thos. Aspinwall
Richard Bentley

[*Jacket notation reads: Col. Aspinwall for W. H. Prescott Abridgment of Ferd. & Isabella*]

AGREEMENT WITH BENTLEY,

August 8, 1843

THIS AGREEMENT made this Eighth day of August one thousand eight hundred and forty three Between Thomas Aspinwall of Bishopsgate Church Yard in the City of London Esquire Consul General for the United States of America in Great Britain as the agent for and on the part and behalf of William Henry Prescott of Boston in the state of Massachusetts in the said United States Esquire of the one part and Richard Bentley of New Burlington Street in the county of Middlesex Bookseller and Publisher of the other part. Whereas the said William Henry Prescott hath lately composed and is the author of a new and unpublished work entitled "The Conquest of Mexico" or however otherwise the same shall be called or entitled and hath contracted and agreed with the said Richard Bentley for the sale to him of all the said William Henry Prescott's right like and interest in the said Work and of and in the copyright and right of publication thereof in the United Kingdom of Great Britain and Ireland under the act passed in the fifth and sixth years of Her present Majesty Queen Victoria Cap 45 to him the said Richard Bentley for the price of six hundred and fifty pounds. Now it is hereby witnessed that in consideration of the said agreement and of the sum of six hundred and fifty pounds of lawful money of the United Kingdom of Great Britain and Ireland current in England to be paid as follows that is to say by three several notes of hand of the said Richard Bentley for the sum of two hundred and sixteen pounds thirteen shillings and four pence each to be dated respectively on the day of publication of the said Work and payable respectively at six, nine and

twelve months after the several dates thereof which said
notes when paid will be for the purchase of the entire
copyright in the said Work. He the said Thomas Aspinwall
for and on the behalf of the said William Henry Prescott
his executors administrators and assigns Doth hereby agree
to bargain sell assign transfer and set over unto the said
Richard Bentley his executors administrators and assigns
All the said work so as aforesaid unpublished and called or
intended to be called ''The Conquest of Mexico'' or however the same shall be called and all and every the copyright therein and all the exclusive and entire right of publication and sale thereof under the said act passed in the
fifth and sixth year of Her present Majesty Queen Victoria
Cap 45 and all and every the profits proceeds and benefit
of the sale thereof To Hold the same with all the benefits
advantages and appurtenances thereof unto the said Richard Bentley his executors administrators and assigns for
his and their absolute benefit and advantage as his and
their goods and chattels for ever And it is hereby further
expressly agreed by the said Thomas Aspinwall for and on
the part of the said William Henry Prescott his executors
administrators and assigns that the said Work shall consist of sufficient matter to make three volumes demy octavo
containing about one hundred pages less matter than the
said William Henry Prescott's History of Ferdinand and
Isabella and that the said work shall be placed in the hands
of the said Richard Bentley in a complete and proper shape
for printing and publication and in sufficient time to enable the said Richard Bentley to publish the said work in
the United Kingdom before it shall be published elsewhere
and that the said Richard Bentley shall be also furnished
with three subjects or designs at least to be engraved from,
illustrative of the said Work and that the said subjects or
designs and the copy of the said Work shall be so placed in
the hands of the said Richard Bentley his executors administrators or assigns free of all charge or expense except
the before mentioned sum of six hundred and fifty pounds.

And further that the said William Henry Prescott his executors and administrators shall and will forthwith on being applied to for that purpose sign the necessary Certificates for entry of the Copyrights of the said Work at Stationers Hall pursuant to the aforesaid act passed in the fifth and sixth years of the reign of Her Majesty Queen Victoria Cap 45 and shall and will also at the request and costs of the said Richard Bentley his executors administrators or assigns well and sufficiently confirm this agreement and every clause matter and thing therein contained by such further acts deeds and assurances in the Law as may be advised by the Counsel of the said Richard Bentley his executors administrators or assigns for the further better and more effectually assigning and assuring the said Work and the copyright thereof upon the terms and conditions aforesaid AS WITNESS our hands the day and year first above written.

Signed by the above named
Thomas Aspinwall in the presence   *Thos. Aspinwall*
of James M. Curley Clk to Col.
Aspinwall

Signed by the above named
Richard Bentley in the presence   *Richard Bentley*
of Alfred Turner

Received the day and year first
above written of and from the above
named Richard Bentley the three
several notes of hand above mentioned which when paid will be in
full for the consideration money
above mentioned to be paid to the
said William Henry Prescott

                                     Thos Aspinwall

WHEREAS since the signing of this agreement it has been ascertained by us that Mr. Prescott's name is William Hickling Prescott. Now, we the Undersigned Do hereby further declare and agree, that the name throughout this agreement should be William Hickling Prescott, and not William Henry Prescott; and that the said agreement shall be, and is to be binding on us in all respects with such amendment and alteration in the name only; and we fully ratify the same accordingly. Dated this twenty first of October one thousand eight hundred and forty three

Thos Aspinwall

WITNESS
Wm. Worseldine
Clerk to Messrs A & W Turner
   32 Red Lion Square
WITNESSES   *Richard Bentley*
I. T. Marsh
Clerk to Mr. Bentley
J. B. Spencer
Clerk to Mr. Bentley

Not to be brought out before 19th Oct. so as to avoid the steamers of that day.

APPENDIX F

———•◆•———

AGREEMENT WITH BENTLEY,
January 7, 1845

MEMORANDUM OF AN AGREEMENT, made this seventh day of January 1845, between Colonel Aspinwall acting on behalf of W. H. Prescott Esq. of Boston, United States on the one Part, and Richard Bentley, of New Burlington Street, Publisher, on the other Part.

It is agreed that the said Richard Bentley shall Publish at his own Expense and Risk, a Collection of Papers written by the said W. H. Prescott Esq. the same to be printed in demy 8vo similar in style to the Editions published by the said Richard Bentley of ''Ferdinand & Isabella'' & ''The Conquest of Mexico'' and, after deducting from the produce of the Sale thereof, the Charges for Printing, Paper, Advertisements, Embellishments, if any, and other Incidental Expenses, including the Allowance of Ten per Cent. on the gross amount of the Sale, for Commission and risk of Bad Debts, the Profits remaining of every Edition that shall be Printed of the Work, are to be divided into two equal Parts, one Moiety to be paid to the said W. H. Prescott Esq. and the other Moiety to belong to the said Richard Bentley.

The Books Sold to be accounted for at the Trade Sale Price, reckoning 25 Copies as 24, unless it be thought advisable to dispose of any Copies, or of the Remainder, at a lower Price, which is left to the Judgment and Discretion of the said Richard Bentley.

IN WITNESS WHEREOF, the said Parties have hereunto set their hands this day. It is further agreed that an engraved Portrait of Mr. Prescott is to be published with the above work, the expense of which is to be defrayed by the said Richard Bentley & is to be charged by him in the general account of the work—but the said engraved plate is to be considered the property of the said W. H. Prescott Esq.

Thos. Aspinwall

[Jacket notation reads: W. H. Prescott pr Col. Aspinwall Essays &c   ½ profits]

THIS AGREEMENT made this Nineteenth day of January, one thousand eight hundred and forty seven—Between Thomas Aspinwall of Bishopsgate Church Yard in the City of London, Esquire, Consul General for the United States of America in Great Britain as the agent for and on the part and behalf of William Hickling Prescott of Boston in the State of Massachusetts in the said United States Esquire of the one part and Richard Bentley of New Burlington Street in the County of Middlesex Bookseller and Publisher of the other part Whereas the said William Hickling Prescott hath lately composed and is the author of a new and unpublished work entitled The History of the Conquest of Peru or howsoever otherwise the same shall be called or entitled and hath contracted and agreed with the said Richard Bentley for the sale to him of all the said William Hickling Prescott's right title and interest in the said work and of and in the copyright and right of publication thereof in the Kingdom of Great Britain and Ireland under the act passed in the fifth and sixth years of Her present Majesty Queen Victoria Cap. 45 to him the said Richard Bentley for the price of Eight hundred pounds. Now it is hereby witnessed that in consideration of the said agreement and of the sum of Eight hundred pounds of lawful money of the United Kingdom of Great Britain and Ireland current in England to be paid as follows that is to say by three several notes of hand of the said Richard Bentley for the sum of Two hundred and sixty six pounds thirteen shillings and four pence each to be dated respectively on the day of publication of the said work and payable respectively at six nine and twelve months after the several dates thereof which said notes when paid will be for the purchase of the entire copyright in the said work. He the said Thomas Aspinwall for and on the behalf of the said William Hickling Prescott his Executors administrators and assigns Doth hereby agree to bargain sell assign transfer and set over unto the said Richard Bentley his Executors administrators and assigns all the said work as aforesaid unpublished and called or intended to be called The History of the Conquest of Peru, or however the same shall be called and all and every the copyright therein and all the exclusive and entire right of publication and sale thereof under the said act passed in the fifth and sixth year of Her present Majesty Queen Victoria Cap. 45 and all and every the profits proceeds and benefit of the sale thereof to hold the same with all the benefits advantages and appurtenances thereof unto the said Richard Bentley his executors administrators and assigns for his and their absolute benefit and advantage as his and their goods and chattels for ever and it is hereby further expressly agreed by the said Thomas Aspinwall for and on the part of the said William Hickling Prescott his executors administrators and assigns that the said work shall contain within one hundred and sixty pages the same amount of matter as in the said William Hickling Prescott's History of the Conquest of Mexico and that the said work shall be placed in the hands of the said Richard Bentley in a complete and proper shape for printing and publication and in sufficient time to enable the said Richard Bentley to publish the said work in the United Kingdom before it shall be published elsewhere and that the said Richard Bentley shall be also furnished with [blank] subjects or designs at least to be engraved from illustrative of the said work and that the said subjects or designs and the copy of the said work shall be so placed in the hands of the said Richard Bentley his executors administrators or assigns free of all charge or expence except the before-mentioned sum of eight hundred pounds. And further that the said William Hickling Prescott his executors and administrators shall and will forthwith on being applied to for that purpose sign the necessary Certificates for entry of the copyright of the said work at Stationers Hall pursuant to the aforesaid act passed in the fifth and sixth years of the reign of Her Majesty Queen Victoria Cap. 45 and shall and will also at the request and costs of the said Richard Bentley his executors administrators or assigns well and sufficiently confirm this agreement and every clause matter and thing therein contained by such further acts deeds and assurances in the law as may be advised by the counsel of the said Richard Bentley his executors administrators or assigns for the further better and more effectually assigning and assuring the said work and the copyright thereof upon the terms and conditions aforesaid —As Witness our hands this day and year first above written

Thos. Aspinwall

Received the 27th of May, 1847 of and from the abovenamed Richard Bentley the three several notes of hand above mentioned which when paid will be in full for the consideration money abovementioned to be paid to the said William Hickling Prescott

Thos Aspinwall

[*Jacket notation reads: W. H. Prescott pr Col. Aspinwall Conquest of Peru Entire Copyt. £800*]

AGREEMENT WITH PHILLIPS, SAMPSON & CO.

August 5, 1854

AN AGREEMENT has been made, this fifth day of August
in the year of Our Lord one thousand eight hundred and
fifty-four, between William H. Prescott, of Boston in the
State of Massachusetts, of the one part, and Phillips, Sampson, and Co. of said Boston, of the other part, respecting
the publication of certain books which the said Prescott
has written or is now writing; and the parties abovenamed hereby respectively bind themselves to conform to
the stipulations of this agreement, which are as follows:—

First. Mr. Prescott shall cause to be made, at his own expense, within one year from the date of this contract, stereotype plates of the first and second volumes of a historical
work, which he is now engaged in writing, entitled "The
History of the Reign of Philip the Second" and shall grant
and allow to Messrs Phillips, Sampson & Co. the use of said
stereotype plates, to print therefrom twelve thousand copies of each of said volumes in octavo, with the right to publish and sell the same during a period of three years from
the first day of the publication of said volumes; and during
the said period of three years no other person shall have
the right to print the said volumes; and Messrs. Phillips,
Sampson & Co. shall pay to Mr. Prescott, for the said right
to print and publish the said twelve thousand copies of
the said volumes, twelve thousand dollars on the first day
of the publication thereof, one half in cash, and the other
half in a note at six months.

Second. Messrs. Phillips, Sampson, & Co. shall further
have the right to print and publish, during the said three

years, any additional number of copies that they please, over and above the said twelve thousand copies, of the said volumes, by paying to Mr. Prescott fifty cents per volume for each of such additional copies, accounting to him semi-annually therefore, and paying him in cash.

Third. At the expiration of the said three years Messrs. Phillips, Sampson & Co. shall have a like exclusive right to print and publish any number of the said first and second volumes of the said work that they please, by paying to Mr. Prescott fifty cents per volume for each copy, accounting to him semi-annually therefore, and paying him in cash; And this right shall continue as long as Messrs. Phillips, Sampson & Co. shall be entitled by the terms of this contract to print and publish certain other works of said Prescott, hereinafter described, in 12mo.

Fourth. Mr. Prescott shall also grant to Messrs. Phillips, Sampson & Co. the like exclusive right to print and publish, during a like period of three years, from stereotype plates to be furnished by Mr. Prescott, twelve thousand copies of each and every, succeeding volume of the said History of Philip the Second which Mr. Prescott may hereafter write; Messrs. Phillips, Sampson & Co. paying him therefor the sum of six thousand dollars for each volume on the first day of the publication of such volume, one half in cash and the other half in a note at six months; Provided however, that at the expiration of the right hereinafter granted Messrs. Phillips, Sampson & Co. to print and publish the said works hereinafter described in 12mo. Mr. Prescott shall be released from the obligation to grant to Messrs. Phillips, Sampson & Co. the right to print and publish such volumes, if any, of the said History of Philip the Second as may then still remain to be written.

Fifth. Mr. Prescott shall further grant to Messrs. Phillips, Sampson & Co. the right to print and publish, during the said three years and after the expiration of the said three years as long as they shall be entitled by the terms of this contract to print and publish the said works hereinafter described in 12mo. any additional copies of each of the said succeeding volumes of the said History of Philip the Second that they please, over and above the said twelve thousand copies, by paying Mr. Prescott fifty cents for each of such additional copies of each volume, accounting to him semi-annually therefor, and paying him in cash.

Sixth. Mr. Prescott shall further furnish to Messrs. Phillips, Sampson & Co., within one year from the date of this contract, stereotype plates of three other historical works, of which he is the author, and which have been already published, to wit: "The History of the Reign of Ferdinand and Isabella," in three volumes 8vo, "The History of the Conquest of Mexico," in three volumes 8vo, and "The History of the Conquest of Peru," in two volumes 8vo; and shall grant to Messrs. Phillips, Sampson & Co. the exclusive right to print and publish any number of copies of each and all of the said works in 8vo that they please, they paying to Mr. Prescott fifty cents per volume for each copy, accounting to him semi-annually therefor and paying him in cash; And this right shall continue until the expiration of the right hereinafter granted to Messrs. Phillips, Sampson & Co. to print and publish the same works in 12mo.

Seventh. Mr. Prescott shall further cause to be made, within one year after the first publication of the said first and second volumes of the said History of Philip the Second, stereotype plates of the three above-mentioned works already published, and shall furnish to Messrs. Phillips, Sampson & Co. the use of said stereotype plates to print therefrom copies of the said works in 12mo; that is to say, "The History of the Reign of Ferdinand & Isabella," in 3 vols. 12mo; "The History of the Conquest of Mexico" in 3 vols. 12 mo; and "The History of the Conquest of Peru" in 2 vols. 12 mo; and shall grant to Messrs. Phillips, Sampson & Co. the right to print and publish three thousand copies of each and all of the said works in 12mo, in each and every year during a period of six years from the first publication thereof; And Messrs. Phillips, Sampson & Co. shall pay to Mr. Prescott, for the said right to print and publish the above-mentioned copies of the said works in 12mo, six thousand dollars in each and every year of the said period of six years; accounting to him quarter-yearly, and paying him in cash; the first payment to be made at the end of three months from the first day of publication.

Eighth. Mr. Prescott shall grant to Messrs. Phillips, Sampson & Co. the right to print and publish, in each and every year of the said period of six years, any additional copies of the said three works, in 12mo, that they please, over and above the said three thousand copies; And Messrs. Phillips, Sampson, & Co. shall pay to Mr. Prescott twenty-five cents per volume for each of such additional copies of said works in 12mo, accounting to him annually, and paying him in cash; But so that if in any year of the said period of six years Messrs. Phillips, Sampson & Co. shall not exercise their right to print and publish three thousand copies of each and all of the three said works in 12mo, they shall nevertheless pay to Mr. Prescott, in each and every year of the said period of six years, the above-mentioned sum of six thousand dollars in equal quarterly payments; and if in any year of the said period of six years Messrs. Phillips, Sampson & Co. shall print and publish any additional copies of any or all of the said works in 12mo, over and above the said three thousand copies, then they shall pay to Mr. Prescott twenty-five cents per volume of each of such additional copies.

Ninth. Mr. Prescott shall further furnish to Messrs. Phillips, Sampson & Co, within one year from the date of this contract, stereotype plates of a certain other work of which he is the author, and which has been already published in one volume 8vo, entitled "Literary and Biographical Miscellanies," and shall grant to Messrs. Phillips, Sampson & Co. the exclusive right to print and publish any number of copies of the said work that they please, in one volume 8vo; they paying him therefor fifty cents a copy, accounting to him semi-annually and paying him in cash; And this right shall continue until the expiration of the right hereinafter granted to Messrs. Phillips, Sampson & Co. to print and publish the three above-mentioned historical works in 12mo.

Tenth. Mr. Prescott shall further cause to be made, within one year after the first publication of the said first and second volumes of the said History of Philip the Second, stereotype plates of the said "Literary and Biographical Miscellanies," and shall furnish to Messrs. Phillips, Sampson & Co. the use of said stereotype plates to print therefrom copies of the said work in one volume 12mo. and shall grant to Messrs. Phillips, Sampson & Co. the exclusive right to print and publish, during six years from the first publication thereof, two thousand four hundred copies of the said work in 12mo, they paying him therefor six hundred dollars, one half at the end of one year, and the other half at the end of two years, from the first day of the publication thereof.

Eleventh. Messrs. Phillips, Sampson & Co. shall further have the right to print and publish, during the said six years, any additional number of copies of the said "Literary and Biographical Miscellanies" in 12mo, by paying to Mr. Prescott twenty-five cents for each of such additional copies, accounting to him semi-annually, and paying him in cash.

Twelfth. After the expiration of the said period of six years from the first publication of said works in 12mo, Messrs. Phillips, Sampson & Co. may continue to print and publish all of the above-mentioned works, by paying to

Mr. Prescott fifty cents for each copy in 8vo, and twenty-five cents for each copy in 12mo, of each volume, until Mr. Prescott shall give them notice to discontinue printing and publishing the said works; and after such notice they shall not print any more copies, but they shall be allowed a term not exceeding six months to sell the copies which they may have on hand.

Thirteenth. Messrs. Phillips, Sampson & Co. shall begin to publish all the above-mentioned works within a reasonable time after the stereotype plates shall have been delivered to them, and shall use all proper diligence in publishing and selling the same; and the retail price of said works shall be fixed at two dollars a volume for the copies in 8vo. and one dollar a volume for the copies in 12mo.

Fourteenth. The right granted by Mr. Prescott to Messrs. Phillips, Sampson & Co. in the terms of this contract, to print and publish the above-mentioned works extends only to the publication of said works in the United States; And the right to print and publish said works shall not be assigned or transferred by Messrs. Phillips, Sampson & Co. to any other person or persons without Mr. Prescott's consent.

Fifteenth. Messrs. Phillips, Sampson & Co. shall deliver to Mr. Prescott twenty-five copies of the first edition of each volume of the said History of Philip the Second gratis; and as many copies of any of the above-mentioned works as he may request at sixty-six cents for each volume in 8vo, and thirty-three cents for each volume in 12mo.

Sixteenth. Whenever the right of Messrs. Phillips, Sampson & Co. to print the above-mentioned works shall cease or expire, they shall deliver back to Mr. Prescott the stereotype plates of the said works, in as good condition as they receive them, reasonable wear and tear excepted; and if the said stereotype plates shall be injured or destroyed, by fire or other casualty, while in the possession of Messrs. Phillips, Sampson & Co., they shall indemnify Mr. Prescott for such damage or destruction.

Seventeenth. If Mr. Prescott shall be prevented by ill health, or any other cause, from completing the first and second volumes of the said History of Philip the Second within such a time as will enable him to have the stereotype plates made within one year from the date of this contract, this shall not be considered as a breach of this contract on his part, but he shall complete the said volumes as soon as he is able, and deliver the plates to Messrs. Phillips, Sampson & Co. who shall publish the said volumes in a reasonable time thereafter.

Eighteenth. Messrs. Phillips, Sampson & Co. shall defray the whole expense of any engravings that may be made for the illustration of any or all of the above-mentioned works.

Nineteenth. If Messrs. Phillips, Sampson & Co. shall fail to pay for any of the copies of any of the above-mentioned works at the time, and in the manner, specified by the terms of this contract or shall fail to fulfill any of their obligations under this contract, then their right to print and publish or sell any or all of the above-mentioned works shall thereupon cease and be void, at the election of Mr. Prescott; and all unsold copies shall belong to Mr. Prescott as security and indemnity for such breach of contract.

IN WITNESS WHEREOF the parties aforesaid have hereto set their hands the day and year aforesaid.

Wm. H. Prescott
Phillips, Sampson & Co.

In presence of
J. F. Kirk
Witness to Wm. H. Prescott
In presence of
H. E. Flint
Witness to Phillips, Sampson & Co.

[Marginal note: Mr. Prescott releases Messrs. Phillips, Sampson & Co. from so much of this contract as binds them to defray the expenses of any engraved plates that may be made to illustrate the works.

Wm. H. Prescott]

APPENDIX I

————•—•————

AGREEMENT WITH BENTLEY

(*unexecuted*), *1854*

AN AGREEMENT made this _____ day of ____ One thousand eight hundred and fifty four Between William Hickling Prescott of Boston in the State of Massachusetts in the United States of America of the one part and Richard Bentley of New Burlington Street in the County of Middlesex Bookseller and Publisher of the other part Whereas the said William Hickling Prescott hath composed and is the author of a new and unpublished work at present intended by him to be called "The History of Philip the Second" and hath agreed with the said Richard Bentley for the Sale to him of all the said William Hickling Prescott's right title and interest in the said work and of and in the copyright and right of Publication thereof in the United Kingdom of Great Britain and Ireland and in any other Part of the British Dominions under the Act passed in the Session of Parliament held in the 5th and 6th years of the Reign of Queen Victoria Chapter 45 and of and in the right of translating the said work for the Price of One thousand pounds for each Volume of which the said Work shall consist it being understood that the said Work shall not exceed 5 Volumes and that each Volume shall contain at least four hundred and fifty printed pages in demy 8vo similar in size to the Page adopted in the first Editions published by the said Richard Bentley of the said William Hickling Prescott's former historical works until the whole work shall be completed. Now it is hereby agreed that in consideration of the Sum of One thousand pounds of lawful British money to be paid for each Volume of the said work in manner following (that is to say) £400 in the said Richard Bentley's draft on his Bankers to be transmitted to the said William Hickling Prescott within six weeks from the day of first Publication thereof respectively subject to the deduction of Five pounds per Cent for discount and in three several promissory Notes of the said Richard Bentley for the Sum of two hundred pounds each to be dated respectively on the day of first Publication of each Volume of the said work and payable respectively to the said William Hickling Prescott or order at 4, 6 and 9 months after the several dates thereof which said Draft and promissory Notes when paid will be for the purchase of the Copyright and Right of Publication and right of translating as aforesaid of and in each Volume of the said work whether published singly or two or more Volumes at one and the same time as the said William Hickling Prescott may determine. He the said William Hickling Prescott doth hereby agree to grant assign and set over unto the said Richard Bentley his executors administrators and assigns all the said work so as aforesaid unpublished and called or intended to be called "The History of Philip the Second" or however the same shall be called and all and every the copyright therein and all the exclusive and entire right of publication and Sale thereof in the United Kingdom of Great Britain and Ireland and in other Part of the British Dominions under the said Act or any other Act or Law and all and every the profits proceeds and benefit of the Sale thereof and all the right of translating the said Work and the profits proceeds and benefit to be derived therefrom To hold all and every the premises with all the benefits advantages and appurtenances thereof respectively unto the said Richard Bentley his executors administrators and assigns for his and their absolute benefit and advantage as his and their goods and chattels forever. And it is hereby further agreed by the said William Hickling Prescott that the complete copy of each Volume of the said work shall be placed in the hands of the said Richard Bentley in sufficient time to enable him to publish the same in the United Kingdom at least ten days before it shall be published elsewhere. And further that the said William Hickling Prescott his executors and administrators will on being applied to for that purpose forthwith sign every necessary Certificate or other Document for entry of the Copyright of the said Work at Stationers' Hall pursuant to the aforesaid Act of Queen Victoria Chapter 45 and will also at the request and costs of the said Richard Bentley his executors administrators and assigns well and sufficiently corroborate and confirm this Agreement and every clause matter and thing hereinbefore and hereinafter contained by such further acts and deeds and assurances in the Law as may be reasonably required by the said Richard Bentley his executors administrators or assigns for the further better and more effectually assigning and assuring the said work and the Copyright and right of Publication thereof and right of translating the said work upon the Terms and Conditions aforesaid Provided always that if the right or power of the said William Hickling Prescott to make an effectual grant and assignment of the Copyright hereby agreed to be granted and assigned should by Statute or judicial decision or otherwise be rendered or become unavailing at Law or in Equity to the said Richard Bentley his executors administrators or assigns according to the true meaning hereof Then the said William Hickling Prescott shall repay to the said Richard Bentley the Sum of £500 in respect of each of the first two Volumes of the said work and the Sum of Seven hundred and fifty pounds in respect of each of the succeeding Volumes on account of such of the same Volumes as shall have been paid for and the complete copy of each Volume or of each remaining Volume of the said work shall be placed in the Hands of the said Richard Bentley in sufficient time to enable him to publish the same in the United Kingdom at least six weeks before it shall be published elsewhere and he shall pay for the exclusive Right and Power to Publish the same during that Period prior to any other publication thereof and such payment shall be made at the rates and in manner hereinafter specified (that is to say) £500 for each of the first two Volumes as follows (namely) £125 for each Volume in the said Richard Bentley's draft on his Bankers to be transmitted to the said William Hickling Prescott within six weeks from the day of first publication thereof respectively subject to the deduction of five pounds per Cent. for discount and three several Promissory Notes of the said Richard Bentley of £125 each for each of the said first two Volumes to be dated respectively on the day of first Publication at 4 months 6 months and 9 months and for the remaining Volumes after the publication of the first two Volumes the Sum of Two hundred and fifty pounds each payable as follows (that is to say) one moiety in the said Richard Bentley's draft on his Banker to be transmitted to the said William Hickling Prescott within six weeks from the day of publication subject to the deduction of five pounds per Cent. for discount and the other moiety in his Promissory Note at six months date from the said day of Publication all such Promissory Notes to be payable to the said William Hickling Prescott or Order. And the said Richard Bentley shall supply the said William Hickling Prescott free of charge with 24 copies of the said work of the largest sized Volumes to be published by the said Richard Bentley—

WITNESS OUR HANDS

A special word is in order about the manuscript sources upon which so much of the present work rests.

The Massachusetts Historical Society holds the most extensive and most significant collection of Prescott materials. The property of Mr. Roger Wolcott, a great-grandson of the historian, these records include, in addition to massive quantities of correspondence, diaries, notebooks of literary memoranda, clippings, business records, and drafts of manuscripts. Here are the communications addressed to the historian, as well as draft copies of many sent by him. The materials range from Prescott's pre-college days to and beyond the day of his death. Among other holdings of the same society, the papers of George Bancroft, Edward Everett, and the Rev. Mr. George E. Ellis significantly impinge on Prescott's career.

In the Houghton Library at Harvard University the following manuscript materials were significantly helpful: the papers of William Hickling Prescott, which include correspondence between the historian and a number of persons; the papers of Jared Sparks and Charles Sumner, both of whom were lifelong friends and confidants of Prescott; and the papers of Richard Bentley, acquired in 1945, which embrace ninety-seven letters from Prescott to his English publisher during the period 1837-58.

The British Museum possesses scores of manuscript volumes of important business records—including correspondence and contracts—of the publishing house of Richard Bentley. This extensive collection covers the entire period of Prescott's relations with Bentley. From it come certain of the contracts reproduced in the Appendix.

The literary records of the house of Bentley, purchased in 1951, are at the University of Illinois.

The Huntington Library contains a small number of significant items among the papers of Francis Lieber.

A very small number of papers relevant to the present study are scattered in the Manuscripts Division of the Library of Congress among the papers of Joseph Story, Oliver Wendell Holmes, James K. Polk, and in the Bancroft-Bliss collection.

The significant data held by the Hispanic Society of America has been reproduced in C. L. Penney (ed.), *Prescott; Unpublished Letters to Gayangos* (New York, 1927). Marginal contributions have come from the papers of Washington Irving at the New York Public Library. The Historical Society of Pennsylvania holds, in the papers of Joel Roberts Poinsett, material of limited relevance to the present study.

Little, Brown & Company of Boston and J. B. Lippincott Company of Philadelphia hold copies of Prescott contracts, the latter one negotiated between the historian and Phillips, Sampson, and Company. These documents are reproduced in the Appendix.

The system employed in citing the overwhelming majority of these manuscript materials calls for special comment. In the use of correspondence, memoranda, financial accountings, etc., full information as to writer, recipient, date, and nature of document is regularly incorporated in the text. Accordingly, it is necessary to indicate here only the collections in which the various categories of papers repose:

Incoming. All correspondence received by Prescott and his immediate family is in the William Hickling Prescott Papers in the Massachusetts Historical Society.

Outgoing. (*1*) Prescott to Bentley, in the Bentley Papers in the Houghton Library; (*2*) Prescott to Sparks, in the Sparks Papers in the Houghton Library; (*3*) Prescott to Sumner, in the Sumner Papers in the Houghton Library; (*4*) Prescott to his American printers, in the Prescott Papers in the Houghton Library; (*5*) Prescott to Lieber, in the Lieber Papers in the Huntington Library; (*6*) Prescott to Bancroft, in the Bancroft Papers in the Massachusetts Historical Society; (*7*) Prescott to Everett, in the Everett Papers in the Massachusetts Historical Society; and (*8*) Prescott to Phillips, Sampson, and Company, in the rare book collection of Boston Public Library.

Note. The existence of the noctograph drafts at the Massachusetts Historical Society of many of Prescott's letters, the original fair copies of which were lost, permit the reconstruction of both sides of certain areas of his correspondence. Such is true with reference to Harper & Brothers, agent Thomas Aspinwall, and English publishers Routledge, Murray, and Longmans.

All references to printed materials are made in the notes and are listed in the following sources.

Abbott, Jacob. *The Harper Establishment.* New York, [1956].

Adams, Herbert B., ed. *The Life and Writings of Jared Sparks.* 2 vols. Boston and New York, 1893.

Allibone, S. Austin. *A Critical Dictionary of English Literature and British and American Authors.* 3 vols. Philadelphia, 1871–74.

Austin, James C. *Fields of the Atlantic Monthly.* San Marino, Calif., 1953.

"Authors and Publishers. Opinions of Some Publishers," *Publishers' Weekly,* xxxi, No. 15 (April 9, 1887), 511–15.

Ayer, Edward E. "How I Bought My First Book," *The Newberry Library Bulletin,* Second Series, No. 5 (December 1950), 143–45.

Bader, Arno L. "Frederick Saunders and the Early History of the International Copyright Movement in America," *The Library Quarterly,* viii (January 1938), 25–39.

[Bancroft, George]. ''Prescott's Ferdinand and Isabella'' (review), *The United States Magazine and Democratic Review*, ii, No. 6 (May 1838), 160–66.

B[entley], R[ichard]. *Some Leaves from the Past.* [London], 1896.

Richard Bentley & Son. Reprinted from *Le Livre* of October, 1855, with Some Additional Notes. n.p., 1886.

[Richard Bentley & Son]. *A List of the Principal Publications Issued from New Burlington Street during the Year 1838.* London, 1894.

———. *A List of the Principal Publications Issued from New Burlington Street during the Year 1839.* London, 1894.

———. *A List of the Principal Publications Issued from New Burlington Street during the Year 1842.* London, 1895.

———. *A List of the Principal Publications Issued from New Burlington Street during the Year 1843.* London, 1896.

———. *A List of the Principal Publications Issued from New Burlington Street during the Year 1845.* London, 1896.

———. *A List of the Principal Publications Issued from New Burlington Street during the Year 1847.* London, 1896.

———. *A List of the Principal Publications Issued from New Burlington Street during the Year 1849.* London, 1897.

———. *A List of the Principal Publications Issued from New Burlington Street during the Year 1851.* London, 1902.

———. *A List of the Principal Publications Issued from New Burlington Street during the Year 1852.* London, 1903.

———. *A List of the Principal Publications Issued from New Burlington Street during the Year 1854.* London, 1918.

————. *A List of the Principal Publications Issued from New Burlington Street during the Year 1855*. London, 1903.

————. *A List of the Principal Publications Issued from New Burlington Street during the Year 1869*. London, 1912.

[Bowen, Francis]. "History of the Conquest of Peru" (review), *North American Review*, LXV (October 1847), 366–400.

Bowker, R. R. *Copyright. Its Law and Its Literature*. New York, 1886.

Boynton, Henry Walcott. *Annals of American Bookselling 1638–1850*. New York, 1932.

Brooks, Van Wyck. *The Flowering of New England, 1815–1865*. New York, 1936.

Brussel, I. R. *Anglo-American First Editions. Part Two: West to East 1786–1930*. New York, 1936.

Cannon, Carl L. *American Book Collectors and Collecting from Colonial Times to the Present*. New York, 1941.

Carter, John, and Brooke Crutchley. *The Printed Book*. Cambridge, 1951.

Charvat, William. "James T. Fields and the Beginnings of Book Promotion, 1840–1855," *The Huntington Library Quarterly*, VIII, No. 1 (November 1944), 75–94.

————. "Prescott's Political and Social Attitudes," *American Literature*, XIII (January 1942), 320–30.

Charvat, William, and Michael Kraus. *William Hickling Prescott. Representative Selections*. New York, [1943].

Clark, Harry Hayden. "Literary Criticism in the *North American Review*, 1815–1835," *Transactions of the Wisconsin Academy of Sciences, Arts, and Letters*, XXXII (1940), 299–350.

————, ed. *Transitions in American Literary History*. Durham, North Carolina, 1953.

Commager, H. S. *Theodore Parker*. Boston, 1936.

Cooper, James Fenimore, ed. *Correspondence of James Fenimore Cooper*. 2 vols. New Haven, Conn. 1922.

C[utler], A[bram] E. *Autograph Letter and Engraved Portraits of William H. Prescott the Historian*. Boston, 1891.

Correspondence of William H. Prescott, Esq. with Richard Bentley, from August, 1856, to November, 1858. [London, 1859].

Derby, J. C. *Fifty Years among Authors, Books and Publishers*. Hartford, Conn., 1886.

Dickinson, Asa Don. *The World's Best Books: Homer to Hemingway*. New York, 1953.

Eaton, Andrew J. "The American Movement for International Copyright, 1837–60," *The Library Quarterly*, XV, No. 2 (April 1945), 95–122.

Emerson, Edward Waldo. *The Early Years of the Saturday Club 1855–1870*. Boston and New York, 1918.

Fay, Theodore Sedgwick. *Statement Relative to Some Business Transactions with the Messrs Harper & Brothers of New York, with Correspondence*. Berlin, 1845.

Fielding, Mantle. "Joseph Andrews," *The Pennsylvania Magazine of History and Biography*, XXXI, No. 1 (1907), 103–13; No. 2 (1907), 207–31.

Fields, James T. *Yesterdays with Authors*. Boston and New York, [1900].

"Fifty Years of Harper's Magazine," *Harper's New Monthly Magazine*, C, No. 600 (May 1900), 947–62.

Foley, P. K. *American Authors 1795–1895*. Boston, 1897.

[Ford, Richard]. "History of the Reign of Ferdinand and Isabella" (review), *Quarterly Review*, LXIV (June 1839), 1–58.

Forster, John. *The Life of Charles Dickens*. 2 vols. Philadelphia, 1872.

Freidel, Frank. "Lieber's Contribution to the International Copyright Movement," *The Huntington Library Quarterly*, VIII (February 1945), 200–206.

Gardiner, C. Harvey. *William Hickling Prescott. An Annotated Bibliography of Published Works*. Washington D.C., 1958.

———. "Promoting a Book: Prescott to Bancroft, December 20, 1837," *The Papers of the Bibliographical Society of America,* LI (Fourth Quarter, 1957), 335–39.

[Gardiner, William H.]. "History of the Reign of Ferdinand and Isabella, the Catholic" (review), *North American Review,* XLVI (January 1838), 203–91.

[Gayangos, Pascual de]. "The History of the Reign of Ferdinand and Isabella" (review), *Edinburgh Review,* LXVIII (January 1839), 376–405.

Gohdes, Clarence. *American Literature in Nineteenth-Century England.* New York, 1944.

———. "Longfellow and His Authorized British Publishers," *Publications of the Modern Language Association of America,* LV (December 1940), 1165–79.

Goodfellow, Donald M. "The Sources of *Mercedes of Castile,*" *American Literature,* XIII (November 1940), 318–28.

Goodrich, S. G. *Recollections of a Lifetime, or Men and Things I Have Seen.* 2 vols. New York and Auburn, 1856.

[Greenwood, Francis William Pitt]. "History of the Reign of Ferdinand and Isabella" (review), *The Christian Examiner and General Review,* XXIV (March 1838), 99–111.

Griswold, W. M., ed. *Passages from the Correspondence . . . of Rufus W. Griswold.* Cambridge, 1898.

Grossman, James. *James Fenimore Cooper.* New York, [1949].

Growoll, Adolph. *Book Trade Bibliography in the United States in the Nineteenth Century.* New York, [1939].

[Guizot, F. P. G.]. "History of Reign of Philip the Second" (review), *Edinburgh Review,* CV (January 1857), 1–24.

Harper, J. Henry. *The House of Harper. A Century of Publishing in Franklin Square.* New York, 1912.

[Hillard, George S.]. "History of the Conquest of Mexico" (review), *North American Review,* LVIII (January 1844), 157–210.

————, ed. *Life, Letters, and Journals of George Ticknor.* 2 vols. (5th ed.) Boston, 1876.

"History of the Conquest of Mexico" (anon. rev.) *Quarterly Review,* LXXXI (September 1847), 317–51.

"History of the Reign of Philip the Second" (anon. rev.), *North American Review,* LXXXIII (July 1856), 96–103.

Houtchens, Lawrence H. "Charles Dickens and International Copyright," *American Literature,* XIII (March 1941), 18–28.

Howe, M. A. DeWolfe. *The Life and Letters of George Bancroft.* 2 vols. New York, 1908.

Johnson, Merle de Vore. *Merle Johnson's American First Editions.* (4th ed.) New York, 1942.

Kaser, David. *Messrs. Carey & Lea of Philadelphia. A Study in the History of the Booktrade.* Philadelphia, [1957].

————. "The Origin of the Book Trade Sales," *The Papers of the Bibliographical Society of America,* L (Third Quarter, 1956), 296–302.

"The Late Mr. George Routledge," *The Illustrated London News,* XCIV, No. 2595 (January 12, 1889), 38.

Lehmann-Haupt, Hellmut, *et al. The Book in America: A History of the Making and Selling of Books in the United States.* New York, 1951.

Library of Congress. *A. L. A. Portrait Index.* Washington, D.C., 1906.

[Little, Charles C., and James Brown]. *A Catalogue of Miscellaneous Books.* Boston, 1839.

[Little, Brown & Co.]. *Catalogue of Books.* Boston, 1854.

————. *One Hundred Years of Publishing 1837–1937.* Boston, [1937].

Longfellow, Samuel, ed. *Life of Henry Wadsworth Longfellow, with Extracts from His Journals and Correspondence.* 3 vols. Boston, 1893.

McGann, Thomas F. "Prescott's Conquests," *American Heritage,* VIII, No. 6 (October 1957), 4–9, 109–11.

Means, Philip Ainsworth. "A Re-examination of Prescott's

Account of Early Peru," *New England Quarterly,* IV
(October 1931), 645–62.

"Memorial of a number of citizens of Boston, *Praying The
passage of an International copyright law,*" Sen. Doc.
No. 398, 25 Cong., 2 Sess. (1838), Ser. 318.

"Memorial of a number of citizens of New York, *Praying
The passage of an international copyright law,*" Sen.
Doc. No. 399, 25 Cong., 2 Sess. (1838), Ser. 318.

"Memorial of a number of citizens of Philadelphia, *Against
the passage of an international copyright law,*" Sen. Doc.
No. 102, 25 Cong., 2 Sess. (1838), Ser. 315.

"Memorial of a number of citizens of Philadelphia, *Praying The passage of an international copyright law,*" Sen.
Doc. No. 400, 25 Cong., 2 Sess. (1838), Ser. 318.

"Memorial of a Number of Citizens of the United States,
*Praying an alteration of the Laws regulating Copy-
rights,*" Sen. Doc. No. 141, 24 Cong., 2 Sess. (1837), Ser.
298.

"Memorial of G. Furman and Other Public Writers, *Praying the passage of an International Law of Copy-right,*"
Sen. Doc. No. 192, 24 Cong., 2 Sess. (1837), Ser. 298.

"Memorial of Peter S. Du Ponceau and others, *Praying
Congress to appoint committees of inquiry on the subject
of copyright, and to await their report before acting on
the subject,*" Sen. Doc. No. 309, 25 Cong., 2 Sess. (1838),
Ser. 317.

"Memorial of Richard Penn Smith and others. *Against
The passage of the bill to establish an international copy-
right law,*" Sen. Doc. No. 369, 25 Cong., 2 Sess. (1838),
Ser. 317.

"Memorial of the Book-sellers of Boston, Massachusetts,
*against The passage of the International Copy-right
Law,*" H. Doc. No. 340, 25 Cong., 2 Sess. (1838), Ser. 330.

"Memorial of the Columbia Typographical Society, of the
City of Washington, *against the enactment of an inter-
national copy-right law,*" Sen. Doc. No. 190, 25 Cong., 2
Sess. (1838), Ser. 316.

"Memorial of the New York Typographical Society, *Against The passage of an international copyright law,*" Sen. Doc. No. 296, 25 Cong., 2 Sess. (1838), Ser. 317.

"Memorials of John Jay and William C. Bryant and Others, in favor of *An International Copyright Law,*" H. Misc. Doc. No. 76, 30 Cong., 1 Sess. (1847), Ser. 523.

Merriman, Roger Bigelow. *The Rise of the Spanish Empire in the Old World and in the New.* 4 vols. New York, 1918–34.

[Milman, H. H.]. "History of the Conquest of Mexico" (review), *Quarterly Review,* LXXIII (December 1843), 187–235.

Morison, Samuel Eliot. "Prescott the American Thucydides," *The Atlantic Monthly,* CC, No. 5 (November 1957), 165–68, 170, 172.

————, ed. *History of the Conquest of Peru.* New York, 1957.

Mott, Frank Luther. *Golden Multitudes: The Story of Best Sellers in the United States.* New York, 1947.

Mumby, F. A. *The House of Routledge 1834–1934.* London, 1934.

Nevins, Allan, ed. *The Diary of Philip Hone 1828–1851.* 2 vols. New York, 1927.

Nevins, Allan, and Milton Halsey Thomas, eds. *The Diary of George Templeton Strong: The Turbulent Fifties 1850–1859.* New York, 1952.

Ogden, Rollo. *William Hickling Prescott.* Boston and New York, 1904.

Oswald, John Clyde. *Printing in the Americas.* New York, [1937].

Peck, Harry Thurston. *William Hickling Prescott.* New York, 1905.

Penney, Clara Louisa, ed. *Prescott; Unpublished Letters to Gayangos in the Library of the Hispanic Society of America.* New York, 1927.

"Petition of the Professors of the University of Virginia, *Praying an Alteration of the Laws respecting Copy-*

rights," Sen. Doc. No. 193, 24 Cong., 2 Sess. (1837), Ser. 298.

"Petition of Thomas Moore, and Other Authors of Great Britain, *Praying Congress to grant them the Exclusive Benefit of their Writings within the United States,"* Sen. Doc. No. 134, 24 Cong., 2 Sess. (1837), Ser. 298.

[Phillips, S. M.]. "History of the Conquest of Mexico" (review), *Edinburgh Review,* LXXXI (April 1845), 434–73.

[Pickering, John]. "Prescott's Reign of Ferdinand and Isabella" (review), *The New-York Review,* II (April 1838), 308–41.

Plomer, Henry R. *A Short History of English Printing 1476–1900.* London, 1927.

[Prescott, William H.]. "The Battle of Lepanto," *The Atlantic Monthly,* I, No. 2 (December 1857), 138–48.

Prescott Memorial. Extra-illustrated copy in Boston Public Library. n.p., n.d.

"Prescott's Peru" (anon. rev.), *Blackwood's Edinburgh Review,* LXII (July 1847), 1–20.

Prothero, Rowland E., ed. *The Letters of Richard Ford 1797–1858.* New York, 1905.

Publishers' Weekly, Vol. IV, No. 12 (September 20, 1873), 293.

Putnam, George Haven. *George Palmer Putnam: A Memoir.* New York, 1912.

P[utnam], G[eorge] H[aven] and J. B[ishop] P[utnam]. *Authors and Publishers.* (7th ed.) New York, 1900.

Quérard, Joseph Marie. *La Littérature française contemporaine.* 6 vols. Paris, 1842–57.

Rawley, James A. "An Early History of the International Copyright Movement," *The Library Quarterly,* XI (April 1941), 200–206.

Ray, Gordon N. "The Bentley Papers," *The Library,* Fifth Series, VII, No. 3 (September 1952), 178–200.

———, ed. *The Letters and Private Papers of William Makepeace Thackery.* 4 vols. Cambridge, 1946.

"Remonstrance of Inhabitants of Massachusetts, *Against the passage of an International Copyright Law,*" H. Doc. No. 416, 25 Cong., 2 Sess. (1838), Ser. 330.

"Report by Ruggles [*To accompany Senate Bill No. 32*]," Sen. Doc. No. 494, 25 Cong., 2 Sess. (1838), Ser. 319.

"Report made by Mr. Clay, *with Senate Bill No. 223,*" Sen. Doc. No. 179, 24 Cong., 2 Sess. (1837), Ser. 298.

Rice, Allen Thorndike, ed. *Essays from the North American Review.* New York, 1879.

Rives, John C., ed. *The Congressional Globe.* Vol. xxiv, Pt. iii, (Washington, D.C., 1852), 1832.

"Rough Notes of Thirty Years in the Trade," *The American Publishers' Circular and Literary Gazette,* Octavo Series, i, No. 6 (July 15, 1863), 242–45.

Rusk, Ralph L., ed. *The Letters of Ralph Waldo Emerson.* 6 vols. New York, 1939.

Sheehan, Donald. *This Was Publishing: A Chronicle of the Book Trade in the Gilded Age.* Bloomington, Indiana, 1952.

Smiles, Samuel. *A Publisher and His Friends: Memoir and Correspondence of the late John Murray, with an Account of the Origin and Progress of the House, 1768–1843.* 2 vols. London, 1891.

Solberg, Thorvald. "The Bibliography of International Copyright in the Congress of the United States, 1837–1891," *Publisher's Weekly,* xxxix, No. 23 (June 6, 1891), 788–93.

Spiller, Robert E. *Fenimore Cooper: Critic of His Times.* New York, 1931.

Spiller, Robert E., and Philip C. Blackburn. *A Descriptive Bibliography of the Writings of James Fenimore Cooper.* New York, 1934.

Spiller, Robert E., Willard Thorp, Thomas H. Johnson, Henry Seidel Canby, *et al,* eds. *Literary History of the United States.* New York, 1953.

Stone, Herbert Stuart, comp. *First Editions of American Authors.* Cambridge, 1893.

Stuart Wortley, Lady Emmeline. *Travels in the United States, etc., during 1849 and 1850.* New York, 1851.

Ticknor, George. *Life of William Hickling Prescott.* Philadelphia, 1895.

Trowbridge, John Townsend. *My Own Story.* Boston and New York, 1903.

Tryon, W. S. "Book Distribution in Mid-Nineteenth Century America," *The Papers of the Bibliographical Society of America,* XLI (Third Quarter, 1947), 210–30.

————. "Nationalism and International Copyright: Tennyson and Longfellow in America," *American Literature,* XXIV (November 1952), 301–9.

Tryon, Warren S. and William Charvat, eds. *The Cost Books of Ticknor and Fields and Their Predecessors, 1832–1858.* New York, 1949.

[Van Nostrand]. *A Century of Book Publishing, 1848–1948.* New York, 1948.

Von Hagen, Victor Wolfgang. *Maya Explorer: John Lloyd Stephens and the Lost Cities of Central America and Yucatán.* Norman, Oklahoma, 1948.

Wagenknecht, Edward, ed. *Mrs. Longfellow: Selected Letters and Journals of Fanny Appleton Longfellow (1817–1861).* New York, 1956.

Wagner, Henry R. "Henri Ternaux Compans: The First Collector of Hispanic-Americana," *Inter-American Review of Bibliography,* IV, No. 4 (Octubre–Diciembre 1954), 283–98.

Waugh, Arthur. *A Hundred Years of Publishing. Being the Story of Chapman & Hall, Ltd.* London, 1930.

Williams, Stanley T. *The Spanish Background of American Literature.* 2 vols. New Haven, Conn., 1955.

Winsor, Justin, ed. *The Memorial History of Boston.* 4 vols. Boston, 1881.

Wolcott, Roger, ed. *The Correspondence of William Hickling Prescott 1833–1847.* Boston and New York, 1925.

"A Word at the Start," *Harper's New Monthly Magazine,* I, No. 1 (June 1850), 1–2.

Chapter 1

1. Ogden, *Prescott*, pp. 91–92.
2. Wolcott, *Correspondence of Prescott*, p. 173.
3. Cooper, *Correspondence*, II, 431.
4. Kaser, *Messrs. Carey & Lea*, p. 157.
5. For a general account of Prescott's life, see Ticknor, *Prescott;* Ogden, *Prescott;* and Peck, *Prescott*.
6. Ogden, *Prescott*, p. 78.
7. Wagenknecht, *Mrs. Longfellow*, pp. 103–4.
8. Nevins, *Diary of Philip Hone*, p. 816.
9. For a complete bibliography of Prescott's works, see Gardiner, *Annotated Bibliography*.

Chapter 2

1. See "Rough Notes of Thirty Years in the Trade," p. 243. See also Carter and Crutchley, *Printed Book*, p. 50; and Plomer, *Short History of English Printing*, p. 243.
2. Wolcott, *Correspondence of Prescott*, p. 13; and Ticknor, *Prescott*, p. 99.
3. Goodrich, *Recollections*, II, 254. See also Oswald, *Printing in the Americas*, p. 87.
4. Ogden, *Prescott*, p. 90.
5. See Appendix B.
6. Wolcott, *Correspondence of Prescott*, p. 341.
7. *Ibid.*, p. 419. The physical process at the Harpers is described in Abbott, *Harper Establishment*.

8. See Appendix H. This contract of August 5, 1854, is held by the J. B. Lippincott Company, Philadelphia.

9. Wolcott, *Correspondence of Prescott,* p. 14.

10. Ibid., p. 17.

11. See *Publishers' Weekly,* IV, No. 12 (September 20, 1873), 293.

12. Wolcott, *Correspondence of Prescott,* p. 98.

13. Ibid., p. 56.

Chapter 3

1. For a detailed view of one of Prescott's aides, see a forthcoming article by C. Harvey Gardiner, "Prescott's Most Indispensable Aide: Pascual de Gayangos," in the February, 1959, *Hispanic American Historical Review.*

2. Wolcott, *Correspondence of Prescott,* p. 8.

3. Ibid., pp. 11–12.

4. Ibid., p. 13.

5. Ibid., p. 14.

6. For text, see Appendix A, reproduced from Bentley Papers, Vol. LIV, foll. 7–8, in Add. Mss. 46613 BM.

7. Little, Brown & Co., *One Hundred Years,* p. 13.

8. For text, see Appendix B.

9. Wolcott, *Correspondence of Prescott,* p. 234.

10. Ibid., p. 240.

11. Von Hagen, *Maya Explorer,* pp. 197, 200.

12. Wolcott, *Correspondence of Prescott,* p. 339.

13. Ibid., p. 342.

14. See Sheehan, *This Was Publishing,* pp. 21, 23.

15. Wolcott, *Correspondence of Prescott,* p. 348.

16. Ibid., p. 350.

17. Ibid., pp. 310, 343.

18. See, for example, Forster, *Dickens,* for an area of Dickens' career which has drawn increasing attention.

19. Wolcott, *Correspondence of Prescott,* pp. 343–45.

20. Ibid., p. 351.

21. *Ibid.,* p. 354.

22. *Ibid.,* p. 355.

23. *Ibid.,* p. 357.

24. *Ibid.,* pp. 362, 363.

25. *Ibid.,* p. 371.

26. *Ibid.,* pp. 371–72. For text, See Appendix E, reproduced from Bentley Papers, Vol. LV, foll. 186–87, in Add. Mss. 46614 BM.

27. Wolcott, *Correspondence of Prescott,* p. 372.

28. See endorsement in Appendix B.

29. For text, see Appendix F, reproduced from Bentley Papers, Vol. LV, foll. 254–55, in Add. Mss. 46614 BM.

30. Wolcott, *Correspondence of Prescott,* p. 547.

31. See "Authors and Publishers," p. 511.

32. See Fay, *Statement.*

33. Wolcott, *Correspondence of Prescott,* pp. 613–14.

34. *Ibid.,* p. 618.

35. Harper, *House of Harper,* pp. 139–40.

36. Derby, *Fifty Years,* pp. 521–22.

37. For text, see Appendix H.

38. Van Nostrand, *A Century of Book Publishing,* p. 9.

Chapter 4

1. See Bowker, *Copyright,* p. 25.

2. "Petition of Thomas Moore, and Other Authors of Great Britain."

3. "Memorial of a Number of Citizens of the United States."

4. "Report made by Mr. Clay."

5. "Memorial of G. Furman and Other Public Writers"; and "Petition of the Professors of the University of Virginia."

6. See "Memorial of a number of citizens of Philadelphia"; *Boston Daily Evening Transcript,* January 4, 1838; "Memorial of the Columbia Typographical Society";

"Memorial of the New York Typographical Society"; "Memorial of Richard Penn Smith and others"; "Memorial of the Book-sellers of Boston"; and "Remonstrance of Inhabitants of Massachusetts."

7. "Memorial of a number of citizens of Boston."

8. "Memorial of a number of citizens of New York"; and "Memorial of a number of citizens of Philadelphia."

9. "Memorial of Peter S. Du Ponceau and others."

10. "Report by Ruggles."

11. Eaton, "The American Movement for International Copyright, 1837–60," p. 111.

12. Ticknor, *Prescott*, p. 166.

13. See Freidel, "Lieber's Contribution to the International Copyright Movement," p. 204.

14. Forster, *Dickens*, I, 319. The twenty-five American signers are named in Houtchens, "Charles Dickens and International Copyright," pp. 19–20.

15. Wolcott, *Correspondence of Prescott*, p. 54.

16. Ibid., p. 316. Neither of the two students of Prescott's political attitudes treats his relationship to the copyright question. See Ogden, *Prescott*, pp. 197–207; and Charvat, "Prescott's Political and Social Attitudes," pp. 320–30.

17. Wolcott, *Correspondence of Prescott*, p. 323.

18. "Memorials of John Jay and of William C. Bryant."

19. Wolcott, *Correspondence of Prescott*, p. 13.

20. Ibid., p. 19.

21. Ibid., pp. 329–30.

22. Ibid., pp. 382, 384.

23. Ibid., pp. 415–16.

24. See endorsement, Appendix B.

25. See Quérard, *La Littérature*, VI, 78.

26. Wolcott, *Correspondence of Prescott*, pp. 469–70.

27. Rives, *Congressional Globe*, p. 1832.

28. See Bowker, *Copyright*, p. 28.

29. Correspondence of William H. Prescott, Esq. with Richard Bentley, pp. 14, 15–16.

30. Wolcott, *Correspondence of Prescott*, p. 327.

Chapter 5

1. Wolcott, *Correspondence of Prescott,* p. 16.
2. *Ibid.,* pp. 37, 98.
3. *Ibid.,* p. 144.
4. For text, See Appendix C.
5. Wolcott, *Correspondence of Prescott,* p. 344.
6. *Ibid.,* p. 523.
7. *Ibid.,* p. 534.
8. *Ibid.,* p. 614.
9. *Ibid.,* p. 623.
10. .*Ibid.,* p. 552.
11. See Appendix B.
12. Wolcott, *Correspondence of Prescott,* p. 37.
13. *Ibid.,* p. 98.
14. *Ibid.,* p. 9.
15. See Wolcott, *ibid.,* pp. 2, 18, 96n, 141, 274–75, 284, 318, 332–33, 347.
16. *Ibid.,* p. 137.
17. See Ogden, *Prescott,* p. 90; and Wolcott, *Correspondence of Prescott,* p. 189.
18. Wolcott, *Correspondence of Prescott,* p. 388.
19. *Ibid.,* p. 56.
20. *Ibid.,* p. 388.
21. *Ibid.,* p. 534.
22. *Ibid.,* p. 511.
23. *Ibid.,* p. 9.
24. *Ibid.,* p. 14.
25. *Ibid.,* p. 12.
26. For text, see Appendix H.
27. See Ogden, *Prescott,* p. 90.

Chapter 6

1. See Tryon, "Book Distribution in Mid-Nineteenth Century America," pp. 210–30, for a general treatment of this period.

2. In the Widener Library, Harvard University, a copy of this prospectus is bound with Count Adolphe de Circourt's lengthy review of *Ferdinand and Isabella*, classified as Span 503.40.

3. For a general discussion of this matter, see Tryon, "Book Distribution in Mid-Nineteenth Century America," pp. 222–25.

4. One revealing career in book promotion in this period is treated in Charvat, "James T. Fields and the Beginnings of Book Promotion, 1840–1855," pp. 75–94.

5. Wolcott, *Correspondence of Prescott,* p. 387.

6. Ibid., p. 513.

7. Ibid., p. 339.

8. See Charvat, "James T. Fields and the Beginnings of Book Promotion, 1840–1855," pp. 78, 79.

9. See Prescott to Bentley, June 14 and November 30, 1843; Prescott to Harpers, December 14, 1843, November 22 and 26, 1847; and Prescott to F. Harper, December 8, 1845. See also Wolcott, *Correspondence of Prescott,* p. 400.

10. Unsigned but bearing the initials of von Raumer, the review of the Leipzig edition appeared in *Blätter für Literarische Unterhaltung* in 1843. Circourt's five-part review appeared in the *Bibliothèque Universelle de Genève* between July, 1838 and January, 1840.

11. Hillard, *Ticknor,* II, 142–43.

12. Wolcott, *Correspondence of Prescott,* p. 25.

13. Ibid., pp. 31, 32.

14. Ibid., pp. 35–36, 55, 59, 60–61, 74–75, 220, 279, 291, 317. For a fuller view of Prescott's relations with Ternaux Compans, see Wagner, "Henri Ternaux Compans," pp. 289–97.

15. Ticknor, *Prescott,* pp. 109–10.

16. Ibid., p. 113.

17. Wolcott, *Correspondence of Prescott,* p. 400.

18. Harper, *House of Harper,* p. 138.

19. Wolcott, *Correspondence of Prescott,* pp. 62–63, 84.

20. See, for example, Prescott to Bentley, May 30, 1844; and Prescott to the Harpers, November 22, 1847.

Chapter 7

1. See Ogden, *Prescott,* p. 95.

2. Ibid., pp. 90–91.

3. Ibid., pp. 91–92.

4. For a full explanation of tokens, see Tryon and Charvat, *Cost Books of Ticknor and Fields,* pp. xxxix–xli.

5. See endorsements, Appendix B.

6. Ogden, *Prescott,* p. 141.

7. Ibid., pp. 156–57.

8. Derby, *Fifty Years,* p. 518.

9. Ibid., p. 518. After the bankruptcy of Phillips, Sampson, in 1859, some authors, doubting the firm's honesty, inspected the records and sustained their suspicions of fraud. See Rusk, *Letters of Emerson,* V, 177.

10. Wolcott, *Correspondence of Prescott,* p. 144.

11. For Cooper's later estimate of Bentley's financial integrity, see Putnam, *Putnam: A Memoir,* p. 156. A modern expression of skepticism of Bentley's financial integrity is Gohdes, "Longfellow and His Authorized British Publishers," p. 1166.

12. Wolcott, *Correspondence of Prescott,* p. 330.

13. Ibid., p. 343.

14. Bentley's records suggest two different figures for Prescott's English income: £2,230 and £2,507 1*s* 6*d.* See Bentley ledger entry for Nov. 25, 1858, in Bentley Papers Add. Mss. 46,595 BM. See also Richard Bentley and Son, *List . . . 1854.* The company records offer the smaller figure as total earnings and the larger figure as Prescott's earnings down to 1854.

Prescott was not the highest paid American author on Bentley's list. Bentley paid James Fenimore Cooper a total of £9,040 during Cooper's lifetime, with payments ranging from £1,300 to £100 per work, or on the average of £350 to £500 per work. For George Bancroft's three-volume *History of the American Revolution,* Bentley paid the author £900 in the period 1852–54. See Spiller, *Cooper,* pp. 105–6, 203–4.

15. Efforts to establish Prescott's popularity have emphasized the volumes published rather than the income received. Ticknor inaugurated this pattern by giving totals for the number of Prescott's books published down to 1860, figures which Allibone and Morison have repeated. However, statements of income up to now have centered on initial contract terms and occasional receipts and copyright valuations. Some of the figures, such as those of Morison, are confusing and inexact. See Ticknor, *Prescott;* Allibone, *Critical Dictionary,* II, 1665–72; Ogden, *Prescott,* p. 156; and Morison, *History of the Conquest of Peru,* p. xl.

While sharing the view of Tryon (in "Nationalism and International Copyright," pp. 301–9), that the works of good American authors could and did survive the competition of cheap reprints of English works in days prior to American adherence to international copyright, the writer believes it impossible to associate Prescott with any "laboratory experiment" capable of meaningful statistical support of the idea.

16. See Tryon and Charvat, *Cost Books of Ticknor and Fields,* pp. xxxvii–xxxviii.

17. Mott, *Golden Multitudes,* pp. 306, 307, suggests a sale of 175,000 copies of the *Conquest of Mexico.* Pure unadulterated fabrication!

Chapter 8

1. Edward Everett to Lord John Russell, May 20, 1850, and Edward Everett to Lord Ashburton, May 20, 1850.

2. See Little, Brown & Co., *One Hundred Years,* p. 22.

3. Putnam and Putnam, *Authors and Publishers,* p. 21.

4. See Little, Brown & Co., *Catalogue of Books,* pp. 134, 226.

5. See Sheehan, *This Was Publishing,* p. 125; and Harper, *House of Harper,* pp. 54, 138.

6. Harper, *House of Harper,* p. 139.

7. Ibid., p. 140.

8. Ibid., pp. 140–41.

9. Derby, *Fifty Years,* p. 522.

10. Wolcott, *Correspondence of Prescott,* p. 17.

11. Ibid., pp. 540–41.

12. Ibid., p. 630.

13. See Richard Bentley and Son, *List . . . 1869.*

14. Goodrich, *Recollections,* II, 275.

INDEX

Abridgment: right to make, 56; reason for, 58; provision for, 288. *See also* Contracts; *Ferdinand and Isabella*

Academic honors: on title pages, 193–95

Advertising: in newspapers, 168; importance of, 174; standardization of, 175; best medium, 185; bill-of-fare type, 190; borrowed, 191; by Fletcher Harper, 192

Agent: in London, 47. *See also* Aspinwall, Colonel Thomas; Lawrence, Colonel, T. B.; Sturgis, Russell

Alamán, Lucas: presentation copy to, 184

The American Monthly: review in, 171

American Stationers' Co.: failure of, 22, 54, 173; nature of, 53; promotion by, 167–69; distribution by, 172; review copies, 178; author's copies, 180; income from, 203; personal relations with, 248; mentioned, 40, 176, 279

Amory, William, 20, 246

Andrews, J., 136, 149, 151

Artists: Catherwood, Frederick, 70, 77; Carderera y Solano, Valentín, 150; Gutierrez de la Vega, José, 150; Madrazo y Agudo, José, 150

Aspinwall, Colonel Thomas: negotiations for *Ferdinand and Isabella*, 48, 49, 175; Prescott's arrangement with, 51–52; commission of, 52, 227–39 *passim;* aids Stephens, 60; negotiations for *Conquest of Mexico*, 63–69, 158; negotiations for *Miscellanies*, 73, 140, 151; negotiations for *Conquest of Peru*, 79–80, 141; departs London, 239; mentioned, 47, 88, 260, 269

The Athenaeum: review in, 171

The Atlantic Monthly: Prescott's contribution to, 257–58

Author's copies: number of, 56, 180–81; from American Stationers' Co., 180; from Bentley, 180, 181; from Harpers, 180, 181; from Little, Brown & Co., 180

Author-publisher relations: changing nature of, 4, 80; aspects of, 14; records of, 14; stereotype plates in, 44–45; state of, 52–53; nature of, 83, 255–56; break in, 132–33

Bancroft, George: review by, 10, 136; Prescott consults, 20–21; promotion by, 169, 170, 171–